HOW TO GET RICH
WITH A 1–800 NUMBER

HOW TO GET RICH WITH A 1-800 NUMBER

NAPOLEON BARRAGAN

CEO DIAL-A-MATTRESS

with Maxine and Frank Brady

ReganBooks

An Imprint of HarperCollinsPublishers

Permissions

"What is a Customer" credo on page 71 reprinted courtesy of L.L. Bean; "Personal Traits Important to a Business Proprietor" pages 56–57 from the Small Business Administration; sample 1–800 numbers on page 114 from *The New York Times Magazine*, December 1996; Maslow's Pyramid reprinted from *Motivation and Personality*, 3rd ed., by Abraham H. Maslow. Copyright © 1970 by Abraham H. Maslow. Reprinted by permission of Addison-Wesley Educational Publishers, Inc.; "Who You Sleep With Is Your Business" on page 130 and "Top Ten Reasons To Buy a Mattress from Dial-A-Mattress with Your American Express® Card" on page 131 reprinted courtesy of Mulryan/Nash; "Dial-A-Mattress is Now Delivering on Broadway" advertisement on page 134 courtesy of D.K.B. and Partners, Inc.; "Convenient & Fast" advertisement on page 141 courtesy of Modografics; Shea Stadium photograph on page 142 courtesy of the New York Mets; "Our Credo" on page 212 courtesy of Johnson & Johnson; Graebel policies on page 225 courtesy of Graebel Van Lines Company.

For information on how to purchase copies of this book by phone and to find out about discounts on quantity purchases of this book for businesses, schools or groups, call 1–800–DIAL–A–BOOK.

HarperCollins books may be purchased for educational, business, or sales promotional use. For information please write: Special Markets Department, HarperCollins *Publishers*, Inc., 10 East 53rd Street, New York, NY 10022.

FIRST EDITION

Designed by Irving Perkins Associates, Inc.

Library of Congress Cataloging-in-Publication Data

Barragan, Napoleon.
How to get rich with a 1–800 number / Napoleon Barragan with Frank and Maxine Brady. 1st ed.
p. cm.
ISBN 0–06–098714–6
1. Telemarketing. 2. Success in business. 3. Toll-free telephone calls. I. Brady, Frank, 1934– . II. Brady, Maxine. III. Title.
HF5415.126.B335 1997   97200
658.8'4—dc21

97 98 99 00 01 ❖/RRD 10 9 8 7 6 5 4 3 2 1

CONTENTS

ACKNOWLEDGMENTS   vii

PREFACE   xiii

1. HOW IT ALL BEGAN   1

2. HOW TO MAKE YOUR BUSINESS GROW   19

3. TELEMARKETING—HOW TO SELL BY PHONE   59

4. HOW TO MARKET, ADVERTISE, AND PROMOTE YOUR
   PRODUCT OR SERVICE   105

5. HOW TO DELIVER THE GOODS, AND TACTICS FOR
   HANDLING YOUR INVENTORY   161

6. BUILD EXCELLENT COMMUNICATIONS—
   INSIDE AND OUTSIDE YOUR COMPANY   204

7. THE FUTURE OF TELEMARKETING   227

   APPENDIX A: FURTHER RESOURCES FROM
   DIAL-A-MATTRESS   255

   APPENDIX B: USEFUL FACTS ABOUT 1–800 SERVICE   257

   INDEX   277

ACKNOWLEDGMENTS

The success of a corporation is largely dependent on the abilities and enthusiasm of its employees. Throughout its existence, Dial-A-Mattress has been fortunate enough to have an exemplary staff. Each person does his or her job, but with an awareness and concern for the needs of the company as a whole.

It is my pleasure to take this opportunity to thank all of the current employees, as well as all of the fine people who used to work for me. Their excellent work has been instrumental to the growth and success of Dial-A-Mattress.

Agnihotri, Anagha
Agreda, Byron
Alessi, Paul P.
Arnio, Ted A.
Arroyo, Brenda
Barragan, Kay
Barragan, Luis
Barragan, Eddie
Baughman, Mary C.
Becerra, Harold
Boissiere, Sabrina T.
Bolton, Ruth
Bonilla, Ernesto J.
Britton, Jennifer
Buckrham, Karen
Butler, Oonagh
Caicedo, Roberto
Calderon, Jane P.
Calhoun, Karen

Canales, Elizabeth
Canterbury, Jamaal
Carballo, Michael
Carrasquilla, Liza M.
Castromonte, Judy
Chevere, Leticia
Chicco, Gian Carlo
Chinman, Leslie
Ciamaga, Madonna
Cinque, Nanette P.
Cook, Zoraida
Cooper-Snell, Phildelis
Cooperman, Neil
Coriano, Christina
Craig, Jaqueline A.
Cusa, Albert John
Daniggelis, Christopher
David, Virginia A.
Dayson, Kevin M.

Defranceschi, Maristela
Deopaul, Yubraj
Desmond-Toomey,
	Kathleen
Duffy, Francis G.
Easterling, David E.
Ehrhardt, Allan C.
Ende, Richard C.
Eskononts, Mordecai
Farigua, Mauricio
Fernandez, Anthony
Fernandez, Orlando
Figueroa, Lourdes
Fleishman, Camellia
Fraschi, Julie
French, Andrea
Friedland, Donald
Garcia, David
Garfield, Alexis M.
Geller, Evan
Goldstein, Jeffery
Gomez, Edgar
Gonzalez, Helen
Goodman, Susan E.
Gordon, Greg S.
Gordon, Lisa M.
Grassano, Jennifer
Grassano, Kenneth
Green, Francisca M.
Halstead, Cara B.
Harripersaud, Tullwatie
Harris, Bernilyn
Haverty, Michael
Herrera, Raul L.
Hoffberg, Nellie G.
Horge, Ericka

Horowitz, Steven
Isler, Robert A.
Jackson, Hazel
James, Herbert
Johnson, Ruby
Jones, Francis E.
Jones, Glenn
Jones, Lisa H.
Joseph, Rachel S.
Kabatsky, Steven
Katz, Donna
Keblas, Robert
Kee, Jasmine
Kelberg, Paul
Kidd, Samuel
Kurpis, Louis W.
Leon, Juan Manuel
Leon, York S.
Loewenstein, Michael
Lopez, Albert
Lopez, Jovier
Lozano, Edgar A.
Lugo, Domingo
Ma, Patrick
Manno, Robert J.
Marquez, Rafael
Massell, Paul
Mastrangeli, Paul
Matos, Natalie
McBride, Patricia J.
McCarthy, Christopher S.
McCormick, Ellen
McGuire, Dan
McKeon, Patrick
McLaughlin, Michael
Mejia, Dario

Mélendez, Wilberto
Minguillon, Adolf
Mizell, Christan W.
Molina, Ramon
Montes, Maribel
Morales, John Gary
Nagler, Jeffery
Nati, Joanne
Neira, Ernesto A.
Nooney, Gregory
Pacaud, Raymonde
Pacheco, Maria
Padilla, George
Padilla, Laurice
Palacios, Harold
Pastrano, Marcelo
Patino, Claudia
Patino, Zoraida
Paultre, Jacques
Paultre, Steven E.
Pena, Ralph A.
Persaud, Samuel
Peterson, Terry
Pimentel, Jose E.
Pinto, Maria E.
Pistis, George J.
Pollonais, Nigel M.
Prokop, Paul J.
Pucha, Juan
Rabinowitz, Joshua
Rahne, Raymond E.
Ramirez, Frances
Rayher, Jack
Renneberg, Maureen
Rizzo, Dawn
Rizzo, Ralph

Rizzuto, Doreen
Rocco, David A.
Rodas, Veronica P.
Rodgers, Arlene
Rodriguez, Angela
Rodriguez, Orlando
Rosa, Martin
Rovello, James
Rueda, Ana
Rueda, Gloria
Russo, Vince
Rust, Bernard
Sagar, Mona
Salvio, Alicia M.
Sanchez, David
Sanchez, Vivian
Sanchez, Viviana C.
Sanders, Michelle
Santiago, Hilda
Sbarra, Jean
Scalogna, Bart
Schoppmann, Kurt
Scott, Lansford
Seidenberg, Richard
Senfeld, S. William
Serrano, Michael
Shev, Jeffery
Shoten, Fran
Siegel, Mira
Siracusano, Louise
Smalls, Bernard
Starr, Philip
Stern, Michael S.
Swain, Traci L.
Tang, Bob B.
Taylor, Darryl

Tiongson, Rodney
Tong, Basil F.
Toro, Jorge A.
Trujilo, Luis H.
Tucker, Ashley
Valdivieso, William
Valentin, Carmen
Valentin, Jose
Valentin, Ruby
Vera, Jair Alberto

Vicens, Jose
Villalona, Elvin
Villalona, Kimberly
Vintimilia, Luisa
Vitolo Jr, Ernest
Waters, James J.
West, Shirley Ann
Wheelock, Gary
Winfield, John
Zweidinger, Ray

No company exists in a vacuum. I feel that the companies I do business with don't merely supply me with products or services; they are virtually partners in my business. If I succeed, it will help *them* grow. If they succeed, it will help *me*.

I would like to thank the companies with which Dial-A-Mattress has a particularly important relationship, and acknowledge them as my Partners in Business.

Allwood Furniture
American Express
AT&T
Bicor Processing
   Corporation
Bloomberg
Borden Avenue Associates
Boyd Flotation Inc.
Capital Distributors
Channel 41
Channel 47
Channel 66
CUC International
D & E Business Forms Inc.
David Kaufman
DHL Worldwide Express

Dowling College
Dun & Bradstreet
Federal Express
   Corporation
Foremost Furniture
Frank Nahser & Associates
Franklin Quest
Furniture Today
Geller & Wind
General Electric Capital
   Corp.
Global Computer Supplies
Global Equipment
   Company
Goldbond
Hewlett-Packard

Howard Rubinstein &
  Associates
Howard Stern
IBM Corporation
Imus
International Sleep
  Products Association
King Freeze
Kinko's
Knickerbocker Bed
  Company
Kostelanetz & Fink
KPMG Peat Merwick
Legget & Platt
Louisville Bedding
LPA Associates, Inc.
MCI Telecommunications
Mendelsohn Kary & Bell
Metrocall
Metromedia Technologies,
  Inc.
Microsoft
Milnat Associates
MKB&N
Motorola Inc.
NY Broadcast
NYNEX
Perfect Fit Industries
Phoenix Down Corp.
Queens Child Guidance
  Center
Restonic Corp.
Rowe Furniture Corp.
Sealy Mattress Company
Serta Mattress Company
Simmons Company

Sleepcare Inc.
SleepCo
Spanish Broadcasting
  System
Spring Air Mattress
  Company
Sprint
St. John's University
Staples, Inc.
Steve Parker/1–800–
  IDEAS
TOPS Appliances
Two Hour Trucking
United Parcel Service
US Healthcare
Viacom Computer
  Associates
WABC TV
WCBS TV
Western International
  Media Corp.
WNBC TV

FRANCHISES:

Consolidated Mattress,
  Boston
J&W Bedding, Maryland
Sunshine Bedding,
  Florida

TRUCKING COMPANIES:

Eleven Truckers Inc.
Fast Freight Trucking
ISH's Trucking
Singh Trucking
T.D.&J. Santiago Trucking

Current and past employees, vendors, product and service providers, all of the people who are the lifeblood of Dial-A-Mattress: You have all earned my deepest respect and admiration.

NAPOLEON BARRAGAN

PREFACE

More new information has been produced in the last 30 years than in the previous 5,000. The amount of available information now doubles every five years. By the turn of the century—only a few years away—the doubling time will be every 20 months.

MASTERING THE INFORMATION AGE
MICHAEL J. McCARTHY, 1991

When I started Dial-A-Mattress in 1976, it was just a small, experimental offshoot of my real business—a modest furniture store on Jamaica Avenue in Queens, a borough of New York City. Most people doubted that we would sell many mattresses by phone, but my instinct told me to go ahead with the idea. By 1995, we were grossing $55 million in annual sales, and I had long since given up the furniture store. Not long ago, we sold more than $350,000 worth of mattresses *in one day*.

Today, Dial-A-Mattress is one of the nation's most successful direct marketing companies. It gained fame selling hundreds of millions of dollars worth of mattresses by phone, and in the process we developed and refined revolutionary new systems for telecommunications, sales, inventory, delivery, and other business procedures that can be used to sell many other types of products or services directly to consumers. Selling by telephone and computer has become pervasive, in part, because of our success. In the latter half of the 1990s, and as we enter the turn of the century, this new method of selling will be an increasingly more significant part of consumers lives.

In a sense, telemarketing actually began with the invention of the telephone, and it has continued ever since. You are already using telemarketing in your personal life, even if you don't know it. People have used and continue to use the telephone to negotiate or market all manner of things: not only commercial items such as products, services, lessons, information, news, reports, or other aspects of business, but social items as well—things such as friendship, affection, love, advice, enlightenment, and confidences.

Toll-free telemarketing has become a $10 billion-a-year market in this country, alone. AT&T, one of the companies providing toll-free telephone service, carries more than 20 billion toll-free calls each year. That is roughly 40 percent of the more than 200 million long-distance calls that they carry *daily*.

The vast majority of toll-free calling is for business purposes. As you can see, if you are not yet using a toll-free number for your business or service, or not taking advantage of your already existing toll-free number, you may be depriving yourself of a vast amount of sales.

To say that selling by telephone is a marketing revolution is almost an understatement—it is a total transformation. Retailing now occurs at the *consumer's* convenience. In conventional retailing, a customer can go shopping only when a store is open. Through telemarketing, customers can call Dial-A-Mattress—or any other retailer—using a toll-free number 24 hours a day, at *their* convenience. This provides a transfer of power to the consumer. It also fills the shopping needs of modern society, where people's greatest lack is *time*.

Although at present the telephone is the principle conduit of selling in this new technology, the concept goes well beyond just telephones, with the use of fax machines and computers. In essence, the technology is enabling us to develop new ways of communicating with each other. Those changes that have been brought about so far, and the further advances in communications that will undoubtedly be perfected, are as important and profound as the invention of movable type and the printing press.

Revolutions are not made; they come about because of *need*. And telemarketing arose because consumers needed an efficient, cost-effective, and equitable way to buy products and avail themselves of the services they need and want. Businesses need telemarketing as much as the consumer: The old fashioned door-to-door salesman, or the department store with soaring real-estate rates and personnel demanding ever-increasing salaries, just has to be abandoned.

More and more families now have more than one telephone line in their homes; and with the explosion of fax machines and cell phones, we are finding that customers are calling or faxing us from their offices or homes, from country houses or sailboats, from automobiles or airplanes.

My intention in writing this book is to share my knowledge of this new technology of selling. When I lived in South America, I used to be a teacher, and teaching is still my great love. So I think of this book as a textbook, a manual that will have immediate application to your business—or the business you may be thinking of starting. The how-to aspect of this book provides principles and techniques that Dial-A-Mattress and other experienced telemarketers have found to be successful.

You can apply what you learn in this book to *any* product or service. Whenever I am telling a story about Dial-A-Mattress or discussing Dial-A-Mattress operations, simply mentally replace the word mattress with the name of the product or service you want to sell by phone. Everything in this book can be applied to the selling of hairpieces or horse shoes, holiday vacations or harlequin costumes. . . *whatever* you might want to sell by phone.

I've also included stories about how Dial-A-Mattress began and grew, to let you see how *we* did it. Hopefully, these anecdotes will be both amusing and inspirational, and help you get ideas on ways to develop your own business. My intention is that this book will enable my readers to apply these new telemarketing systems and dynamics to your own companies, and that you will have the same success that I have had.

NAPOLEON BARRAGAN
LONG ISLAND CITY, NEW YORK

1

HOW IT ALL BEGAN

Swim upstream. Go the other way. Ignore the conventional wisdom. If everybody else is doing it one way, there's a good chance
you can find your niche by going in exactly the opposite direction. But be prepared for a lot of folks to wave you down and tell
you you're headed the wrong way. I guess in all my years, what I
heard more often than anything was: a town of less than 50,000
population cannot support a discount store for very long.

Made in America
Sam Walton, 1992

When I arrived in New York in 1968 as a new immigrant from
Ecuador, I had a wife and a child, and about $10 in my pocket.
Though I had been a teacher in Colombia, and had even run my
own school there, I had no license to teach in New York, and my
command of English was very poor. To support my family, I
worked in small factories in Queens, one of the five boroughs of
New York City, where we had settled. Then in 1973 I began to
work as a salesman in a furniture store. In a short time, I had
worked my way up to sales manager. I learned the business from
the inside out, and shortly afterwards, I decided to open my own
furniture store.

Selecting a site for a business has always been somewhat tricky,
although those who have followed Marshall Field's maxim for

retail success, "Location, location, location," couldn't go all that wrong, all other business factors being equal. The problem, however, is that the small businessman, just starting out, can rarely afford the prime location that he needs to guarantee himself a sufficient number of customers to come into his store to buy his products or avail themselves of his services. That is the beauty of *telephone sales:* In effect, you are bringing your store or operation right into the consumer's home. The telephone instrument— yours and the consumer's—becomes the greatest "location, location, location" in the world. It took me several years to realize this essential piece of business lore.

At first, though, I started out quite traditionally. My first business in this country began in an area of Queens that is called Jamaica. Because I lived in Queens and had a chance to become familiar with it, I'd seen that Jamaica was one of the major retail and transportation hubs of the borough. For more than a half a century, Jamaica was known to the residents of Queens as one of the main shopping centers of the area. Department stores such as Macy's, Gertz, May's, and Grant's drew customers, and once there, people shopped in the smaller stores as well.

Way before I became a businessman in Jamaica, it had a bustling downtown district that was the third largest in New York City. There were first-run movie theaters and hundreds of shops and offices. For years, Queens was considered a microcosm of New York. It was used as a signpost, as an indicator of the financial health of New York City.

When I set up shop in 1974, Jamaica had been losing retail business to the suburban shopping malls, but a new group of potential customers was beginning to move in. They were immigrants, mostly Hispanic as well as people from various Asian countries. These people were still a minority population, but a significant new consumer base. Partly because of them, Jamaica was in a retail upswing, especially for the small to mid-size value-price retailer or "niche store." Because Spanish was my first language, I felt comfortable selling to the Hispanic and multi-cultural community, calculated that I knew and understood the culture, and believed that Jamaica would make an ideal spot for my tiny, undercapitalized retail operation.

My first store was located on Jamaica Avenue, a 100-foot wide commercial street that had a proud tradition, going back all the way to 1704 when it was constructed by the British; it stretched from South Ferry in Brooklyn, east to the village of Jamaica. In l974 it was a thriving retail corridor, and I believed in the adage that in retailing you must go where the traffic is. A new subway line was under construction, buildings were being renovated and reconstructed, and there seemed to be a commitment—a buzz of optimism—by the businessman in Jamaica to redevelop the area. New York's two airports were only 15 equidistant miles away, and the area was the focus of no less than 40 bus routes. There were also thousands of curbside and off-the-street parking spaces available. Two million people resided in Queens, and I wanted them all as customers. "Location, location, location," I thought.

Cost was on my mind, too. When I arrived in Jamaica to seek out a retail site, rents for office and retail space were quite low, immensely more affordable than they were in Manhattan. I must admit that the savings that I could realize on rent was foremost in my mind when I began to look for a store. When I learned that York College, a division of the City University system, was literally down the block from an empty store, and that the city planned to greatly expand the college, I chose to lease that tiny store, within the shadow of the large building. The shop was barely 1,200 square feet, roughly comparable to the size of a comfortable apartment.

Knowing myself, it's probable that my experience as a teacher and educational entrepreneur in Colombia, South America, attracted me to the college. My feeling, almost subliminal, was that perhaps I could someday become involved in the college, as a teacher, consultant, or whatever. On a more practical level, though, I realized that faculty members would be moving into the area to teach, and they would need furniture for their new homes and apartments. All of this was spinning in my head when I came upon the name for my first store. It was magic. The name fit like a perfectly fitted sheet the moment I thought of it: *College Furniture Discounters.*

Although the title of the store came to me instinctively, and I can't truly say that I had any kind of brilliant inspiration, *College Furniture Discounters* was a strong and valuable name. Consumers' shopping values, attitudes, and behavior are all influenced by many factors, not the least of which is *where* they shop. By using the word "college" in my store's title, I was saying that my merchandise was directed toward higher-class buyers, whereas the word "discounters" indicated that we were also offering bargains, which is attractive to any kind of buyer, no matter what their socioeconomic background.

I crammed my minuscule store with as much merchandise as it could possibly hold and I could afford to purchase with my limited funds, gained from a small nest egg of a few thousand dollars. In a matter of days, I turned the key on the front door and, as they say, the rest is history.

Although my location was optimum and business was relatively brisk, for the first few years I really had to struggle to pay my expenses and overhead, put even the most meager amount of food on my family's table, and clothe my four children. The problem lay in the fact that I had little or no reserve cash (let alone credit!) should business slack off for a day or two, or a week or two, due to weather or other conditions or difficulties. I tried everything I could think of to keep customers coming in, to please them with the price and the merchandise, and to keep my overhead as low as possible. I handed out leaflets to passersby, and I concocted all manner of sales, giveaways, discounts, and offers. Once, because my display space was so small, I even convinced the owner of a nearby fruit and vegetable store to prop up one of my mattresses in front of his store, bearing a hand-lettered sign that said "Buy This Mattress!" with an arrow pointing to my store down the block. For every mattress I sold in this way, and there were quite a few, I gave the greengrocer a percentage of the retail price.

On Sundays, when my store was closed, I often loaded my car with tables, stuffed chairs, and lamps, and drove to local flea markets, arranged the furniture in some heavily trafficked spot (Remember: "location, location, location!") and spent hours trying to make a few dollars, while also reducing my inventory so that I could make way for new merchandise in the store.

Somewhere in the back of my mind I knew there had to be a more high-performance way to reach the consumer, and a more efficient way for the consumer to shop. What if the weather was inclement and the potential customer could not leave the house that day? Perhaps he would change his mind and decide not to purchase at all when the sun was shining the next day. I would lose a sale and he would be minus the product. Supposing a customer came to my store at an odd hour when it was closed, or on a holiday when our shutters were down. Again, I thought, I would lose that theoretical sale. And yet I couldn't remain open 24 hours a day, seven days a week: It would cost me too much in salaries and overhead. Also, what about the fact that I might have had the exact piece of furniture that a potential customer wanted and at the price he thought fair, but he lived in the Bronx, for example, and my store was in Queens. It would be the rare bargain-hunter who would travel all that distance just to buy from me. How could I connect buyer and product in a satisfactory and productive way where everyone would benefit?

The problem percolated in my head and filtered slowly, and I remembered an old maxim that I heard when I was growing up in Ecuador. *Ideas are like beards: Men do not have them until they grow up.* Perhaps I was maturing, or maybe the world of retailing simply *needed* a new idea. Eventually the solution came to me in one of the most unlikely places—in a New York City subway train. One day in September of 1976, I had had some business in Manhattan and was traveling back to the store. To while away the time on the subway, I read *The New York Post*, which I often did to keep up with the day's events, to improve my English, and to learn what the competition—furniture stores—were doing. I spotted a small advertisement for *Dial-A-Steak*, a company that would have a filet mignon or a porterhouse (or whatever kind of steak you wanted) delivered, piping hot, to your home in a matter of 40 minutes or so. What an incredible idea, I thought! When the importance of the idea came to me, I felt a rush of exuberance.

By the time I had arrived back on Jamaica Avenue, I had pretty much decided that I had to try *Dial-A-Steak's* innovative (to me) retailing strategy. I shared my enthusiasm for the idea with one of my employees: Just think of it, I said, *Dial-A-Steak* has removed all of the fuss and bother in this retailing exchange. No getting in the car to go to a butcher shop or supermarket to buy the steak (eliminating lines and the time spent), no having to prepare it, cook it, or even clean up the skillet or grill afterward. The transaction was pure and simple: Pick up the phone, dial the number, tell the order-taker what you want, and in a short while, enjoy the results without leaving the comfort and safety of your own home!

The notion of telemarketing fascinated me. Would people really buy steaks by phone? What else could you sell that way? Instinctively, I immediately thought of mattresses, but I forced myself to slow down and carefully consider each of the products I carried. I walked slowly through my small store, looking at the merchandise, wondering about selling any of it by phone. I stopped at the section where the mattresses were displayed. Somehow, although they had never before been sold by phone, sight unseen, the idea seemed inevitable. A mattress. Something just about everyone needs to buy, and buys several times during their lifetime. It also rang of gentle symbolism: warmth, luxury, security, support, comfort. A mattress.

After all, mattresses play an extremely important role in our lives. We spend approximately eight hours a day—a third of our lives—on a mattress. Most of us are conceived on a mattress, most of us are born on one, most of us will die on one. The significance was overwhelming.

With hardly a second thought, I composed an advertisement that offered my least expensive mattresses—a $29 twin-size, a $39 full-size, and a $49 queen-size—wrote out the details on a piece of paper that gave my store's telephone number, handed it to Terry Peterson, an assistant to one of my delivery men (who is now one of my security guards), and instructed him to take it to *The Village Voice*, then the country's largest circulating weekly newspaper, with a group of upscale, adventuresome readers who just might be open to experiment in purchasing a mattress by telephone. In the ad I wrote that we would provide speedy delivery, and I also offered to remove the customer's old mattress at no extra cost. The ad ran on September 11th, and in a matter of days, my phone started ringing and the orders began, if not to pour in, at least to come quickly and successfully. After two weeks time, the telephone was still ringing enthusiastically, and I was having trouble fulfilling all of the orders that were coming in, even though I was restricting my delivery area to Jamaica, Flushing, and Richmond Hill—three nearby neighborhoods in Queens, plus an occasional foray into nearby areas of Brooklyn. It was clear, though, that I was on to something significant, and I knew that in some way my career as a retailer was about to change.

It didn't all go perfectly smoothly, however. Telephone sales were still just a tiny fraction of my business, and things were touch and go for a few years. By 1980, I had moved my small furniture store in Queens to a larger store nearby, on Steinway Street, and I had opened a second small shop in Manhattan. Actually, I had rented the street level of three connected apartment houses on Third Avenue and 118th Street, in the section called Harlem. We used one of the sites as a small store, and the other space was turned into a warehouse, which handled deliveries for both stores.

My sales staff had expanded. Instead of one salesperson, there were now two other people, plus myself, working out of the Steinway Street store. Whenever a customer called, one of us would run to the telephone at the back of the floor and try to make the sale. The bulk of our sales still came in the traditional way—from people who came into the store. But I was encouraged enough by the steady trickle of phone calls to increase my advertising. Now we ran ads on the radio, as well as in newspapers.

In 1978 we created our first TV commercial. We couldn't afford the huge prices for prime-time television, or even for spots to run during the day. So we experimented by placing this commercial on late-night TV. It worked far better than I'd ever dreamed it would. It turned out that many people watch late-night television, and some of them were more than happy to be able to do some shopping from their homes. In fact, many of our telephone orders came late at night, right after we ran each TV ad. We didn't have salespeople working nights, during those early years. (Now we're open around the clock.) So we set up an answering machine in a cramped, makeshift area at the front of our Third Avenue store and returned the calls the next morning. (Chapter 4, How to Market, Advertise, and Promote Your Product or Service, tells more about our advertising strategy and provides guidelines you can use in your own company.)

Joe Vicens, who is now General Manager of my entire company, started out working in the Third Avenue store. At first, he was doing the routing for deliveries, and some of the loading. He scheduled deliveries for sales we had made the day before. We had expanded our delivery area to include all five boroughs of New York City. After the trucks made their deliveries, they returned to our warehouse, empty. If it was early enough in the day, they often loaded up with *that day's* orders, and then went out again. We were doing same-day delivery at a time when Macy's made its customers wait six weeks. To reassure customers, who were not used to buying a product sight unseen, we guaranteed them delivery *on approval*. If a customer didn't like the product, or it was "no good," for any reason, the truck would simply take it right back to the warehouse—no questions asked.

The drivers kept telling me how much our customers appreciated our delivery service. I began to realize that the *service* we provided was at least as important as the product. It was at this moment that the true concept of Dial-A-Mattress began. We started making "emergency" deliveries, at customers' requests. If someone needed a mattress in the evening, after our store had closed, we sometimes made deliveries on the top of my blue Granada or on someone else's car. Joe delivered some mattresses on his way home at night, especially if the customers were in our neighborhood. One day, a woman called in desperation and begged us to deliver a mattress that night. Unfortunately for us, she lived way out on Long Island, more than two hours away. So Joe called his wife to explain that he would be home late—*very* late—and he and Jose, one of the first drivers, drove the mattress out on the top of Jose's car.

Normally, of course, we relied on trucks to deliver our merchandise. For a while, Dial-A-Mattress owned one truck and one van. But very early in our corporate history, we started dealing with independent contractors who owned their own trucks. We paid for each delivery according to its distance from the warehouse. Our limit, at first, was a 25-mile radius from the warehouse.

Our record-keeping system wasn't quite as sophisticated as it is today. Instead of computers, we used pieces of paper to keep track of the amount each trucker was due. Every time a driver made a delivery, we gave him one of our advertising fliers (or one-half of a flier, for a short trip or a service call). He would write the Invoice Number on each flier, and put it away somewhere. At the end of the week, the drivers would bring in their fliers, and we'd count the papers and pay each man what he had earned for that week.

One day, Joe strained his back badly. He clearly wouldn't be able to lift a mattress for a while. Even though I hadn't hired him to be a salesperson, I said to him: "Why don't you try the phones?" The first day Joe began selling over the phone was the best day we'd ever had for the telephone part of my company. We sold 14 mattress sets. Thereafter, Joe would play back the answering machine every morning, listen to the messages, screen out the crank calls and wrong numbers, and call back the people who sounded like potentially serious customers.

We didn't offer the top quality brands we carry now. In 1980, we carried only inexpensive mattresses. That's why we were surprised that some of our callers told us that although they had seen mattress commercials by expensive stores such as Bloomingdale's, they had decided to call us instead. These responses validated my assumption that telephone sales would work.

Since Joe Vicens was doing such a good job on the telephone, we had him return all the calls that had come in during the night. When calls came in during the daytime, either Joe took them, or if he was already busy on a call, another salesperson answered the phone and took the caller's name and number, so Joe could phone them back. In time, though, the floor salespeople began learning some of Joe's techniques, and then they, too, made some phone sales.

Joe's technique of telephone sales, which seemed to spring from the head of Zeus, was both brilliant and simple:

- Truly listen to the customer, and ask enough questions to determine exactly what the *customer wants*, not necessarily what you want to sell him or her.
- Try to empathize with the customer's problems and attempt to alleviate them.
- Understand what you are selling so that the customer has confidence in your knowledge.
- Act in a friendly way and do not be afraid to make small talk so as to build instant rapport.

After a while, when it became clear that the telephone portion of my business was growing even faster than the retail store division, I moved the phone business to the Queens store, which was my headquarters. At that time, I applied to AT&T for a "vanity" phone number. A vanity number includes your company's name, logo, or slogan—it's not just numerals. I chose vanity numbers in five different regions: *212–Mattres* (New York City), *201–Mattres* (New Jersey), *914–Mattres* (Westchester County), and *516– Mattres* (Long Island). The first four were our selling and delivery areas—all locations within a reasonable radius of our stores and warehouse. (We also obtained *305–Mattres*, for southern Florida, where many of our customers went on vacation. When we got an order from there, we simply shipped a mattress down.) Owning these vanity numbers meant that customers in each location could reach us through a *local* phone call. People are much less likely to telephone you if it means they have to spend the money to make a long-distance phone call.

By 1983–84, although I still thought of myself as selling furniture, we were in fact selling more mattresses than all of our furniture combined. We didn't carry name brands yet, but we were selling 15 to 16 of our "house brands" per day. It was obvious, though, that some customers wanted quality mattresses. And that was a problem: We couldn't *get* leading brands. Manufacturers of top-of-the-line mattresses didn't want to sell to a telephone marketer, because they were afraid of angering the department stores and large retail stores that were their key clients. And those stores were afraid that their customers would think less of a brand that was carried by a company that sold by telephone, so they pressured the manufacturers not to do business with us.

So we started "jobbing" name brands. There was a store named Jack's Furniture in Manhattan. We started buying top brand mattresses from Jack's, and later on, from Cosmo's Furniture in Queens. They didn't mind selling to us at all—they reduced their mark-up a bit because we were buying in quantity, but they still made a profit. And as we were soon buying relatively large numbers of mattresses from them, both stores were very happy indeed. So were we. We made a little less profit when we sold their mattresses, since we hadn't bought them at the full manufacturer's discount price, but it still gave us the brand names that some of our customers specifically requested.

Joe Vicens would go to Macy's, and to Jack's Furniture, to see what mattresses were out there. Then he'd create a Comparison List of different mattress brands, sizes, prices, and qualities such as firmness, padding, and so forth. (Those one-page lists were the basis for the extensive Comparison Lists we now have on our computers, which are updated constantly.) This list enabled us to decide which specific mattresses to carry—that is, to buy from our jobbers.

We bought so many mattresses this way that the three key manufacturers began to wonder why Jack's Furniture and Cosmo's Furniture were suddenly doing so well. I was sure they knew, sure they were aware that Dial-A-Mattress was becoming a significant retailer of their products. But even as recently as 1986, the representative of a key manufacturer would not come to my store to meet with me. He wouldn't even return my phone calls. That year, however, I was finally able to persuade this company that it was to its advantage to sell directly to us. Nonetheless, the representative was still so worried about alienating his key retail clients that he was afraid to be seen entering my store. So, in true secret agent or spy-thriller style, we met surreptitiously at a coffee shop around the corner and made the arrangements for my company to buy mattresses directly from them. Within the next two years, not only this company but the two other leading manufacturers, as well, reluctantly made the same arrangement with me. All three manufacturers wound up making huge profits as a result of the vast numbers of their mattresses we sell.

The TV commercials were bringing in more business than the newspaper ads, so we expanded our media mix to include local radio shows, to see if they would work for us. By 1986, almost 100 percent of our advertising was electronic, either late-night TV or radio. As an experiment, I hired talk-show host Howard Stern to talk about Dial-A-Mattress on his radio show. The first day his one-man commercial ran, it was enormously successful, and Howard has continued to be the best spokesman for our company. Following the pattern we had now come to expect, our phones were flooded with calls right after we ran a commercial. This meant it was possible for us to anticipate when the major amounts of calls would come in. To my surprise, though, some of the calls came from areas of New York and New Jersey that I had never considered my sales territory. Clearly there were customers in those locations who were willing to buy from me! So in 1986, we doubled our territory, expanding our delivery area to a 50-mile radius.

In 1987 we stopped selling furniture at the Steinway Street store. Instead, we loaded it up with mattresses. Bedding filled the storeroom in the back, and the entire selling floor. It even reached up to the very front, where the phones were. Only a few years before, my salespeople had preferred selling on the sales floor; they considered the telephone calls a distraction. By this time, everyone preferred selling by phone. It had become so effective that they could see the profit potential. Sometimes, however, we needed to sell on the floor, too, because some customers continued to shop in the traditional way—they would come into the store and choose which mattress they wanted. These were becoming the exceptions, though. The telephone portion of my business became so busy that I moved it to my "Brazil" store. I had rented another nearby store in Queens, at 2355 Broadway, where I originally intended to sell the boatload of Brazilian furniture I had purchased. As usual, mattresses outsold everything else, so the "Brazil" store, a five-minute walk away from our main store, became our telephone sales headquarters.

Joe and some of the telephone salespeople moved to the "Brazil" store. I kept one employee at the Steinway Street store, to sell to customers who came in to the store. Greg Nooney, who had started out delivering for us, found himself taking messages while the others were busy with callers. Sometimes he would try to make a sale himself, patterning his telephone technique on Joe's. He did so well that I soon assigned him to telephone selling, full time.

As the business evolved, it seemed a better idea to keep my sales staff together. So in 1988 I turned the Broadway store into a warehouse, and brought everyone back to the Steinway Street, to do floor and phone sales. We had learned that customers needed to be served days and evenings, weekdays and weekends, so the sales staff was divided to cover all shifts.

We continued to run out of room and the company continued to grow, so in late 1987 we moved to 5934 Myrtle Avenue, in the Ridgewood section of Queens. It was 5,000 square feet—a much larger space than I'd ever had, but it hadn't originally been intended for commercial use. In fact, it was really a series of connecting apartments in three attached brownstones that had seen better days. We wound up with a maze of connecting rooms. I divided it into a Call Center, a warehouse, and a small showroom. That sounds much grander than it actually looked. The Call Center was a two-bedroom apartment in the back; we held sales meetings in the kitchen; and phones were set up in the living room, dining room, and bedrooms for incoming calls from customers. The basement held stock and also functioned as our showroom for those customers who were only comfortable buying what they could see and touch. There was a second floor, but since it didn't have a very strong floor, we stored only light, foam mattresses up there. As an indication of our progress, we were now carrying only name brand merchandise.

At this point, though the building was far from glamorous, we had become a "real" company—a significant business that was professionally run. Then we did something that created our greatest sales increase: I obtained a *toll-free* telephone number, *1–800–Mattres*. This simplified all our advertising, since the same ad could now run anywhere in the country, in any newspaper, radio, or television station. No matter where customers saw or heard our ad, they could respond, calling us at no expense to themselves. We started promoting this toll-free number in October of 1988, and sales rocketed dramatically. Our enlarged sales staff—eight people, working under Joe Vicens—were hard pressed to keep up with all the calls. At that time, we also established a Customer Service division, to help us deal with our customers' needs. We installed our first computer system, to enable us to keep track of inventory, sales, deliveries, and all the other details of what had become an extremely complex company. We made $4 million in sales in 1988.

Business flourished, causing an unexpected problem. There

were trucks outside constantly, either delivering merchandise to us, or picking up merchandise to deliver to our customers. Neighbors complained that we were tying up all the parking spaces. And we were, too. Our merchandise "turned" so rapidly that half of it never even got into our warehouse. We simply unloaded the pieces from the manufacturer's trucks and put them right into the trucks making our deliveries.

It was obvious that we needed more space to handle inventory. *Much* more. I rented a big warehouse on Kingsland Avenue in the Greenpoint section of Brooklyn. It was 50,500 square feet—enormous, for us—but I leased it for a very reasonable price, because it was right next door to a city sanitation facility. There were days when the smell was, well, a bit hard to handle. But the greater amount of space enabled us to keep pace with the continually growing number of sales, and the constant need for more and more merchandise. We were finally able to keep all our inventory in this single location and to ship out all our deliveries from there.

Moving the inventory out of the Ridgewood store allowed us to expand our telephone sales division in that location. We still maintained a small showroom, but telephone sales took predominance. I hired many new salespeople to handle the phones, which were now not only on the main floor, but in the basement and upstairs as well. The entire operation had grown so large that we needed to establish some clear division of labor. So we set up departments to handle financial matters, administration, and confirmation. We became an efficient operation.

I was still unhappy having different parts of the company in different locations, however. In 1991, therefore, I moved all the divisions to our current location, in Long Island City in the borough of Queens, and closed all other sites. This allowed me to merge Sales, Warehouse, Distribution, and Operations for the first time since the company began.

Dial-A-Mattress has provided both a product and a service that continues to fill a customer need. This is reflected in our sales figures:

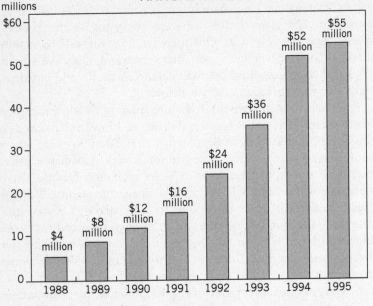

ANNUAL SALES

TELEMARKETING TODAY

When IBM and L.L. Bean followed the catalog companies in using toll-free numbers to sell their products, even traditionalists had to recognize the enormous potential of selling by phone. At that point, vast numbers of companies—from large retailers to manufacturers to entrepreneurs with little more than a plan and a prayer—quickly acquired their own 800 numbers and began setting up telemarketing enterprises. Telemarketing has really become the retailing Big Bang of the twenty-first century, and for those who recognize its power, its validity, and its reach, success is a certainty.

In essence, the technology is enabling us to develop new ways of communicating with each other. The present state-of-the-art of telemarketing, and the inevitable changes that will occur in the future, are as important and profound as any marketing innovation since the introduction of the first mail order catalog. Since telemarketing is dependent on the trends in technology and customer service, it is constantly evolving. As its popularity grew during the 1970s and 1980s, pioneer telemarketers added databases, automatic dialers, computer-based scripts, and least-cost call routing. The creation of computerized databases in the network allowed businesses to advertise a single toll-free number—which people referred to as an 800 number—that could be located anywhere in the U.S. and called from anywhere else in the U.S., at no cost to the caller. The single nationwide number freed businesses from needing different phone numbers in different states. These databases also allowed toll-free calls to be routed to different offices or call centers based on the time of day, the day or the week, or the call's point of origin. The emerging capabilities helped businesses expand their markets and hours of service at a minimal cost.

As the popularity of toll-free calling increased, national advertising began to routinely include 800 telephone numbers. Blue-chip corporations jumped on the toll-free bandwagon; startup businesses learned of its power. Consumers, affluent baby boomers, and women entering the nation's work force discovered a fast, convenient way to shop and, in the process, helped spend the U.S. economy out of recession in the 1970.

The shrinking of leisure time is one of the key factors affecting all aspects of retailing today. It has increasingly led consumers to shop by phone as a timesaving way to obtain products and services. According to a recent survey, American consumers, on the average, have made four toll-free calls in the past three months, and over half of them have made a toll-free purchase during that same time. Annually, 75 percent of American consumers make more than 17 calls to businesses that offer toll-free telephone numbers. Realizing this, retailers and catalog companies of all types are adding telephone and computer sales to their marketing repertoire.

In some ways, telemarketing—selling via the phone—is not the same as traditional retail selling. The most obvious difference is that the customer can't see the merchandise and certainly can't touch it or examine it. Telephone salespeople need to be carefully trained, not only to describe merchandise well, but to determine through carefully conducted conversations precisely what the customer wants and needs so that salespeople can recommend products that customers will like and will *keep,* once delivered.

Person-to-person communication is enhanced. Two people involved in a satisfying one-to-one dialogue are a cost-effective and appealing way to grant the consumer the personalized attention that he or she demands, and deserves.

Immediacy and flexibility are other advantages of the telephone. It enables the telemarketer to gain almost instant feedback. The retailer can make quick management changes in strategy, price, and product because of the constant information flow. Businesses do not have to wait for weeks, or even months, for the accountants to tally up the profit and loss columns. Market research is an incremental by-product of each telephone conversation, and specific market research questions can be woven into the telemarketer's script. The retailer has the flexibility to test different offers (price, size, quantity, etc.), using various creative strategies, and make immediate and inexpensive marketing or pricing changes, without high printing or production costs. This also gives the retailer the opportunity to structure multiple product offerings.

The telephone has a complementary effect when used with other media. It is more effective combined with television than is a television commercial alone, and it is the most immediate cost-accountable direct-response medium, since for every conversation there is an easily quantifiable response.

2

HOW TO MAKE YOUR BUSINESS GROW

Every organization must be competitive and cooperative to succeed. With the many choices available to customers and constituents today, if an organization isn't continuously and aggressively examining its competitive strategy, it can't hope to be successful. In addition, cooperation is becoming even more critical as organizations forge closer relationships with their suppliers and other organizations to compete more effectively while serving customers in the best possible manner.

THRIVING IN CHAOS
TOM PETERS

Some readers may be thinking about or planning to start a new telemarketing business for the first time. Others may already have established companies but wish to add, expand, or improve a telemarketing component. I've tried to write this book to serve both types of needs, so as you read, focus your attention on the portions of each chapter that pertain to your questions. But I suggest that you skim even those parts that don't seem to relate to you. They just may contain information that will be important for your company and your telemarketing operation—if not today, then in the future.

HOW TO GET YOUR 1–800 NUMBER

Expanding your business, or launching a new one, can be as simple as getting a 1–800 number. Here's how you get it: AT&T's system for acquiring and connecting a 1–800 number is essentially easy to do. Call AT&T and request the toll-free hook-up. There is no application to fill out, nor is there an installation fee. Everything can be done through your telephone and AT&T's computers. Your incoming 1–800 calls can ring on your already existing line, or you can have a new phone line installed to receive these calls.

At this writing, the regular service fee is $5 per month to maintain the toll-free line. In addition, each incoming call will cost your company 19 cents per minute from anywhere in the U.S. during normal business hours (8 A.M.–5 P.M. Monday–Friday), and 15 cents per minute at other times. AT&T can have the line connected within 24 hours of your call, and there is no on-site service required. You can also reserve as many vanity numbers as you like, for no additional charge. A vanity number usually consists of seven letters, which can spell out your company's name or slogan. It takes AT&T a few days to clear your request for a vanity number. Please bear in mind that many have already been taken, but thousands are still available.

Before you call AT&T, make a list of vanity numbers that best represent either the name of your company, your logo, or a word or phrase that your customers can easily remember and identify with your company. A vanity number must be a minimum of seven letters (or a combination of letters and numbers), but a few *extra* letters or numbers will work, too.

Some companies need to use eight or nine letters to create a meaningful word. That's okay—the telephone system only pays attention to the first seven digits. Just don't make your vanity number too much longer than seven.

MCI and Sprint also provide toll-free numbers, and as phone companies continue to merge, separate, and remerge into new companies, there may well be additional providers of toll-free service. Before you select one for your use, do some careful comparison shopping to find which company provides the service you need at the best possible prices. You might also ask if the phone company allows you to have vanity numbers, or only numeric telephone numbers.

Some toll-free phone companies also offer *volume discounts* to businesses. A 1–800 call from Los Angeles to New York, for example, may cost a business a certain amount per minute after 10 hours of use, but less per minute after 100 hours of use.

With International Toll-Free Service via AT&T Direct, you can offer the convenience of toll-free calling from more than 130 countries. Calling your domestic toll-free numbers from outside of the U.S. is now as easy as calling from around the corner. International Toll-Free Service via AT&T Direct delivers worldwide telecommunications efficiency with one toll-free number around the world.

Most customers want the convenience of international toll-free calling. You can select the countries from which your company accepts toll-free calls. If you select the option of toll-free calling from a country, your callers first reach AT&T Direct Service by dialing a local access number (toll-free) or by calling from specially marked phones located in airports, hotels, and other convenient locations. They are then greeted by either an English-language voice prompt or an English-speaking AT&T operator who requests the AT&T toll-free number to be reached. (In some countries, pay phones require depositing coins for dial tone.)

If you only need a toll-free *presence* from some countries, you may select countries in which the *caller* is required to pay for the international portion of the call. Callers will be able to reach your AT&T toll-free number via AT&T Direct Service access, and they will be charged AT&T Direct Service international rates for the call. Your company will be charged only for the U.S. AT&T Toll-Free Service portion of the call.

If there are countries from which your company does not want to accept calls, an intercept message can be provided indicating that your toll-free number cannot be reached from the caller's country.

You can use your existing U.S. AT&T toll-free number, and no new equipment is needed. The same toll-free number can be used both in the U.S. and throughout the world. International Toll-Free Service via AT&T Direct is available with most AT&T toll-free services and, in most cases, can be up and running in less than a week.

Because the possible numerical combinations of 800 numbers began to run out early in 1996, after 29 years of increasing use, "888" joined "800" as an additional prefix for toll-free calling. This new 888 prefix has created the availability of eight million new toll-free numbers. If you accept an 888 number to launch or add to your telemarketing campaign, remember that the public is still yet not totally aware that "888" means "toll-free." They *are* familiar with the concept that "800" *does* mean "toll-free."

Therefore, if you begin using an "888" number in your advertising, it is my suggestion that you always—and I mean *always*—add the phrase "toll-free" to your advertising copy so that it is completely clear to the consumer that if he dials "888," there will be no charge to him for the call.

SELECTING A PRODUCT OR SERVICE

Selecting a product or a service for telemarketing is relatively similar to selecting a product or a service for any kind of retailing: the quality of your product is your most important element in deciding what to choose. No matter how dynamic your marketing, promotion, and publicity are, you cannot build a foundation for a business on shoddy or inferior merchandise, or on laggard or deceptive service.

In many ways, a service-oriented business, such as a travel agency or a resume writing and printing company, could be easier and less risky to start than a traditional retail business that sells a product. Because you have little or no inventory in a service, your business will probably require less of a capital investment and no warehousing costs. Such services are usually payment-upon-completion set-ups, anyway, so you don't have to wait 30 or 60 or 90 days in order to get paid.

Although service companies are usually not as prone to be forced out of business by larger competing corporations, even here you must know and appraise what might occur. Think of what happened to many of the smaller copy services when Kinko's went national with 24-hours-a-day service.

I cannot overemphasize the importance of *knowing* about the product or service you want to sell. For example, if you want to sell books by telephone, work in a bookstore for a while before you start your telemarketing operation and learn everything you can about books, including such things as: what sells and what doesn't; what amount of stock is needed for specific titles; what seasonal factors affect sales; what kinds of discounts you should allow in order to remain competitive; the relationship of advertising and publicity to sales; how unsold books are returned to the publishers. In short, through observation and experience, know your product or service *before* you try to sell it by telephone.

If you cannot gain direct experience with your potential product or service, then attempt to read, study, investigate and analyze as much as you can about what you intend to sell.

In selecting a product or a service for telemarketers, be wary of fads. Although you might be able to sell tens of thousands of Tickle Me Elmo dolls or Pet Rocks, once the fad disappears, what do you have? In starting out with a telemarketing business, you need a product or service that has permanence, or staying or repeat power.

That is why selling mattresses by phone has proven to be as lucrative to me as it has. Virtually everyone in the world sleeps on some sort of mattress; it is a high-ticket item that costs an average of $500 or $600 or more; and people replace their mattresses six or more times during the course of their lifetimes.

In general, you might want to consider such recurrent products:

for example, computer software, flowers, health foods, appliances, automobiles, health and beauty products, clothing, furniture, videos, CDs, books, sporting equipment, or food, wine, and spirits.

For a telemarketing business that specializes in service, you might want to consider, for example, a wake-up service, a travel agency, car rentals, tours, an employment agency, a resume service, legal counseling, psychological counseling, carpet and upholstery cleaning, dance instruction, or exercise training.

Of course there are tens of thousands of possible products or services, and combinations thereof, that you can sell by telephone. It is through research on your part, combined with your own passion for the product or service being considered, that you will be able to choose what to sell.

But which product or service, of the hundreds or dozens that you might sell should be the right one to select for testing in a telemarketing campaign? Or if you do not yet have a product or service, how can you come up with a successful telemarketing idea?

The answers to these two questions are not simple at all, but you might consider the following evaluative strategies: If you already have products or services, or perhaps just one product or service, consider talking to your sales personnel and other members of your firm as to what *they* think might be a specific, possible telemarketing venture to begin with. The people in your sales "trenches" might be armed with a great deal of experience and knowledge as to what kind of product or service a customer will respond to and order by phone.

Also, I think it is obvious, although perhaps not readily apparent, that if you have a marketing department or marketing staff, they *must* be involved in helping you to select the product or service for a telemarketing test, and in advising you as to the possible potential of your idea.

Remember that sales progress in this day and age cannot be accomplished without change, and that the first thing you are going to have to do—in addition to radically changing your own view of telemarketing—is to change the minds of your salespeople if they believe, as many do, that your product or service is so unique, so abstract, so unusual, that it just *cannot* be sold over the telephone.

Ask yourself, is the idea realistic? Do you have enough stock or can you reorder or manufacture enough, quickly enough, and with the highest possible quality to fulfill demand? One successful commercial on national television could bring in thousands of calls and hundreds of sales. Will you be ready for them? Can you inspire your personnel to become enthusiastic about selling this product or service over the telephone? Is the product or service that you intend to sell simple enough in concept that it *can* be easily explained over the telephone so that the potential customer can understand it? If your product or service *is* complicated, how can you explain it or describe it in simpler terms?

If you produce enough positive answers to these questions, all of which should be posed to yourself and to your colleagues, you might be able to narrow the field of choice as to which product or service you will begin to test.

What specific product or service do I recommend as a starting point for a telemarketing effort? I may be the wrong person to answer that question, since I truly believe that virtually *any* product or service can be sold over the telephone, from penny candy to multimillion-dollar aircraft, from silverware to rare silver coins.

Of course *certain* services cannot be *conducted* over the telephone. How could a dentist, speaking over the telephone, help anyone with a throbbing toothache (other than by recommending aspirin or some other painkiller)? No, eventually the patient will have to come to the dentist's office for a filling, an extraction, a root canal, and so on. So how could dentists possibly increase their business or their practice with telemarketing? There are many ways. Dentists could:

- Place their 1–800 number on their stationery and in all of their advertising and on a sign that is prominently displayed at their office.
- Call existing patients to remind them of their annual cleanings or check-ups.

- Call past patients to talk about any dental problems that they might be having.
- Place advertisements in newspapers or commercials on radio or television indicating the range of dental services that are available, and invite readers and/or listeners to call.
- Make direct-mail efforts to people in the local community, inviting them to call to learn more about the dental services that are available.
- Call other dentists to determine whether any referrals can be arranged.
- Call patients for payment of overdue bills.
- Hang up a 1–800–DENTIST sign and become part of the national network of dentists, a generic nationwide organization.

Using *your own* imagination and experience geared to the vagaries of your own product or service, and applying some commonsense logic, you will unearth many other ways to telemarket.

Further, although it is not always necessary by any means, if you can provide a clear and attractive photograph of your product, say in a catalog, a direct-mail piece, a newspaper or magazine advertisement, or on television, then when your customer calls, he or she already knows what the product is going to *look* like, and presumably some of the benefits or qualities of that product.

You might even have a videotape developed for your product. When you are attempting to sell a high-ticket item such as a piece of real estate, an automobile, enrollment at a university, or a cruise around the world, for example, a $2 or $3 cost for sending out a videotape extolling and showing the virtues of your product or service, sent to a legitimate prospect, is really an infinitesimal investment.

Should your product be relatively generic—say bananas, bagels, or binoculars—you really don't need a photograph to describe it. When your potential customer calls, all you need do is paint a word picture of your product and answer any specific questions that he or she may have. Obviously, if you are selling a service—such as an educational course or a financial newsletter or a certain type of counseling, for example—you probably don't need an illustration to make the sale, as much as you need a clear explanation of the objectives, goals, and possible result of your service.

Some people feel that the only products that should be considered as telemarketing vehicles are those—such as the mattresses that I sell—for which it doesn't matter what the product looks like. Obviously, if you are dealing with pet food, car batteries, shingles, or diapers, you're lucky. Most people don't care what they *look* like. So from the perspective of a telemarketer, you may have a slight edge on products such as expensive rugs, paintings, or other home furnishings. When shopping for items in the latter group, people usually make their selection based on what the furnishings look like and whether they will fit into their decor. But even here, if you provide *some* illustrative material, you can still sell the product over the telephone.

You might be amazed at what currently sells by telephone. Here is just a partial, random sampling of products and services, as a catalyst, perhaps, to your own idea search. There are tens, if not hundreds, of thousands of other possibilities:

Advertising
1–800–AD–AGENCY

Advertising
1–800–4–BLIMPS
1–800–458–EDGE

Air conditioners
1–800–4–CORIAN

Airline tickets
1–800–FLY–CHEAP

Automobiles
1–800–NEXT–CAR

Bagels
1–800–USA–BAGEL

Banking
1–800–KEY–BANK

Bathroom accessories
1–800–BUS–IKEA

Bed and breakfast
    accommodations
1–800–NY–PALACE

Beverages
1–800–GET–COKE

Bookcases
1–800–43–HERGO

Computers
1–800–E–TECH–SYSTEMS

Counseling
1–800–DIAL–GAY

Cosmetics
1–800–FOR–AVON

Country music
1–800–NASHVILLE

Cruises
1–800–CRUISES

Diamonds
1–800–SAVE–HALF

Discount shopping service
1–800–TELESHOP

Doors
1–800–22–STYLE

Electronic components
1–800–238–ASCI

Elevators
1–800–TRI–STEEL

Envelopes
1–800–ASK–XEROX

Fax paper
1–800–THRU–FAX

Fences
1–800–4–FENCES

Film
1–800–258–IMAGE

Firewood
1–800–FIREWOOD

Flowers
1–800–FLOWERS

Gift baskets
1–800–BASKETS

Gourmet food
1–800–76–CAJUN

Groceries
1–800–U–TEL–BP

Hay
1–800–ANY–SUBJECT

Healthcare products
1–800–90–METRX

Hotel reservations
1–800–243–NYNY

Life insurance
1–800–METLIFE

Investment services
1–800–342–FUND

Labels and tags
1–800–288–IDEA

Language training
1–800–TEACH–12

Legal services
1–800–LAWYERS

Limousines
1–800–LIMOUSINE

Loans
1–800–LOAN–YES

Mattresses
1–800–MATTRESS
1–800–TELEBED
1–800–DIAL–A–MAT
1–800–BUY–SLEEP

Meats
1–800–YUMMY–88

Medical advice
1–800–CHARTER

Mortgages
1–800–CHAMPION

Money market funds
1–800–REPUBLIC

Moving and storage
1–800–DIAL–G.O.D.

NY Yankees merchandise
1–800–YANKEES

Newsletters
1–800–TIE–DOWN

Oxygen tanks
1–800–GRILL–PARTS

Paging systems
1–800–BEEPWEAR

Paint
1–800–937–STYLE

Pet food
1–800–321–PETS

Real estate
1–800–FOR–SALE

Secretarial services
1–800–WORK–NOW

Skiing supplies
1–800–ASK–MODELL'S

T-shirts
1–800–2–ETHNIC

Telephonic Yellow Pages
1–800–POPULAR

Tours
1–800–ATLANTIS

Translators
1–800–227–4–FUN

Trucking service
1–800–TWO–HOUR

Uniforms
1–800–UNIFORMS

Videos
1–800–3–LINKUP

Warehousing
1–800–GO–RYDER

A great many products and services that are introduced into today's economy fail for a variety of reasons, not the least of which is the cost of development. Start-up costs, marketing expenses, promotion, and overhead all seem to mount up before you know it, and sometimes the only way to keep from getting deeper and deeper into the hole, and to avoid sinking below the bottom line, is to abandon what might be otherwise a stellar idea. Usually, one simply does not have the capital to play a lengthy waiting game to determine success.

This is where telemarketing can be of the greatest help: If you plan carefully, train your telemarketers well, select your media with great precision, consider that no matter what your product may be, it is the *service* that is most valuable to your customers— and their feeling of wanting to be given special treatment. If you strive for reliability and quality, and test, test, and test again, and apply some of the techniques and strategies that you've learned from this book, you might have the possibility of a successful telemarketing launch.

As your operation becomes successful, as will other sell-by-phone companies, a growing confidence in the entire telemarketing process will occur among consumers, which, in turn, will help to increase sales in a constantly evolving and revolving syndrome. That is why I believe in sharing as much information about Dial-A-Mattress as I can: The more companies that go into telemarketing, whatever the product or service—and become successful—the more consumers will begin to rely on the telephone for ordering their purchases. All of us in the telemarketing business will prosper, and the customer can only benefit.

And what happens if you fail? Failure can often be highly instructive. It is a sign that you have attempted to surpass yourself. Learn as much or more from your failed experiences as you have from your successes. It is not a disgrace to fail if you truly analyze the causes behind your failures, and then go on from there. But I truly believe, from my own experiences and experiments at Dial-A-Mattress, that an innovative and well-executed telemarketing campaign cannot help but to succeed.

STARTING UP A TELEMARKETING BUSINESS

Starting up a telemarketing business is as difficult or as simple as any other business in terms of legalization. Depending on your city's or state's (and sometimes county's) laws, you will probably need a business license or a Doing Business As (D.B.A.) certificate, which you can secure at your city clerk's office (or ask your bank at which your company has its account where to get a D.B.A. certificate.)

You can set up your telemarketing business in one of several ways, all of which will have an effect on your company's tax structure and also your personal liability, and perhaps even how your company will grow:

1. **Sole Proprietorship:** This is a business that is owned by a single person (presumably you), who controls all of the money and finances. As a sole owner of a business, you will probably make all of the business decisions for your company (working with the advice, perhaps, of your lawyer, your accountant, and your bank loan officer). You will garner all of the profits, and you will also be responsible for all the debts that the business incurs.

    It's important to note that as the sole proprietor of your business, should it go under, you will not be able to collect unemployment insurance.

2. **Partnership:** If you establish your business with another person or persons, you and your partners will be individually responsible for all debts that the company incurs. Usually a partnership is set up with two or more people who pool the money that is necessary to begin the business, and they often share their experience, abilities, and skills, as well. One of the greatest disadvantages of a partnership can occur if one or more of the partners want to buy out one or more of the others, who may or may not want to sell, and agreement cannot be reached as to the worth of the business. Before

entering into a partnership, it is essential that you all determine and agree upon the details of a possible future dissolution, and put them—in writing—into your partnership agreement.

3. **Corporation:** If you incorporate your business under your state's charter, you will not be held personally responsible for any debts incurred. You must charter your corporation, file your company's name with the state's secretary, write up a set of by-laws, name the officers of the corporation, and, if you wish, issue shares of stock.

Although the incorporation process can be a bit complicated, the major advantage is that in a corporation no stockholder is liable for more than the limits of its assets, so no personal liability can fall upon you or the other shareholders.

In addition to issuing and selling shares, a corporation can own property, can sue, and can be sued. An additional advantage is the possibility of "going public," putting your company on the stock market. This provides a means to gain additional financing by selling shares of the corporation. Remember, though, if you sell 50 percent or more of the company, you can lose partial or total control, and may have to bow to the votes of your shareholders.

LEGAL ISSUES

Selling over the telephone really has no special legal issues that are different from any other kind of retail business. As in any business, you cannot break the law, so if you follow all legal requirements pertaining to general businesses, you should have no problems. As with any business, as I've said, you should obtain the counsel of a good lawyer and accountant, who can advise you on all specific issues.

Certain products, such as fireworks and explosives, cannot be shipped by mail in most states, and may have other transportation restrictions as well. Some states have laws governing the transportation of agricultural products across their boundaries, too. Check with the U.S. Post Office and your attorney to determine any restrictions on what you might want to ship.

One possible legal problem might occur in your telemarketing business. It is extremely rare, but I bring it to your attention just to alert you to its possibilities: sexual harassment by one of your sales representatives toward a customer on the phone.

A scenario such as this *could* occur: A woman calls your 1–800 number to place an order. The sales representative likes the sound of her voice, a pleasant conversation results, and he begins to flirt, finally asking her to meet him. Some women will just ignore the advances of the sales representative, order what they called for (or not order, in annoyance), and hang up the phone as quickly as possible. Other women, however, might suffer severe emotional stress and might file a complaint against your company and possibly sue you for sexual harassment.

As the employer of a telemarketing business, you must be aware that this crime—sexual harassment is covered by federal law—could occur. Screen your applicants for telemarketing jobs carefully, to make sure they are emotionally well-balanced, and make sure that all of your telemarketers know that they will be randomly monitored by a supervisor listening to their calls. If you sense that a telemarketer is getting a bit too personal in his or her approach to customers, warn them to formalize their sales strategy in the future. If they persist in this inappropriate approach, terminate them.

In telemarketing, as in any business, you can be found guilty of fraud, which is an intentional deception, a misrepresentation, a concealment, or nondisclosure of facts about your product or service. *Always* deliver to your customer *exactly* what you have advertised, and exactly what the customer has ordered.

I think it is essential for any telemarketing operation to offer a money-back guarantee. Remember, your customer might have some hesitancy in buying your product because he or she can't see it, kick its tires, smell its aroma, or whatever. By providing an unconditional guarantee, or a limited guarantee requiring the customer to return unwanted merchandise within a limited amount of time, you will *greatly* add to your sales, since you will make the customer feel more confident that, in case he has ordered something he doesn't like, he will be able to get his money back. This establishes a certain credibility for your operation. Make sure that your guarantee is prominently stated in every advertisement. Unless you are deliberately selling defective products (in which case you shouldn't be in business anyway), you should stand by what you sell. And if your merchandise is of good quality, the rate of customer return through the use of the guarantee will be relatively light.

Talk to your lawyer and your accountant as to what kind of insurance, and how much, you need to cover all exigencies. You want protection for such things as your equipment, your employees (in case of accidents), your investment, and also for the vehicles that you might use in delivering your product or service. Don't go overboard with too much insurance; it's expensive. But don't buy too little, either; make sure you have enough to protect yourself. Too much coverage will crunch your financial resources with high monthly or quarterly premiums. Too little coverage will give you no real help if a catastrophe or a crisis occurs. And remember, too, that insurance such as workman's compensation is required by law.

CASH OR CREDIT?

In most retail businesses, hard cash is the best transaction. Someone comes into a restaurant, eats his meal, pays the cashier, and leaves. It is simple and uncomplicated. The restaurant owner needn't wait for anything to be processed, and aside from the eventual tax he will have to pay on that transaction and his concern that the cash he just collected might be counterfeit, it is a completed deal.

But cash is *not* the best system in a telemarketing business, unless you are delivering the product in person for a cash-on-delivery transaction. In telemarketing, you save the customer the time and bother of making out a check and filling out a coupon or an order form if you accept his or her credit card number. True, you must pay a percentage to the credit card company, but the credit card has become so pervasive, so international, that there are consumers who simply will not do business with you unless they can use their credit cards.

If you are going to go into the telemarketing business on a serious level, then I suggest that you establish accounts with all of the four major credit card companies: American Express, MasterCard, Visa, and the Discover Card. In the case of MasterCard and Visa, you must deal with a bank in order to set up an account. American Express and the Discover Card are handled directly, and you must apply to them to set up an account.

If for any reason you do not care to, or cannot, establish a business relationship with one of the credit card companies and prefer to take checks as payment for your product or service, then I heartily recommend that you subscribe to Telecheck Service, a company that, for a small percentage, will determine the reliability of the check (whether there is enough money in the bank, *at that time*, to cover it) *before* you ship your merchandise.

But there are other reasons why establishing a non-credit card, check-only business is a poor business move for a telemarketing operation. Suppose a potential customer calls your 1–800 number and orders your product. Unless you can establish a C.O.D. situation, you must wait for the customer to mail in his or her check. Taking the scenario a bit further, suppose the customer never gets around to sending in the check, or decides to buy elsewhere during the interim. You will have lost a sale.

With the use of the credit card, however, the sale is usually completed after the customer gives you his or her credit card number and expiration date. The possibility of your customers' changing their minds—and your losing a sale—has been greatly diminished with credit card sales.

STAFFING A TELEMARKETING OPERATION

How many people do you need to run your company? That answer is as variable as the sizes and types of possible companies. If you're just starting out or have a very small company with a very limited advertising budget, you *could* simply list your toll-free telephone number in your advertisements. Then, when customers phone, you could handle the calls yourself or ask other members of your existing staff to handle them.

If, however, you are going to energetically promote and advertise your business and your toll-free number, try to develop at least a reasonable guesstimate as to how many people you are going to need for your staff.

You will need to provide your telemarketers—your telephone salespeople—with all the knowledge they will need as to price, quality, sizes, and so forth of your new product or service, and the competitors' products or services. (See Chapter Three, Telemarketing: How to Sell by Phone.) Leave enough time for training before you begin advertising your toll-free number, or before you permit a sales representative to handle a call.

It is difficult for me to give you a rule-of-thumb appraisal of how many telemarketers you will need. But your final decision will depend on three key factors: the amount of money you will spend on advertising, the price of the product or service, and how much your potential customers need or want this product or service. For example, if you publish a 200-page catalog of different appliances and you mail out millions of these catalogs to potential buyers, and if your prices are competitive and the quality of your merchandise is high, you might receive thousands of telephone calls within the first week or two that the catalog is received. So you will need hundreds of telemarketers to answer your phones. In addition, since the catalog will remain "live" for perhaps a month, sometimes longer, people could open it up, find an item they want to buy, and telephone your company as long as several months after you send out the catalog.

Similarly, if you buy a half-dozen television commercials

prominently displaying your toll-free number, during a prime viewing time such as the Superbowl, which is watched by hundreds of millions of viewers, you might also receive thousands of responses, but these will come within minutes of the airing of the commercial. By comparison, a small classified ad in a local newspaper might produce only two or three calls in total, depending, of course, on your product, its price, availability, and so on.

Perhaps the following information, based on my own experience, may be of help to you in attempting to calculate your staffing needs for a telemarketing operation. For every $1,000 I spend in advertising, whether it be print or broadcast, billboard or direct mail, I hope to generate $10,000 in sales. From experience, I have found that for each $1,000 spent in advertising, I receive approximately 133 calls. My general closing ratio (that is, the percentage of callers who actually buy my product) is usually 15 percent. That means that for every $1,000 I spend in advertising, my telemarketers will make approximately 20 sales (out of the 133 calls that come in), at an approximate income per sale of $500.

Obviously, if your product or service sells for substantially *less* than $500 (for example, if you're selling blue jeans or audio-cassettes or compact disks), then all other things being equal you would probably receive *more* than the 133 calls per $1,000 ratio. And conversely, if your product or service costs substantially *more* than $500 (for example, if you're selling private jet planes), you will probably receive *less* than the 133 calls per $1,000 ratio.

For the sake of this example, however, if you did receive approximately 133 calls in response to your $1,000 investment in advertising, how many telemarketers would you need on staff? First, bear in mind that each telephone call must be handled politely and responsibly by your telemarketers, *even though it might not necessarily result in a sale at that time.* You will get several different kinds of non-sale calls on your toll-free number:

- Wrong numbers
- General inquiries about the product or service

- Follow-up calls from a *previous* customer (which do not lead to a sale)
- Crank calls
- Calls that do not result in a purchase by the potential customer, for a variety of factors
- Calls from competitors, who are surreptitiously trying to find out what your company is doing

So, of 133 calls that come in, fully 113 or so will not produce any income for you, but will nonetheless consume a good deal of time on the part of your telemarketers.

How long does it take to complete a sale, or to complete a non-sale call? For mattresses, it usually takes us seven minutes to complete a sale (figuring the time it takes to answer the customer's questions, explain the details of the product and alternative styles, sizes, and prices, to take the customer's credit card number, arrange for delivery, etc.). To order Chinese food, by comparison, it might take only five minutes—or less—a call.

Ironically, a call that doesn't result in a sale (other than a wrong number call, which could take only seconds to answer) often takes longer to deal with than one in which the caller makes a purchase. Such calls often take 15 to 20 minutes. Why? Because if the telemarketer senses that it is a legitimate inquiry, and if the caller seems to be interested in buying but has some concerns or doubts that prevent him or her from finally deciding to make the purchase, the telemarketer will continue to try to close that sale as long as it seems feasible. That can take more time than a sale to a customer who is more certain.

The number of telephone salespeople you'll need will also depend on the frequency of those phone calls. Do those hypothetical 133 calls come in at a leisurely rate, perhaps 10 or 12 an hour, during the course of a day? Or do they flood in within minutes of the time your commercial airs on television? The frequency of the calls will depend on the success of your advertisement or commercial, and the medium that you have chosen. With a highly successful radio or TV commercial, you might need as many as 20 operators to handle the influx of calls.

What does this all mean as to your staffing needs? Well, if you placed a $1,000 advertisement in a newspaper, your 133 hypothetical calls might come in over a period of 12 to 16 hours, since people read and respond to a newspaper advertisement at different times during the day. In this case, you might need only one or two operators to handle the entire day's responses.

On the other hand, television and radio advertising usually produces an immediate response, and most of your 133 calls will come in within one hour of the time the commercial will air, forcing you to have a relatively large number of operators to be appropriately staffed.

If your operation is going to rely on direct-mail responses (from catalogs or mailing pieces), the responses may be stretched out over a period of weeks or months, and you can staff your Call Center accordingly. Perhaps you will need only a few telemarketers to handle a large volume of calls, if they're stretched out over a long period of time.

There is another factor that will affect the number of calls you can anticipate. In addition to the amount of money you spend on current advertising, there will be a residual response due to your previous ads, as well as your company's reputation and the brand-name recognition of the products you sell. For example, every once in a while, I eliminate *all* of my advertising for a period of time, and I notice that at first it has little effect on the number of calls that I receive, or on my sales figures! You may ask how this can possibly occur.

Well, the reason is that I have spent many, many millions of dollars in promoting my 1–800–MATTRESS number, and it is imprinted on the minds and in the memories of thousands of potential customers. So when those people want to buy a mattress, they think of Dial-A-Mattress, recall the toll-free number, and call in. They don't *need* an advertisement or a commercial to induce them to call us.

Then why should we advertise at all, you might continue to inquire. The answer is that the residual effect lasts only a short time—perhaps only a few days, certainly not more than weeks. I bring up this point only because it does prove the strength of the remembrance of a toll-free number (especially a vanity number that includes the company's logo or slogan, which makes it easier to remember), and also to warn you that if the name of your product or service is sufficiently well-known, you may have to continue to staff your telemarketing operation, even if you are not running any advertising on a specific day.

There are other factors concerning staffing. For example, there may be certain holidays or seasons in which, no matter how much you advertise, the number of calls will be less than usual. For instance, people usually order virtually nothing by telephone on Christmas Day. Undoubtedly many people are celebrating the holiday with their families, or traveling to see those families, but even those who are not Christian somehow don't shop on Christmas. Yet the days immediately before or after Christmas can be fairly voluminous as far as telesales are concerned. You will have to staff your company accordingly.

Also, during certain times of crisis or tragedy, as in the assassination of a national or world leader, people rarely purchase by telephone. (They don't tend to shop in traditional retail stores, either.) Often, however, during times of adverse weather conditions, such as a blizzard, in which people are housebound, telephone sales figures can shoot up astronomically. Retail stores curse bad weather. Telemarketers love it. Remember that under such conditions, you will need to adjust your telemarketing staff accordingly.

GET ADVICE FROM EXPERTS

In establishing or building a telemarketing business, it is essential that you retain the services of an experienced lawyer, a sharp accountant, and a supportive banker. In searching for these people, don't turn to the Yellow Pages and select *any* name that happens to come to light. Talk to friends, relatives, and/or business associates. Don't ask for the name of a lawyer they happen to know and like. Ask what experience they've had with that individual, what they know of his or her abilities.

Not just any lawyer, accountant, or banker will do for you. You need people who have the expertise to assist you with your telemarketing business. For example, a specific accountant may be excellent for a large corporation that specializes in international commerce. But your company might be small and local, so you might be better off with an accountant who can understand and has experience with all of the peculiarities of your telemarketing operation. It is essential that you choose the right professional match for your needs.

Once you have determined who will help you with your banking, legal, and accounting needs, those individuals will probably be able to guide you through most of the details that you need to know in gearing up your business.

Other ways to gain information and seek advice and assistance may be through:

- **Small Business Administration:** Check with your local SBA (or call Washington, D.C.) to determine whether you qualify for loans, if needed, or for any other information they can give you in establishing your telemarketing business.

- **Service Corps of Retired Executives:** This group not only provides free counseling and information of a general business nature but will also put you in touch with a retired executive who has experience in telemarketing and/or with your product or service, and who might be able to give you seasoned advice as to the vagaries of your business.

- **Superintendent of Documents, U.S. Government Printing Office:** This government office publishes hundreds of publications, some free of charge and some at a nominal charge, that provide details and important information for small businesses, and some are geared directly to telemarketing.

- **Telemarketing Magazine and Call Center Magazine:** These monthly publications deal with all aspects of selling by telephone, from establishing and maintaining a Call Center, to tips on how to save money on toll-free calls.

- **AT&T:** This Fortune 500 company, one of the largest in the world, will not only help you set up your specific telemarketing lines but will also work with you on how new trends in communications can affect your business. They will also give you advice on how to use innovative methods in solving any telemarketing problems that you may have.

- **Business Libraries:** Local business libraries, whether public, private, or academic, might be able to provide you with the information you need about your product or service, your competition, and other telemarketers, as well as details on operations, distribution, and marketing.

- **Information Database:** The U.S. Information Database gives you access to tens of thousands of government documents and official information from federal, state, and military sources, with a simple keyword search. The keyword search does not simply direct the user to another Web site, the actual document itself is retrieved. It is located at http://www.usid.com.

KEEP TRACK OF YOUR DATA

When Dial-A-Mattress first started receiving an influx of sales calls on our 1–800 number, I just kept adding telephones; if one line was busy, the calls would simply roll over from one instrument to the other. However, not long after I had reached about

15 telephones, constantly ringing, I realized we had to computerize our operation to keep track of such things as inventory, availability of merchandise, volume of calls, availability of delivery times, and so forth.

Because the needs of every company are highly individual, I can't tell you specifically how to program your computers. Here are some general guidelines, though, that should be adapted to your particular needs. Establish a software program (with the help of computer experts) that will enable you to pull up on your screen:

- **Order entry:** Your sales representative should have a sales template where he or she can enter all kinds of information about the order: the customer's name, address, and delivery time, and the size, price, and other specifics of the merchandise ordered, etc.

- **Inventory Availability:** Your sales representative will have to know whether the item requested is available, when it will be restocked, whether it can be back-ordered, etc.

- **Credit Card Transaction:** The financial transaction between the customer and the sales representative must be recorded as to credit card number, expiration date, etc.

- **Database of Previous Transactions:** Your screen should indicate whether the customer has purchased from you before, when, what he or she bought, and how much he or she spent.

- **Possible Sales Scripts:** You might consider having an actual "canned" script on the screen, so the sales representative can read right from it.

One of the systems that we use at Dial-A-Mattress is AT&T's Accumaster Services Personal Computer (ASPC) software, which allows electronic access to AT&T data, via a personal computer, over a simple, dial-up link. The program is based on Microsoft Windows and is, therefore, easy to use.

The ASPC program provides us with information on each 1–800 call that we have received. The data that are stored can be arranged and displayed in virtually any way that we want: by date, time of day, area, 1–800 number, the callers' phone numbers, the length of the call, and additional data.

We study this data and use it to track the response to our commercials and advertising, which helps us to forecast staffing needs and collect phone numbers for callbacks to complete a sale.

With this data available, especially on the volume of calls, we know within two minutes or so whether we have a vast increase, a "spike." We then have to make arrangements to immediately increase our staff to handle the influx.

There are literally thousands of computer consultants who can help you with your specific programs. Some of them are listed in your Business Yellow Pages. There are also some off-the-shelf programs that you can buy from large computer software stores to help you get started. Software and consultants directly dealing with telemarketing are also listed in the back section of *Telemarketing*, *Target Marketing*, and *Call Center* magazines. If you are about to purchase a fairly large amount of computer hardware, talk to the computer companies—IBM, Apple, or whatever—and see if they can suggest your best software options.

If you are selling diamonds, for example, your entire operation may be kept in a closet-sized vault, and you can ship your gems, perhaps once a day, through a reliable common carrier, such as DHL. Compare that with a company such as mine, which has huge inventory problems, stores mattresses in a number of locations, and deals with dozens of trucks that have to be dispatched all over the tri-state area and beyond, with hundreds of deliveries each day. The differences in computer software needs are vast. You have to tailor-make your software to handle your company's specific needs.

INVENTORY: TO STORE, OR NOT TO STORE?

If you are selling fairly large-size products, such as the mattresses that I sell, you will *probably* have to have someplace to store them: a warehouse or, in the current vernacular, a distribution center. I stress the word "probably" because there are several ways to get around buying or leasing your own warehouse space.

First, what exactly *is* the size of your product? You can probably fit 25,000 lapel pins, one-inch-long, into the average apartment-size closet. I know of an independent book publisher who keeps his entire stock (a few thousand books) in a large walk-in closet in his apartment on Central Park South in Manhattan. If you *are* dealing with a smallish-size product, such as bow ties, dental mirrors, wrist watches or fountain pens, you might consider keeping your inventory in a basement, a spare room, a garage or an attic. You can also lease a small storage space that might be able to hold most or all of your products, usually for less than $100 a month, in a warehouse that rents out space. Then, as you need to ship out products to your customers, you can visit your storage space (or basement or closet) once each week or so, or on demand, to secure the amount of products that you need to ship.

Storing large-size products, such as furniture, office equipment, large appliances such as refrigerators or washing machines, or certain sporting or exercise equipment, often takes ingenuity in determining and fulfilling your space requirements. If you must lease or buy a warehouse, see Chapter Five to learn how to operate it efficiently. Whatever you do, especially if you are just starting your business, look for the most inexpensive space you can find. Remember that your warehouse is not your showroom, and it probably doesn't have to be high-tech, or decorated by a famous designer.

Here are a few other possibilities to consider, too. Determine whether your manufacturer, supplier, or distributor can store your merchandise at *his* facility. Often this can be arranged, especially if he is interested in securing your business on a regular basis. It is also possible that you can arrange to have your supplier drop-ship your product for you. This means, simply, that the supplier himself will ship the products directly to your customers. There are some businesses whose executives and employees in the front offices rarely see the product that the company is selling. It is manufactured, packaged, and shipped at another location, perhaps thousands of miles away, and perhaps by a totally independent company.

Another idea, one that I have been particularly successful with, is leasing or buying a warehouse, and then sub-leasing some of the space to my own suppliers, should they happen to need warehousing in my area. It's also possible, to lease space on an ad hoc basis to any company that needs it. If you can secure commitments (in writing, please!) before the fact, it is possible that a bank will lend you the money you need to buy or lease a fairly large warehousing facility. As your business grows, you then take over more and more of the warehouse yourself, as needed, for your own products.

Bear in mind that if you begin to lease space to others, you will have the responsibilities of a landlord, with all of the headaches that such a role implies. Someone in your company will have to take charge of dealing with the everyday problems of your renters, and that means that person will not be able to be totally involved in the marketing or sales aspects of your business.

A third innovative idea depends on the specific product you sell. Some products, such as videotapes and audiotapes, or special plaques or trophies, are or can be made on demand. When you receive an order, you create a copy of the tape. It is always wise to keep some copies on hand, but there's no need to stock much of an inventory for such items because they can be produced very quickly, as long as you have an adequate source for supplying blanks.

EXPANDING AN EXISTING BUSINESS

If you are satisfied with the scope and activity of your business and are tempted to rest on your laurels, you really *need* to read this book. Satisfaction can mean death to a business. As long as you continue to reach for a goal, and have the wish to succeed or grow, your business will continue to prosper or at least maintain its status quo. There is a direct relationship between how pleased you are with your operation and the erosion of your business. Financial success increases in direct proportion to the amount of energy you put into your company.

Whatever prosperity I have had with Dial-A-Mattress, I owe to my restlessness with what I had achieved. Whenever I began to have a feeling of contentment, or of having "arrived," I equated the sensation with indolence. I simply would not rest, and I continually pushed my business to grow and expand.

Some companies make the mistake of becoming greedy. They become determined to make large profits on each and every sale. That is not what the founders of major retailing establishments, the Macy's and Bloomingdale's of the world, intended. Those mercantile pioneers would be horrified if they knew what a travesty their businesses have become.

The underlying philosophy they set forth from the beginning, of *satisfying the customer*, has been completely scrapped. If only the current retail owners and managers had paid attention to the plans of the founders, they wouldn't be experiencing the financial crises that several of them are experiencing now: Complacency leads to poor service, which leads to the loss of customer loyalty. These problems have caused several department store chains to go bankrupt and others to close many of their branches. They could someday lead to the possible death of traditional retailing.

That's a fear that I have, the fear of growing complacent. You must always recognize complacency in your business and always fight against it. In order to prosper in business, you must be eager to learn from the successes of others and be determined to avoid their errors. Study and understand some of the great merchants, such as Sam Walton, the founder of Wal-Mart. He started off like me, with nothing, and turned into the biggest retailer, not only in history, but in the world. What Sears, Roebuck & Co. took 100 years to build, he did in 20. Sears has now slithered down the same path that Macy's and Bloomingdale's are now wandering. They diversified so much, but never had a clear plan, a *weltanschung* of their own business.

By contrast, Sam Walton's business plan was always about selling wares. He turned his business into a super-hardware store and began adding to his product line, all the while keeping his basic strategies intact. He has now passed the company on to his children.

Take the time to learn all you can about companies that have become famous for their excellence in customer service: Nordstrom, which grew from a chain of local shoe stores to an immensely profitable nationwide chain of department stores; and the top mail-order companies, Lands' End, Fingerhut, L.L. Bean and Spiegel. All of them now have well-organized, well-staffed, and highly profitable multimillion dollar telemarketing divisions that could become excellent models for your own company.

There have been many articles written about these companies. Insert their names into your library's computer for both newspaper and magazine sources to learn more about them. It is possible that these companies will also supply you with additional information if you want to contact their public relations departments.

Many people think that criticism is negative, and they try very hard to avoid being criticized. I thoroughly disagree with that sentiment! If you fail to admit that anything is wrong with your operation, you will never be *able* to correct it. And criticizing the established method or system takes courage and hard work. As difficult as it is to accept, encourage your employees, your suppliers, and your customers to tell you what is wrong. Encourage yourself to do the same thing. Do this on a regular basis. Keep looking for what's wrong, so you can make it better. If you never shake the tree, you'll never enjoy the apple.

Remember that you can't always be on top. I don't see Dial-A-Mattress, for example, as currently being at the summit, but as a renegade trying to upset the proverbial apple cart. That's what I'm going to be doing with the rest of my life, striving for more: achievement and fulfillment for myself, stability and comfort for my family, security and prosperity for my employees. I am also committed to the development of communications, internationally, to improve health care, education, and many other existing social conditions. That's my life's mission.

I believe that in order to even *survive* today, already existing businesses must make fundamental changes in the way that they're run, how their employees are trained and treated, and the ways that corporations can learn to collaborate with each other. Businesses must also learn to contend with the new technology that is changing the way products and services are delivered.

Are you old enough to remember when people bought provisions from the corner grocery store and the owner tallied the cost of the groceries on the back of a brown paper bag? Compare that with the electronic checkout counters at the gigantic supermarkets all over this country today, most of which now use bar-coded transactions. Not only is there less chance of error on behalf of the consumer, but the system allows each store to keep a constantly updated record of its inventory so that it always knows what is selling and what is not. This helps the store market its products better, replace or remove them if needed, and improve their presentation and delivery. The technology helps all concerned: the consumer, the supermarket, the distributor, and ultimately the manufacturer.

You've heard of the term "re-engineering your business." Daniel Morris and Joel Brandon, principals of a Chicago-area management consulting firm, have written a book on that subject, which is an excellent plan for reassessing, repositioning, and restructuring your business for greater market presentation. Although Messrs. Morris and Brandon do not touch upon telemarketing directly, as this book does, what they have to say is important:

Re-engineering is both the fundamental and ultimate tool of change. Re-engineering addresses the business process, which is the means by which work is done, whether by people or machines. In its present state it is helping to adjust business from the old industrial paradigm to a new one of service and information. In the future, it will continue to move business from one paradigm to the next.

As re-engineering is used, it will itself undergo several paradigm shifts. Business is going through one now, but there is at least one more on the horizon: the second paradigm shift—using continuing change for competitive advantage. . . . The businesses that gain the most will be those that can assimilate the most new technology and take advantage of opportunities with the least delay. They will be the businesses that equip themselves to change.

Re-engineering Your Business
Daniel Morris and Joel Brandon, 1991

There are corresponding, and often conflicting, advantages and disadvantages, problems, and opportunities, for business as we near and enter the twenty-first century. Inflation will not disappear, although some economists believe it will lessen. Foreign competition, already besting us in many areas, will probably only increase in its intensity. Employment will continue to shift from our traditional agrarian and industrial society toward a more service-oriented one. Our work, as business people, is to confront the economy, and make the most out of what we have.

I truly believe that the telephone and some of the other technology that is available to us *right now* is the key for the success of most businesses. The telephone is such an incredibly useful instrument, and not only for marketing, of course.

Recently I set up a conference call with eight of my daughter Bibi's doctors, all of whom had been treating her for years, but who had never met each other. In a matter of a few minutes, a diagnosis was confirmed and other information shared about her, saving all kinds of time-consuming and, perhaps, wasteful treatments for her in the future.

Also, during a business trip to Minneapolis, I set up a conference call with my daughter Kay, in Cleveland, and her children Sarah and Luisa, and my son Luis in New York. We had a wonderfully heart-warming family visit that just could not have taken place at that time without the telephone.

What we need in this country are more ways to exploit our *existing* opportunities, not necessarily anything other than what we have. The new technology already exists, it is available to virtually any businessman, and it is beginning to shake the entire retailing and marketing industries to their very foundations.

Often, people cannot recognize what opportunities they have right in front of them. I'm thinking of a young inventor named Chester Carlson, who developed a "black box" capable of reproducing images not on film, but on plain paper. He took his invention to literally dozens of blue-chip manufacturers. And wherever he went, whether it was General Electric or RCA, he was turned down. It wasn't until he had continued to try for ten years that the Haloid Company decided to take a chance on Carlson. The process he'd invented came to be know as "Xerography." Now wouldn't you like to have been in on the beginning of Xerox? Would *you* have recognized its potential?

Presumably, you have a product or service, or an idea for one. Each idea has a life of its own, and as Goethe has written: "Daring ideas are like chessmen moved forward; they may be beaten, but they may start a winning game."

What I am saying is that your product or service is alive in itself, *and how you believe in its growth will strongly determine what it can become.* I believe that telemarketing is going to revolutionize the retailing industry and how services are going to be rendered. It already has started doing this. I can actually *see* it. It takes a bit of creative visualization to conjure up your product or service to an elevated position of possibility, but it is not all that difficult to do so. You must follow your dreams. Not to do so is a form of psychic suicide.

At Dial-A-Mattress I try to teach all of my employees that every experience is a learning opportunity. Some of my closest aides have fought me on this. They are so involved in their daily routines, so pressured to "put out fires," so harassed to hit the daily, weekly, monthly, or annual goal, that they cannot, or will not, allow new experiences, new methods of doing things to enter their realms. They think that I'm too innovative, too eager to try the "new"—especially if they see that it will cost a few dollars and that the immediate income potential is highly speculative. Louis Agazziz, an eminent zoologist and geologist, once said that he could not afford to waste his time making money. I cannot afford to waste my time thinking of ways to hold on to it. Whenever I experiment with something new, I invariably come upon some nugget of information and insight that I did not seek in the first place.

Perhaps some of my colleagues are not comfortable with the new technologies. I must admit that the innovations of software alone can be overwhelming, but we must learn to conquer what is becoming an integral part of the telemarketing process.

Whatever your business, product, or service, telemarketing, if conducted intelligently and carefully using a toll-free number, will add to your progress. Some marketers will tell you that telemarketing is a highly complex field where expensive call centers must be established, intricate equipment purchased, and extensive and costly training employed, before you can even think of adding it to your sales efforts. Although I am well aware of the complicated applications of the field—I live it seven days a week—I believe, nevertheless, that you can start immediately, as I did.

Don't misinterpret what I'm saying: I don't think that in order to be successful all you need do is publish your toll-free number somewhere, have one phone on the corner of your desk, pick it up when it rings, take the order, and let the money roll in.

Nor do I think that the automation of outbound calling—where the consumer receives a message from a computer—really works; nor do I approve of it. It's simple, but perverse, actually: The computer calls numbers from a list. If no one answers, or if the phone is busy, the computer keeps redialing that number.

When the consumer finally picks up the phone, he or she is hit with a computerized message, usually by a booming, male voice. I think that kind of selling gives telemarketing a bad name and should be discouraged, even if it works, which I doubt.

No, telemarketing is much more difficult and sensitive than that, and to be successful in the field, you will have to use the sum totals of all of your imagination, perseverance, common sense, and intelligence in order to make a go of it. The attractiveness of telemarketing, however, is that it can be applied to virtually *any* product, *any* service, from electrolysis to electrodes, from exporting to exterminating. Although I am selling more mattresses by telephone than anyone else in the world, I am experimenting with other products and services as well, all sold over the telephone: from bagels to books to boxes; from $30,000 automobiles to $500,000 homes; from expensive Turkish carpets to cases of pet food.

Although I believe that you can start your telemarketing campaign under easy sail, I do not believe that it should be relegated to a secondary position in your marketing plans. If you are feeling pressure with your existing sales figures, maybe it's time to stop doing more of the same. Your sales might get worse, unless you consider changing your marketing strategy and tactics.

LEADING YOUR COMPANY TO SUCCESS

The Small Business Association suggests that there are four characteristics that are the benchmarks of success: personal drive, ability to deal with people, ability to communicate with others, and the technical knowledge necessary to thoroughly understand and explain your product or service and to run your business smoothly. Nothing is so contagious as personal drive and enthusiasm. To the extent that you can convey your own energy and belief in your product or service to your employees, you will dramatically influence their attitudes and job performance. The model of your personal drive will transform lackluster employees into highly productive personnel. It will charm your already effective people into achieving business victories that they can barely dream of now, as they begin to hitch their individual wagons to your star.

Equally important is your ability to deal with people: with your employees, and with people outside of the company with whom you do—or want to do—business. You must look *into* people as well as *at* them, and realize that almost everyone really has three aspects of personality: that which he exhibits, that which he has, and that which he thinks he has. All three forms of character may be in conflict with each other, and it is your job to try to understand all of them and, as businessman/teacher, help the individual integrate himself in order to achieve all that he can be. Get to know your employees and those who service your company, attempt to find their weaknesses and strengths, and then guide them to help themselves in strengthening their weaknesses.

Your ability to communicate with others is paramount if you really want to succeed. You might have the best intentions in the world and truly understand the dynamics of a problem, for example, but unless you can convince others of what you know and what you want, you'll go nowhere. The recipe for success in communications includes the use of a variety of approaches (for example, put it in writing *and* bring it up at a personal meeting; say it over the telephone *and* demonstrate it in a visual presentation); preparation on your part so that you have facts and purposes straight (you might consider constructing a script that you can use); and repetition. Say it over and over again, occasionally using other words and examples to illustrate your points, until the listener has no other alternative *but* to understand.

Although you may not know all of the intricacies of a situation, study it enough to master at least its basic concepts. For example, you may not have complete knowledge of the most highly complicated computer programs; that's all right, because you can hire experts to install them. But if you are going into the computer business, or are going to use computers in your company, you must understand *something* of their technical dynamics.

I understand all of the intricacies of bedding, but quite frankly, I am not thoroughly conversant with some of the technical details of how my highly sophisticated computer operation works. . . but I *do* understand the basics.

Suppose that you are selling legal services by phone: You must understand the essence of contracts, torts, appeals, and all other elements of the law. If you're selling pizza pies you must know what constitutes the best kind of cheese, where to buy the most flavorful tomatoes, and which brand of oregano your customers prefer. When you don't know something, such as making a television commercial, for example, or building a sloop, setting up an accounting system, or whatever, hire appropriate experts to fulfill your needs. But you must know what you want your experts to accomplish, and be able to convey your requirements to them.

Look at and fill out the worksheet *Personal Traits Important to a Business Proprietor* (pages 56–57), to help you assess your personal and business styles, and see what traits are your strongest. When negativity arises with distributors and suppliers, keep some of these more positive elements in mind and apply them, as tactfully as you can, with the principal decision-maker. You can actually use variations of some of the statements of affirmation in the left-hand column as an introductory script or ice-breaker, followed by an elaboration on your part as to why they are pertinent to having them do business with you.

In effect, look upon your telemarketing business or service as a laboratory, in which you will be learning how to market by integrating your telephone with other forms of technology, and you will have the opportunity to practice and refine, on an ongoing basis, what you need to know in order to make your business a success. One of the definitions of success, to my mind, is the ability to know how long it will take to succeed. Of course, you cannot know precisely how long it will take, but eventually you will succeed. I assure you, however, that you may slip before you can walk confidently.

Although it is not easy to admit, failure, or the making of mistakes, is actually the foundation of success and the means by

PERSONAL TRAITS IMPORTANT TO A BUSINESS PROPRIETOR

Instructions: After each question place a check mark on the line at the point closest to your answer. The check mark need not be placed directly over one of the suggested answers because your rating may lie somewhere between two answers. Be honest with yourself.

Are You a Self-Starter?

I do things my own way. Nobody needs to tell me to get going.	If someone gets me started, I keep going all right.	Easy does it. I don't put myself out until I have to.

How Do You Feel about Other People?

I like people. I can get along with just about anybody.	I have plenty of friends. I don't need anyone else.	Most people bug me.

Can You Lead Others?

I can get most people to go along without much difficulty.	I can get people to do things if I drive them.	I let someone else get things moving.

Can You Take Responsibility?

I like to take charge and see things through.	I'll take over if I have to, but I'd rather let someone else be responsible.	There's always some eager beaver around wanting to show off. I say let him.

How Good a Worker Are You?		
I can keep going as long as necessary. I don't mind working hard.	I'll work hard for a while, but when I've had enough, that's it.	I can't see that hard work gets you anywhere.

Can You Make Decisions?		
I can make up my mind in a hurry, and my decision is usually okay.	I can if I have plenty of time; if I have to make up my mind fast, I usually regret it.	I don't like to be the one who decides things. I'd probably blow it.

Can People Trust What You Say?		
They sure can. I don't say things I don't mean.	I try to be on the level, but sometimes I just say what's easiest.	What's the harm if the other fellow doesn't know the difference?

Can You Stick with It?		
If I make up my mind to do something, I don't let anything stop me.	I usually finish what I start.	If a job doesn't go right, I turn off. Why beat your brains out?

How Good Is Your Health?		
I never run down.	I have enough energy for most things I want to do.	I run out of juice sooner than most of my friends seem to.

(Source: Small Business Administration)

which it is achieved. Errors can be instructive, and if you can sustain a certain alertness and sensitivity toward them, you will learn quite as much from your failures as from your success. I embrace failure. My greatest strides have come after I have taken some steps backward. You can't predict the turning point, but you must be confident that with diligence, constant practice and the accumulation and sharing of information, you will succeed in the telemarketing business.

I cannot overemphasize the need to practice your business, since only through practice will you develop the expertise that you need in order to succeed. To constantly practice your business is one of the most effective means of advancing and preserving your operation. When I'm talking about expertise in telemarketing, I don't mean merely training your sales consultants, the people who talk directly to the customers, but your entire personnel, whether small in numbers or great. The intelligence and training of your work force is your key to succeeding fully in the telemarketing business.

I like to think of Dial-A-Mattress as something of a university, a marketplace of ideas, rather than just a business, and we operate our company more like a campus, not a sales operation or a warehouse for mattresses. We continually attempt to raise our own standards. Just as any university should, Dial-A-Mattress commits ourselves to excellence and the pursuit of knowledge, which flows from free inquiry and our own dedication and experience. Since truth, research and imaginative methodology are the basis for teaching, we pursue these ends in order to enlighten our staff and executives. I suggest that you run your telemarketing operation in the same way.

3

TELEMARKETING— HOW TO SELL BY PHONE

Marketing requires separate work and a distinct group of activities. But it is, first, a central dimension of the entire business. It is the whole business seen from the point of view of its final result, that is, from the customer's point of view.

MANAGEMENT: TASKS, RESPONSIBILITIES, PRACTICES
PETER F. DRUCKER, 1974

Selling by phone requires a different set of skills than selling in person. Since my company began as a retail store, we were familiar with face-to-face communication with customers. We could see how they reacted to the different merchandise and how they responded to the information we gave them about merchandise, prices, and other sale issues, and we could judge pretty well when each customer needed or wanted more information or assistance. It's not that easy to develop and maintain such a close awareness of your customer's reactions when you can't see the person with whom you're talking. And, of course, it's also difficult for potential customers to develop trust in salespeople they can't see, or to feel secure about buying a product they can't see, touch, sit on, or try on.

To overcome these problems, we've developed a system of selling techniques specifically geared for telemarketing—selling by phone. They're based on the best of traditional sales techniques, but they have been adapted for this new retailing method—and they work! To use telemarketing effectively, you'll need to master such techniques and set up a training program to enable your salespeople to learn them. No matter how good a person may be when he or she is selling in a store or any other face-to-face situation, it still requires some study—and some practice—to convert those skills into effective telephone-selling skills.

As you can deduce from our advertising, Dial-A-Mattress gets its customers from people who *call us*. This is called inbound telemarketing. Whether you choose to use this system, or have your salespeople make calls *to* prospective customers (outbound telemarketing), or combine both processes as we may do soon, your salespeople will need to become proficient in this dynamic new method of selling. They will need to become not salespeople, but *telemarketers*; not order-takers, but experts who can really act as advisors to the customer.

One of the most important things in establishing a telemarketing business is to have a strong sales training program, and such a program should exist whether you have dozens or hundreds of telemarketers or just one person answering the telephone. At Dial-A-Mattress we have a very precise method that all of our prospective sales employees go through. The first day of training is dedicated, in part, to an overview of our company. Your salespeople are going to *represent* you, not merely sell your merchandise. We give our new telemarketers a complete overview of Dial-A-Mattress: who we are; where we are going; our organizational structure; even our advertising and marketing programs. We teach them which departments and individuals they'll interact with and explain the functional structure of the company, the *process*—what happens after an order is taken. (For example, the delivery department must put this order onto its schedule, and so on.)

Once the trainees have a strong sense of the company and our objectives, we begin to present our product line-up, which each of them must learn in absolute detail. Then we introduce them to the specifics of telephone selling, which includes general ways to greet a potential telephone customer, ways to improve communication, how to listen so that you understand what customers are *trying* to tell you (the customers may not express themselves clearly), qualifying what the customer seems to want to buy, building rapport (trust), overcoming objections, and developing a closing technique to complete the sale.

Whatever you're selling, it's essential that your salespeople be given a thorough indoctrination before you allow them to handle a customer. We do a lot of "play-acting," with experienced salespeople taking the role of callers, so trainees can practice talking to "potential customers." Real customers can sense how well-prepared a sales consultant is and how much knowledge he or she has about the product. If a salesperson is not sufficiently prepared, not only might he or she lose that specific sale, but an unhappy customer can badly hurt your reputation.

Remember that whatever product or service you are selling has its own specific features, and these influence the way your salespeople should speak to potential customers. A person calling a lawyer for legal advice looks for a different response than a customer wanting to order a bouquet of roses to be delivered on Valentine's Day. Your company needs to develop an understanding of your market and convey this to every salesperson. The requirements for each market—and each customer—must be understood so that they can be dealt with individually to guarantee each sale.

For example, at Dial-A-Mattress we have our Bedding Consultants-in-Training become familiar with an entire glossary of bedding terms, so that, if necessary, they can better explain even the most minute and technical details to the on-the-phone consumer. Create such a glossary of your own products or services. Here are some examples from ours:

Bonnell: A knotted, round-top, hourglass-shaped steel wire coil.

Border Rod: A heavy-gauge wire rod attached to the perimeter of the innerspring unit by means of a helical wire or metal clips.

Flanging: The process whereby a strip of fabric is sewn to the edge of the mattress cover and, in the assembly process, secured to the perimeter of the innerspring unit to prevent the cover and filling materials from shifting.

Torsion Bars: A type of spring system used in box springs, characterized by square-shape wire forms.

As you can see, our terms include a good deal of detail. Yours should, too. Make sure your telemarketers know *everything* there is about your product or service and that they are *au courant* as to the latest, most pertinent terms that could possibly arise as a result of a consumer's questions.

Our initial training is a comprehensive program to deliver the knowledge, skills, and abilities necessary for sales representatives to effectively and efficiently respond to customers' inquiries and concerns. It generally consists of a four-week classroom training structure, followed by 2 to 4 weeks of side-by-side training with advanced salespeople, supervisors, and training support staff.

We incorporate many personal development games, exercises, and videos into our training classes, as well as utilizing video cameras for self-analysis. The instruction is provided by our training staff, who work in close cooperation with many other departments to insure that our trainees get the practical knowledge they'll need.

At Dial-A-Mattress we ask all of our managers and directors to share their respective areas of expertise, and we rely on our vendors to deliver a portion of the product knowledge to the sales-consultant trainee. We move from the general to the specific, as the trainees' knowledge and understanding of the operation and industry deepen and they learn all the details of our merchandise. Here are the key facets of our sales training program. Though we use it to sell mattresses, you will find that the system can be used to sell virtually any product or service—including yours.

By the way, we've found that speaking with customers as a telemarketer is an excellent way to learn what makes consumers happy versus what makes them unhappy and, therefore, what our company needs to do to ensure a continuing good business. So, assuming that your managers and directors thoroughly understand the product or service that you are selling and the dynamic of the customer/sales representative relationship, all managers or directors—no matter what their positions in the company, whether it be computers, delivery, or bookkeeping—should spend at least one day a year selling by phone in order to gain even further insight into the telemarketing process.

We have recently initiated a new system, in which all of the directors of the company, whether from operations or sales, from the legal department or marketing, call a certain number of those customers each day:

- Customers who have purchased our products, to see if they are satisfied with the sales transaction, the delivery, the product, and so forth.
- People who did not buy, to see if we can find out what went wrong, correct the problem, and "convert" this rejection to a sale.
- People who called us and then hung up.

We do this last procedure to separate the crank callers from potentially interested buyers, to try to complete the sale.

The process of having directors make these calls teaches them how to sell, how to deal with customers, and gives them an insight into the business that is invaluable. United Parcel Service and Nordstrom. have similar programs. In the former case, all new executives of UPS must actually work for a short period on their trucks delivering parcels, so that they become knowledgeable about their customers; and in the latter, all executives of Nordstrom spend a minimum of two weeks every year on the floor, selling in various departments, to provide a rapport with the customer and the other employees and so that they can discern the problems of the sales efforts.

One of the points that we stress in our training is The Psychology of a Winner. This consists of leadership and commitment and a Team Methodology that links the salesperson with the customer, so the telemarketer thinks in terms of *We* (himself *and* the customer) and not *Me* (himself *against* the customer). It is extremely important to find out who your customer is during each sales call; what he knows and what he does not know; what he *says* and what he *means*—and they are not necessarily the same. Sometimes a customer does not know how to explain what product he has in mind. The closer the salesperson gets to his customer, the closer he is to a sale.

Another important point that we stress in our training (indeed, an underlying factor in every aspect of training) is "how can we turn the calls we receive into sales." Yet it's also important to realize that not every call will result in a sale.

For example, out of approximately every 1,000 calls, 100 or so are just trying to find information on price, type of mattresses offered, and so on; another 100 or so just call to give the operator a hard time and have no intention of buying anything. (These callers are either what we call "cranks" or children playing with free telephone calls.) There are also, inevitably, a certain number of "abandoned calls"—that is, a call that is answered by the sales representative, but is then hung up or disconnected before any opportunity for conversation begins. Although these calls, too, must be answered by your salespeople, and it takes time to do so, they obviously lead to nothing. I only mention them because you must understand that not every single call will represent a sale, through no fault of your sales representative.

Out of what remains of all the calls we receive, about 500–600 have already decided to buy a mattress and are calling us to see what we have to offer. That group of "core customers" is the prime target market for the salesperson.

DEVELOP A CORPORATE POLICY MANUAL

Before you set your salespeople in front of their phones, they will need to know how your company intends to deal with all foreseeable situations. Decide on all of your policies and procedures, and then incorporate them into a Corporate Policy Manual.

The booklet should include your company's policies and procedures on discounts, returns, guarantees, damaged merchandise, and other situations that your telemarketers will need to deal with. This will ensure that your salespeople will have a standard response for each type of situation. Here are some of the items you should include:

- Payments by cash, check, credit card, layaway
- Manufacturer's warranty/guarantee
- Pro-rated warranties
- Defective merchandise, or merchandise damaged during delivery
- Merchandise replacement or parts replacement
- Thirty-day trial use period
- Exchanges
- Credits and/or refunds
- Delivery fees
- Redelivery fees for merchandise exchanges
- Delivery on approval
- Pick-up policy for unwanted merchandise
- Tips for drivers
- Discounts
- Procedures for using UPS and/or Federal Express

As you explore the ways you do business, you will come up with more items to include in your manual. Periodically, test your salespeople on their knowledge of the Corporate Policy Manual.

It is also helpful to create a set of *Dear Customer* letters, which might be needed to cover any type of foreseeable problem situation. Having such letters already in existence will help to ensure that every customer's complaint will be handled as rapidly as possible, in order to preserve your company's reputation and the goodwill of your customers.

KNOW THE PRODUCTS—
AND THE COMPETITION

Set up a procedure to notify all your salespeople—experienced as well as trainees—about your product line, and what your competitors are carrying. Send them a written update whenever you take on a new product, or when you stop carrying something you used to sell, or whenever there are changes in manufacturers' warranties or in your own company policies or procedures.

Your suppliers are a major source of this data. We sell a product—mattresses—that comes in many different prices, sizes, manufacturers styles, and so on. Our vendors give us printed descriptions of each mattress style that we carry, complete with code numbers and style names.

In addition, we have created a comparison chart of all mattresses, which is updated monthly and distributed to all sales personnel. The chart also provides them with information about merchandise our competitors are carrying, and how those products compare with ours. You see, the national brand mattress manufacturers make certain mattress styles and then sell them to different retailers.

Some of these stores want to give the impression that they carry exclusive merchandise, in part to prevent customers from doing comparison shopping. So for each retailer—such as Bloomingdale's, Macy's, Ikea, etc.—the manufacturer covers the same mattress with a different fabric design or color and sews on a label with a different style name. If a customer calls us and says she saw the "Sierra Firm" mattress and wants to know if we carry it, our salesperson can glance at the comparison chart and tell that it is the same as our "Allegro" model; both are manufactured by Sealy.

We counsel our salespeople to explain this situation to the customer and to point out that it is a policy of the mattress industry, not of our company. The comparison chart also tells us that the version with the "Sierra Firm" label is carried by Macy's and

Burdines. Knowing this provides the salesperson with further information that helps reassure the customer of our professionalism and integrity. And in the rare instances that a competitor has a model that is slightly different from ours, the comparison chart explains what the difference is. Our salesperson can then point out the advantages of our model, or suggest different models that would be more appropriate for this particular customer—based on the *qualifiers* that the conversation has established about the person's specific needs or preferences.

It is our philosophy of marketing that all mattresses are created equal—at first. Although there are hundreds of companies that manufacture mattresses, and thousands and thousands of models, most of the components come from one supplier. How these components are put together, the precision of the craftsmanship, and any additional materials that are used produce a great diversity of excellence and quality. As with all our products, you get what you pay for.

In your business, never, *never* sell a poorly made product—and make sure your sales representatives understand the elements of your product or service.

SET UP A COMPUTER PROGRAM FOR SALES, DELIVERY, INVENTORY, AND MULTIPLE OTHER USES

The computer is not just to record the completed order. It also gives the telemarketer information that will help get the sale, and gives the company information you need to process the order and to keep track of inventory, sales productivity, and many other factors.

As my business has mushroomed, the needs for the telecommunications system have become so complex that we are developing a custom-tailored software system. The existing system already tracks the time and location of each call, nationwide; indicates what mattresses are available in that caller's zip code area; tracks delivery schedules, and maintains an ongoing record of the details and logistics.

Here are some of the data categories your programmers will need to enter into your computer system. Modify them to fit your company's needs:

1. **Salesperson Code:** You will need to know who makes each sale for your ongoing evaluation of your sales personnel, and if you pay by commission. Give each salesperson his or her own log-on name and password to get into the computer system. These log-ons automatically indicate who wrote what invoice.

2. **Zip Code:** Once the salesperson enters the zip code of the customer, your computer should indicate the customer's town, city, and county. It should also show the name of the distributor that takes care of that location, and the distance of the closest warehouse.

3. **Location:** This tells where the customer lives, or where he or she wants the merchandise delivered to—such as New York, Mississippi, Canada, etc.

4. **Type of Customer:** We keep track of the following: male, female, crank calls, and calls directed to Customer Service. There is a category for Options, Female and Options, Male, which cues the salesperson to provide specific information. We also code our calls by Special Type Call, and by the usually friendly group we refer to as Call Back, Male and Call Back, Female.

5. **Category:** This is a merchandise category. For us, we would enter the word "Normal" to indicate a mattress. To indicate a waterbed, we would list "WB." A company such as Staples

might list pens, pencils, and highlighters all in a category called Write. They might list all sizes and shapes of stationery, notebooks, and pads in a category called Paper. Create categories and abbreviations that work for your own computer codes.

Obviously, your computer needs to list every item you sell, in every possible variation in which you sell it (for example, Parker Brothers fountain pens: colors, styles, prices; Parker Brothers ball-point pens: colors, styles, prices; Paper Mate fountain pens: colors, styles, prices; and so on.)

It should indicate the category of each item, its manufacturer, and its current price. For inventory and delivery purposes, we also use a code that tells us how many of that item we have on hand. The computer keeps track of ongoing sales, so we can easily see if we're running dangerously low on a product, and we can quickly reorder it. We're constantly aware that if we run out of a product somebody wants to buy, we can lose that customer forever!

Our telemarketers are told to keep track of *leads*, too. The choices are listed on the screen to prompt the salesperson to ask each customer how they heard of the company. It's very important to know what stimulated people enough to call you. Be specific. For example, when you list Advertising, use several different code numbers—not only for each of the different media, but for every newspaper, radio station, or TV show you place your ads on. That's how you'll determine which work effectively for you.

We also list, as possible lead sources: Walk-in, Old Customer, Referral (referred by another customer), and Truck (the billboard-type ads we have on our trucks draw in many new customers).

6. **Size:** This is a crucial descriptor for our products, different mattress sizes are different product categories. For your company, you might need a different description to be listed here.

7. **Item Number:** This will give you the item name, price, inventory status, and a brief description of the item selected.

8. **Delivery:** This category must prompt your salesperson to enter critical information that your delivery and warehouse people will need to have later on. Include the delivery charge, if any. We include such as data as:

- Home phone (area code first)
- Last name
- First name
- Address
- Apartment number
- City/State
- Zip
- Cross street (This is crucial to ask for!)
- Business phone
- Delivery date
- Delivery time
- Other instructions

9. **Order Date**

10. **Payment Form:** Indicate how the customer will pay: by check, C.O.D., credit card (we enter V for Visa, MC for MasterCard, A for American Express, or D for Discover), or money order (MO). Then have the computer screen prompt your salesperson to fill out the necessary information for each type of transaction.

  Once the telemarketer completes entering all of this information into the computer, a Customer Invoice Number will appear on the screen. The telemarketer should tell the customer his or her number; it will be used to follow the rest of the transaction to its completion—the delivery of the merchandise, and the payment of the bill.

Finally, after the transaction with the customer is completed, the telemarketer should send the order through—by computer—to the next department responsible for processing it.

HOW TO BUILD A GOOD CUSTOMER RELATIONSHIP

The most successful retailing companies, whether they be stores, catalog companies, or telemarketers, are those who establish excellent customer service. This means, in part, giving the customers what they want—and need. It also means treating them with respect and speaking in a courteous, friendly, helpful manner—always.

L.L. Bean, one of the most successful catalog companies in the world, has the following credo prominently displayed in its Freeport, Maine, headquarters:

WHAT IS A CUSTOMER?

A Customer is the most important person ever in this office. . . in person or by mail.

A Customer is not dependent on us. . . we are dependent on him.

A Customer is not an interruption of our work. . . he is the purpose of it. We are not doing a favor by serving him. . . he is doing us a favor by giving us the opportunity to do so.

A Customer is not someone to argue or match wits with. Nobody ever won an argument with a Customer.

A Customer is a person who brings us his wants. It is our job to handle them profitably to him and to ourselves.

—L.L. Bean

KEY TECHNIQUES FOR TELEMARKETERS

The telemarketer's first rule is to *always listen carefully to customers and treat them with dignity*. The salesperson should recognize that if customers fail to buy, you'll be out of business and he'll be out of a job. We issue a handout on the art of listening to all of our new telemarketers. In essence, what we teach, is:

KEYS TO GOOD LISTENING

1. **Limit your own talking:** You can't talk and listen at the same time.

2. **Think like the customer:** Your customer's problems and needs are important and you'll understand and retain them better if you listen to his point of view.

3. **Ask questions:** If you don't understand something or feel you may have missed a point, clear it up now before it embarrasses you later.

4. **Don't interrupt:** A pause doesn't always mean the customer is finished saying everything he or she wants.

5. **Concentrate:** Focus your mind on what he or she is saying. Practice shutting out outside distractions.

6. **Take notes:** This will help you remember important points. But be selective. Trying to note down everything said can result in being left far behind or in retaining irrelevant details.

7. **Listen for ideas. . . not just words:** You want to get the whole picture, not just isolated bits and pieces.

8. **Interjection:** An occasional "Yes," "I see," and so on shows the customer you are still with him or her, but don't overdo or use this as a meaningless comment.

9. **Turn off your own concerns:** This isn't always easy, but personal fears, worries, or problems not connected with the contact form a kind of "static" that can blank out the customer's message.

10. **Prepare in advance:** Remarks and questions prepared in advance, when possible, free your mind for listening.

11. **React to ideas. . . not to the person:** Don't allow irritation at things the customer may say—or his or her manner—to distract you.

12. **Don't jump to conclusions:** Avoid making unwarranted assumptions about what the customer is going to say, or mentally trying to complete the sentence for him or her.

13. **Listen for overtones:** You can learn a great deal about the customer from the way he or she says things and the way he or she reacts to the things you say.

Our Bedding Consultants are extremely well trained, not only as to the nuances and specifics of our mattresses, but also to be *pleasant* to every customer.

For example, one customer, Harry Letzt, called us late one evening, just to obtain some information about prices and sizes for a mattress he thought he might need in about a year or so. He had no intention of buying. Salesperson Richard Seidenberg struck up a conversation with the Mr. Letzt and they found that they had grown up in the same neighborhood. The two men reminisced and "schmoozed" and soon discovered that they both had gone to the same high school, although in different years.

Before long, they were having a friend-to-friend conversation touching upon the nostalgia and trivia of their lives and exploring common interests. The result? Mr. Letzt bought a mattress that evening. He told Richard that he felt he was buying from a friend. And he was.

There's a friendly conclusion to this story, too. While Mr. Letzt was waiting for his new mattress to be delivered, he decided to rearrange some of the furniture in his bedroom. His leather recliner was too heavy to move; even two handymen in his building were unable to lift it.

Then the Dial-A-Mattress truck arrived. The driver and his assistant removed the customer's old mattress, set up the new one, and obligingly picked up the recliner and carried it into the living room. Mr. Letzt called back to thank us for the excellent service.

We were pleased because he was pleased, and he assured us that he would tell all his friends about his "wonderful mattress experience."

Recently, Mira Siegel, one of our salespeople, received a phone call from a woman who had obviously dialed the wrong number. She had actually been attempting to reach an insurance company. Through a friendly conversation with Mira, the woman found out that she was really calling a mattress company. To make a long story longer, the woman, so pleased at the courteous way she had been treated and hearing of our superb personal service, ended up buying a mattress, which was delivered a few days later.

Six Steps to Persuasive Listening

Here are some critical concepts we teach our sales consultants. As some of them point out, this advice is not only helpful for selling, it is also a good way to deal with people in daily life.

1. **Listen carefully to what the customer has to say:** Fight the inclination to argue. You are unlikely to win customers over if you can't or don't understand them.

2. **Don't jump to conclusions about what someone else is thinking, needs, or will say next:** Sometimes this is particularly difficult. It's hard to listen with an open mind to what someone has to say when he or she is irate. But there is a big difference between listening and merely hearing words. If your mind is made up, nothing anyone can say will make a difference. We can also miss something important that someone may say. We very often prejudge what we think will or will not make a difference. As a result we tend to miss a lot of the good stuff that comes along the way.

3. **Respect the thoughts and opinions of others:** Keep your mind open to the possibility that they can say something that is right.

4. **Control your emotions:** This comes into play with the above information.

5. **Common sense:** Repeat what the other person has said to verify that you understand the problem. Be clear.

6. **Acknowledge the other person's point of view:** Take their issue to heart.

We need to remember to acknowledge our own feelings as well. People seldom argue in a rational way.

To build a reputation as a good listener, you must master active listening skills. To do so, try these approaches:

Repeat: In your own words, feed back to the speaker what you heard. Say something such as "Are you saying that. . . " to make sure you got the message right.

Empathize: Put yourself in the customer's shoes and say, for example, "I know how you feel" or "I understand how upsetting this is."

Ask a question: The clearest signal you can send to show that you are listening is to ask a follow-up question, wait for an answer, and follow up with a related question.

Listen "actively": This means that you give customers full attention. To make sure you do, get rid of non-listening habits.

Non-Listening Habits

1. Thinking about what you will say next when a customer finishes.
2. Continuing with your work (writing and reading) while a customer is speaking.
3. Considering how much better you could phrase what the customer is saying (for example, thinking about customer's grammar).
4. Concentrating on getting a chance to interrupt (cannot wait to interrupt, instead of listening for key points).
5. Thinking of a point you want to make. (What I have to say is more important than what you are saying, so I am not going to listen anymore.)

Sometimes people inadvertently fall into ways of thinking that hinder their own effectiveness. Do these and you will *decrease* your effectiveness as a salesperson. We point them out to our sales trainees to highlight what *not* to do. We urge our personnel to become aware of their attitudes and actions and, if they find they're doing any of the following, to stop and focus their minds on more effective selling behaviors.

Instead Focus On:

Write down key points.

Explain how our company works.

Never say what first comes to your mind. You may stray from key points and frustrate the customer.

Listen without interruption. You will have your chance, and a better one, if you first let the customer speak without interrupting.

Keep calm and courteous. Disputes with customers often get out of hand. You will lose money and waste time as a result.

Pause before you respond. If you answer too quickly, you signal that you have not heard, or do not care about what the customer said.

Respond calmly. A curt or sarcastic response makes an irate customer.

Never talk down to a customer. This will only make a situation worse. *The only way to achieve a win-win environment is to properly service and care about your customers.*

TAILOR EACH CONVERSATION TO THE CUSTOMER

Teach your salespeople to talk on the telephone with a smile on their faces. . . literally! Smiling usually affects the way a person speaks so that, in effect, customers can almost magically "see" that smile through the telephone, and it often leads to a sale.

Since you're doing all business on the phone, a common (and potentially fatal) mistake is assuming the customer can't pick up on or discern the attitude of the salesperson. If he or she becomes patronizing or worse, ignoring the customer's queries, your sale will almost invariably be lost. Just because the customer can't see you doesn't mean they won't pick up on subtle voice inflections and attitude. Train your telemarketers to always listen to what the customers have to say, answer any questions they might have succinctly and directly, be as helpful and courteous as possible, and, most importantly, never treat the customer rudely. Customers can always go somewhere else to spend their money, and they will, if they aren't treated with respect.

Karl Albrecht, a management consultant who has spent a lifetime studying the dynamics of customer relations, talks of the spirit of service needed for success, an attitude based on certain values and beliefs about people, life, and work that lead a person to willingly serve others and take pride in his or her life.

Somehow you must instill in your sales personnel this spirit of service, the sense of giving something of themselves, making a connection with the callers, not just taking their orders. There is no place for cynicism in telemarketing. If you discern that a salesperson is impatient or condescending to customers, he or she should be transferred out of sales or removed—quickly—before he or she hurts your valuable reputation.

Treating someone with respect starts the moment your telemarketer picks up the phone. If they answer it in a bored voice, that annoyance is going to be transferred directly to the customer. This is not the way to start a sales call. Whether this is the first call of the day or the hundredth, each one must be answered with a high level of energy, attentiveness, and courteousness. It cannot be stressed enough that a salesperson (or, as we call them, a bedding consultant) must always be on his or her best behavior. They must be polite and courteous and answer all questions clearly and succinctly, and slowly enough so that they can be understood.

Also, to be an outstanding sales consultant a person must be able to separate one call from another: If a telemarketer has a bad experience with one customer, he mustn't let it taint his conversation with the next person. Instruct your people never to sell over the telephone while they are angry. If something like this does happen (and it probably will; as mentioned above, a good percentage of calls that come in may be from cranks or kids who saw the number on TV and decided to have some fun), they should put down the phone, take a deep breath, take a walk, get a cup of coffee, do whatever they have to do to calm down, and not let their attitude about the last call affect their feelings about the next one.

Realize that crank calls are also opportunities. Though people occasionally call us to fool around, if they're treated nicely, some of them will call back months or years later, when they need to buy our product. This has happened to us quite often. Even kids can help; they frequently remind their parents of our phone number—1–800–MATTRESS—and they always remember our slogan. . . "And leave the last 'S' off for Savings."

So don't offend anyone! You never know who will become a customer, or recommend a new one.

According to Richard L. Bencin, in his book *Strategic Telemarketing,* the ideal telephone salesperson should be: educated (some college optional, but preferred); articulate; intelligent; expressive; creative; vocally mature; have a pleasant and well-modulated voice, free of heavy accent, and a moderate speaking pace; be stable and dependable; aggressive/assertive; enthusiastic; resilient and "thick skinned"; curious; and in need of a job.

Gather all customer data quickly and efficiently. At the beginning of a sales call, we tell our salespeople to ask for the customer's zip code and write it down so they don't have to keep asking for it. We have our merchandise coded by zip code. Knowing where the person lives, the telemarketer can immediately know which merchandise is available in his area and can discuss those specific products. And later in the conversation, the telemarketer can refer to that zip code to pull up delivery availability in that area, and then give the customer some alternative delivery dates to choose from. (For example, "We have an opening for delivery on Oak Street this afternoon and one tonight. What time is good for you?") This efficiency translates as consideration and gains appreciation from our customers.

The customer judges you by the voice he hears. It doesn't matter whether your salespeople are wearing formal suits, or blue jeans and T-shirts: The customer can't see them, your office, your showroom, or your products. All he hears is a person's voice. And from that voice he defines the salesperson's knowledgeability, attitude, and trustworthiness. Every salesperson needs to be able to speak in a pleasant, clear manner. Even if he has an excellent knowledge of the product, it won't do a bit of good if he speaks in a whiny or gruff voice, an inappropriate heavy accent or regional dialect, can't be easily understood, or is rude to the customer.

Dance with the customer. You've probably heard the adage "It takes two to tango." Never is it more true than when selling (and buying) by phone. Both the customer and salesperson go round and round until a deal is reached and a sale has been made.

Closely linked to the practice of "letting the customer see your voice," "dancing" is the practice of the salesman being able to think quickly and *adapt to the customer's style,* be it a fox trot or a waltz. For example, more than nine-tenths of the 1–800 number calls are nationwide. That means you may get one caller from Boston, the next from Maine, and the next from Missouri. Your salespeople will have to adapt to the speaking styles of each.

People all over the country speak not only in different dialects, but at different paces. People from the South may talk slower than people from the Northeast. Those from cities like Boston and Chicago will usually ask more technical questions than someone from a small town in the Midwest, who may just want to know the price and if the mattress is comfortable.

A retired person on a fixed income may ask a seemingly endless number of questions concerning price. A person used to comparison shopping might listen to a description of one mattress, then say "I'm not sure that's the best one for me. What else do you have?" And when the salesperson gives them other options, they may want to know in what ways they differ from one another and why that difference is, or is not, important.

Then someone from a big city (either New York or Los Angeles) may call and say, "I need to buy a mattress today, and

I'm in a hurry. I don't want to hear the sales pitch. What do you have and how much is it?"

Telemarketers have to be able to vary their presentation to handle each type of customer.

FIND OUT WHAT THE CUSTOMER WANTS TO BUY

In an ideal situation, customers would tell you exactly what they want to buy. Since the world is less than perfect, it shouldn't surprise you to know that sometimes callers aren't quite sure what they want, or how much it should cost, or even just what it is you sell. That's fine. Just have your salespeople bear in mind that the telemarketer has two equally important functions:

1. Listen to what the customer tells you.
2. Then ask questions to find out what information he *didn't* tell you.

The object isn't just to make a sale. It is to sell merchandise that the customers will like, products that fulfill their wants and needs, items they will be happy to keep once they are delivered. Always remember that if a person is coerced into buying something he doesn't really want, he has a powerful weapon: He can refuse to accept the delivery and refuse to pay for it. That is far more expensive to a company than losing a sale in the first place.

When consumers call us about mattresses, here are some of the "qualifiers" our telemarketers ask, to be sure we know what the customer really wants. *Adapt these questions to your own products,* and develop others to help your sales staff assist callers in defining what they want to buy:

- What kind of mattress are you using now? Do you like it?
- Is this mattress for your master bedroom or your guest room?

- Do you like your mattress to feel hard, soft, or something in between?
- What size do you want?
- Are you interested in a top-of-the-line mattress, or a middle-range, or a basic one?
- Do you have any brand or model preference?
- Are you a first-time caller/shopper to Dial-A-Mattress?

The caller's responses and what he actually says he wants will enable your telemarketer to think of one or more items from your product line that will probably fulfill his needs. Now it's time to describe them.

Use effective descriptive words to create a picture of your products. Opinion words such as "terrific" or "fantastic" don't describe things very well. What color is a "terrific" pen? How soft or hard is a "fantastic" mattress?

Your salespeople need to know your product line thoroughly to be able to describe each item. Terms such as a "soft mattress," a "felt-tipped" pen, a watch with a "quartz battery," a company with "licensed attorneys," are the kind of descriptions that enable the customer to understand what you're selling. Avoid using initials and esoteric terms: "That model is in our Santa Fe group." (*Your what?*) "And it's guaranteed by the E.R.F." (*The who?*)

Company employees tend to use such insider language with one another, because they all understand the terminology. But the object isn't to show that you're smarter than the customer. The goal is to provide him with such a clear, precise description that he'll be able to visualize the product. If your telemarketers don't do that successfully, the customer is going to hang up and buy the product in a store where he can *see* it.

Here are some ways to develop good terms to describe your product or service.

1. Consider its *quality* in terms of its *physical properties:* what it's made of, the workmanship involved. If you sell woolen

sweaters, you might include terms like *natural, handmade,* and *long-wearing.* On the other hand, if your sweaters are made of synthetic fiber, you might describe them as *wrinkle-resistant, moth-proof,* and *shrink-proof.*

Describe the details of the sweaters, too: pearl buttons, lace trim. Or if you sell furniture, describe the leather seats and chrome handles, genuine *Formica* desk top, or *oak* that is hand stained and polished.

2. Consider the product or service in terms of *psychological qualities,* too. Different customers seek different attributes. For some, major brand names are extremely desirable. If you're selling such products, mention that the item is a Swatch watch, or a Champion sweatshirt, or a Sealy mattress. The brand name gives the customer an immediate mind-set of the merchandise. It also provides him with the security of knowing what you're selling, even though he can't actually see it.

No matter what the product or what its price, and whether it is at the top, middle or bottom of that product's price range, you can honestly tell the consumer the virtues of that product.

Unless your product line is very easy to describe verbally, take the time to develop a Product Description List, which should also include the major features and benefits of each type of merchandise.

Brainstorming is an effective way to do this. Hold a meeting with your top salespeople, your company's buyers, and all other personnel who are most knowledgeable about your merchandise (or who are best equipped to describe the service you sell). Talk about one product at a time, and invite everyone to suggest aloud both descriptive terms and selling points. Assign one person (or yourself) to write down their suggestions, and remember that brainstorming works best when it's not critical. Keep the atmosphere open and accept all suggestions. Later on, you—or someone you assign—will edit the list, have it typed up into a Product Description List, and distribute copies to every salesperson. I guarantee that the list will be useful to members of other departments, too.

Have your sales trainees spend extra time becoming familiar with your most popular items. In our case, we even have our trainees select which mattress they prefer from each size and price range. Then they create their own description (using their own words, not manufacturers') for these favorite items.

Then when a customer calls and asks a salesperson to recommend, for example, a twin-size mattress, after the telemarketer has determined the quality level the person wants, he can recommend his favorite mattress in that category and can talk about it with accuracy and enthusiasm, because it's not just an item inside a catalog.

If you are selling a fairly large-ticket item, such as a $2,000 Leica camera or a $40,000 BMW, or a $500,000 condominium, or even a $5,000 sofa, consider producing a videotape of your product that shows its highlights and its strengths and benefits, and having it Federal Expressed, mailed, sent by UPS, or delivered by messenger, perhaps within hours—maybe even minutes—of your receiving the initial inquiry from the consumer.

HOW TO DEAL WITH A CUSTOMER'S OBJECTIONS

Unless you're lucky enough to get a call from someone who knows exactly what he wants to buy and has his credit card out and ready—it does happen occasionally—the majority of customers calling in will have some sort of objection to the sale. The most common customer concern is: "It's too much money," but people also frequently say "I have to check with my wife (or husband)" or "I'm looking to see what's out there." Each of these objections must be answered by the sales consultants, or they won't be able to make a sale. We use a three-step dialogue to overcome such objections:

1. **Make a Softening Statement:** Have the salesperson show that he or she understands the customer's point of view and can relate to it. If the customer says, "The cost is too high," the telemarketer can reply, "Having a fixed income myself, I can understand where you're coming from," or "I'm sure it seems like a lot of money, but, like most items, prices have gone way up since you last purchased a bed." These statements are immediately followed up with point 2.

2. **Reassure, Using New Information:** After expressing understanding of the customer's objections, the salesperson then takes it one step further by adding a qualifier: "You're right about prices going up, but the mattress we've been talking about is built to last and will save you money in the long run." Or "I understand how difficult it is to live within a budget today. That is the reason I am suggesting this model. Besides being very comfortable, it is the least expensive in the long run." Or "You can buy it now and have it delivered anytime you want, without paying until then." In each case, the sales consultant is answering the objections indirectly by providing new information.

3. **Ask a "Closer" Question:** The "close" is the most difficult part of the conversation. After the salesperson has determined what merchandise the customer prefers, it's time to have him buy the product. "Closer questions" lead into that. For example: "May I write up the order and put it on your credit card, or are you interested in our time payment plan?" Or "What day is best for delivery?" Or "Would you like to open an account with us?" The purpose of these questions is to steer the conversation away from the customer's objections and back toward the eventual sale. How the customer reacts to these queries is indicative of where the call is going.

   If a customer responds in a positive way to any of the closer questions—"Tell me about your time-payment plan" or "What kinds of credit cards do you accept?"—he is seriously considering buying. If he brushes off a closer with "Well, I'm not sure this is right for me," your salesperson should go back up to step one and start the process over again, all the while listening carefully to the customer's objections and diplomatically pointing out why this would be a good time to purchase the product. Point out to trainees and full-fledged telemarketers, alike, that *being a sales consultant requires equal proportions of listening, diplomacy, hand-holding, and being able to think quickly and answer any question the customers may come up with.*

Above all, as I've stated earlier, *listen to the customer.* Almost as important as what customers *say* is what they *do not say.* For example, although the first question a customer may ask is "What type of mattress do you carry?" there are probably several unspoken questions he's thinking but does not say out loud, such as "What is this going to cost me?" "Do I really need to buy a mattress right now?" "Is this just another fly-by-night organization?" "Can I trust this guy?" "Is it safe to give him my credit card number?" "How do I know what type of delivery people they're going to send?" "Will my mattress get here in one piece, and if it's broken, what do I do then?"

A good telemarketer must listen to the customer's silence as closely as he listens to his speech. Then, drawing on what has been taught in the training program, and on knowledge of the products the company sells, and on his awareness of the entire process, from taking the order to delivering the merchandise, the telemarketer can answer and overcome customers' objections and concerns.

The rule that "the customer is always right" may not be easy to follow if the customer is asking all sorts of questions that may—in the salesperson's opinion—have no bearing on the sale of the merchandise. However, since it is the customer who is going to be doing the buying—hopefully—it is obviously important that the telemarketer be able to empathize with the person on the other end of the phone, and learn to see things from the customer's point of view.

Dial-A-Mattress uses some optical illustrations in our training program to help the trainees realize that often there are several correct ways to consider the same situation. The instructor holds up various diagrams, and asks different members of the training class what they see. Invariably, half a dozen queries will yield half a dozen different answers.

This illustrates that each person's answer is not necessarily the right one. Indeed, sometimes there is no correct answer.

Just as the different trainees will see different things when observing a diagram of an optical illusion, it can happen that a customer and a salesperson may have different viewpoints about what is important when buying a mattress. And since the customer hasn't taken any kind of training course, it's up to the telemarketer to realize that fact, and to patiently provide additional information whenever the customer needs or wants it.

CREATE A TEAM BETWEEN THE TELEMARKETER AND THE CUSTOMER

If they treat each other as adversaries, it's much less likely that the customer will make the purchase he wants, or that your salesperson will make the sale *he* wants. Here's how we demonstrate the benefit of this approach.

We divide the trainees into small groups, and give each person in each group several small stick figures. The goal is to create five squares of equal size. The only thing the trainees are told is that the sticks they have can be combined to create the appropriate squares. To do so, however, they must share their stick figures. Each person needs pieces the others have. To succeed, the members of each group must work as a team.

As they begin to work together, ideas are tossed around, one person usually emerges as a team leader, another may stand off to one side, a third person may try to force his or her way into the decision process, while a fourth may keep trying to politely suggest his or her solution.

Ultimately, out of this group of separate people, a team comes together and the squares are constructed. Then the instructor points out the positive and negative attributes of each of the team members. This helps the trainees to recognize their own strengths and weaknesses in working with other people, and helps them learn to build up their positive attributes and discard negative ones. The knowledge they gain here can then be used when talking with a customer.

Another important facet we teach our trainees about teamwork is that they have to know when to give up control to one of their teammates. In the same way, when talking to a customer, they have to know when to let him ask questions, and when to let him voice an objection (which the salesperson will then deal with). And just as important, they have to know when to regain control of the conversation.

What to Do When a Customer Stalls

- Always listen carefully.
- Make comments to show the customer you are listening.
- Encourage the customer to express himself fully. Find out what the objection is.
- Use a softening statement.
- Before answering, lower the objection to the sale with a statement that indicates understanding.
- Let the customer know that you understand how he feels and can put yourself in his shoes.
- Reassure the customer.
- Answer, using new information that reassures his decision.
- Let him know it's all right to ask questions.
- Ask another closing question.

What To Do When the Customer Is Annoying or Impolite?

Sometimes we get calls from people who are rude or angry. This is normal—even customers are not always in a good mood. We prepare our trainees to deal with such situations by teaching them how to deal with *themselves* when unpleasant phone conversations occur.

We have all been there: Someone yells at us, and we feel like yelling back—especially if we know we didn't do anything wrong. Role playing is essential in this type of training. Whoever is doing the training of your sales consultants should compile a list of every possible objection a customer may have to your product or service. This can be done through direct experience with customer calling, or by talking to other telemarketers to get their views on the subject.

Have the trainer raise these objections, in a one-on-one practice session, to be answered by the sales trainee. Make sure each trainee understands the answer, makes notes, and can rattle off a positive response to *any* objection, before he or she is permitted to take his first call.

If a customer is grouchy, we teach our trainees to be as patient as possible. They ask the customer what the problem or complaint is and repeat it so that the customer knows the company understands what he feels is wrong.

A salesperson must be aware that making customers feel like he genuinely cares about their feelings is very important. He should honestly try to help them as much as he can and tell them he will help them in the best possible way. If there has been an error, he should assure the customer that it will be corrected. Encourage the trainees to show the customer that he cares—as he should.

A satisfied customer is a return customer, and a person who will recommend your business to new customers. An unsatisfied customer will never give you his or his friend's future business. And from a very personal point of view, his phone call will end on a very down note—which can leave the telemarketer feeling just awful and can adversely affect his selling ability for several hours.

WORK WITH DISSATISFIED CUSTOMERS

Keep calm and confident: It's often a natural reaction to get irate with someone who is angry. Don't get angry or defensive. If you hope to control the situation, you have to first control your temper. Concentrate on keeping your voice calm and nonjudgmental. Sometimes speaking a bit lower helps. Keep your manner attentive and helpful. Remember, the customer is not mad at *you*; the customer is upset with the situation.

Listen: Really listen to what the customer is saying. Customers who are upset need to vent their anger and frustration. Listen carefully and don't interrupt. Give the caller 100 percent of your attention and let him or her fully explain what's wrong.

Acknowledge respect for your customer: Convey that his or her concern is legitimate and deserves your serious consideration. Be careful not to agree with the customer's objection. Acknowledge the emotion, not the facts as presented by the customer.

For example, don't say, "You're right. That's the worst service I've ever heard of." A better way to convey concern without agreeing might be to say, "I certainly understand how upset you are about this situation, and I want to do everything I can to help you."

Make sure customers don't feel they are being troublesome or difficult even if you think they are. Consider changing your perspective from thinking the customer is being unreasonable to thinking of what skills you can use to persuade him or her to behave more sensibly.

Avoid using the word "complaint" or "problem" when talking to customers. These words often set up a defensive reaction. Try substituting the word *situation* or *question* for their problems or complaints. Customers will be more cooperative and less upset if you do. For example, rather than saying "Here's what I can do to solve your problem," say, "Here's what we can do to resolve this situation." Hear the difference?

HANDLING SPOUSE OBJECTION

If, after a strong, qualified presentation, you make your specific recommendations and the customer responds with "I have to speak to my husband, or wife, or mother, or brother, or neighbor, etc." you can try by responding, "Of course!"

Then ask a key question to resolve the problem:

"Assuming your husband agrees with you and says okay, would you expect to need delivery in the next few days?"

If customer responds with a "yes" or "probably," go on to the next suggestion.

Ask when the customer would like to have the mattress delivered. But we don't have our sales representative phrase this as an open-ended question. Instead, we offer the customer several "windows of opportunity" for delivery. The Bedding Consultant first asks:

"Would you prefer to have your mattress delivered today, tomorrow, some other day?"

Once the customer chooses the day, the telemarketer asks:

"Would you like your delivery in the morning, afternoon, or evening?"

And, finally, to narrow down the time preference:

"We have several deliveries in your area. Would you prefer to schedule yours within a four-hour time slot or a two-hour time slot?"

By offering such a broad range of specific delivery options, you will overcome any time problems the customer may have. Once your customer has selected a day and time slot, follow up with:

"Let me get you in on that time slot so that we are able to accommodate you. We'll set it all up for you and call to confirm it all after you speak to your husband. What's your home phone number?"

This technique is often effective. Try it; it works. During the rest of the call keep stressing benefits. Example:

1. How durable a mattress it is
2. How great it will be for your husband's bad back
3. What a difference this will be from your old mattress
4. How easy this process is. . . how convenient and simple
5. We help you select what merchandise is best for you, geared toward your specific needs

Continue to reassure the customer. *Listen* to her buying signals or hesitations and respond accordingly. Reassure her again—by letting her know that if she ever needs anything, you will always make yourself available to help her at any time.

HANDLING DELAY IN ARRANGING DELIVERY

We usually ask our customers to call us back by a certain time to guarantee their delivery time frame after completing the sale. If a wife says, for example, that she can't make an appointment without checking with her husband, we ask when the husband will be home. Suppose she says 5 P.M. Respond with: "Okay, then if we can touch base today before 6 P.M. we'll be able to confirm the time for tomorrow. Can you call back before 6?" (Obviously, use whatever time or day fits into the customer's response). "Great. I'll wait to hear from you. Thank you for calling. . . etc."

Many times, during the course of your conversation, it is possible that customers will cut you short and just go ahead and schedule the delivery on their own. The more convincing you are and the more you simplify and clarify the issue, the easier it will be for customers to complete the transaction. Just because they give you the "spouse objection" does not mean it is true.

An Objection is an Excuse to Get Off the Phone

Put the customer in a position in which the mattress you recommend will mean something special to him. Once you have qualified the customer, you will have a *clear* picture of the type of bed he really needs, in the price range that is realistic for him. Then, if you make a strong presentation, this mattress will not be an abstract item, but the *specific model* that the customer will be most comfortable on and that will help him to get a better night's sleep. He is likely to feel committed to buying the mattress, because this mattress is the answer to his "problem." Create need. Create urgency. Create enthusiasm.

Sometimes methods work, sometimes they don't. If you do not make the attempt, it is a guarantee your approach will not work. If you try with every spouse objection, maybe you'll close two more sales each day. Sometimes when you least expect it, the customer will buy. It's all in your approach, the words you choose to use, and your instinct and courage to pursue the customer. Assume he or she *will* buy, keep it smooth and sincere, and stay in control. It's a good feeling when you know you made that sale happen.

ONGOING SALES SUPPORT AND ADVANCED TRAINING

Our training program gives new salespeople an intensive overview of the most effective techniques to be used in telephone selling, as well as a concentrated introduction to our product line. But even experienced telemarketers can benefit from further instruction and support to help them improve their sales support. Since most salespeople work on commission—in our company as well as in many others—they are usually most happy to avail themselves of the opportunity to sharpen their selling skills through advanced training.

For the first few weeks after the training program, each new salesperson has the constant support of a master telemarketer, who listens in on his calls and provides specific critiques and suggestions on how to make the call more effective. After that period, one of our top salespeople, Jennifer Grassano, provides continuing instruction to our sales staff.

She works in two ways. Telemarketers may make an appointment with her to have her listen in on one or more of their sales calls. She wears a headset that enables her to hear the conversation with the customer, but she doesn't participate in the conversations—though at times she may record them.

Afterward, she will confer with the telemarketer and go over problems that occurred, and what the salesperson might have said or done to overcome those problems. She will point out the strong points of the conversation to encourage the salesperson to continue using certain techniques. She will give hints on speaking style, timing (from when to suggest an alternative product to when to ask the customer the best day to have the order delivered), and how to handle certain types of customer objections.

Because this instruction is completely specific, and not at all theoretical, the salesperson finds it completely applicable to his selling technique, and can begin to apply the results in the very next phone call. In fact, we find it somewhat ironic—though entirely predictable—that the telemarketers who are most likely to seek out this personal advanced training are those who are already earning the highest commissions. And after getting pointers to improve their telephone style, they are invariably rewarded by an even higher sales ratio.

Manager of Sales Maureen Rennenburg strongly supports this ongoing instruction. Recently she has introduced some actual retraining classes for experienced telemarketers. To increase the company's percentage of orders, we evaluate each telemarketer's daily sales against the total number of calls they receive, which are always monitored. We do periodic reviews to find out why a sale is not closed. This tells us whether a given salesperson needs further training or support.

The two-hour retraining classes are held on several different dates and times, allowing the salespeople to sign up for whichever session is most convenient for them. Each session covers some of the most important, or most difficult, topics, such as:

- Properly handling each call
- Increasing the closing percentage of the total calls
- Properly informing the customer of necessary details at the point of sale
- Preventing charge backs
- Anything else the telemarketers might want to review

Retraining reminds each telemarketer to slow down and evaluate what he has or has not covered in a call, before it ends. Very often, at the end of a long sales pitch, the salesperson may forget to tell the customer a piece of important information—perhaps the total price including sales tax, or when the delivery can be made, or a final verification of the address, and most importantly, he may forget to make sure the company has the specific merchandise the customer has requested. (This has to be checked, because even with an up-to-date computer program, what appears on the screen is not always what is in stock.)

In addition, retraining reminds telemarketers that they need to deal with rejection. A fast worker will handle dozens of calls a day, and a large percentage of those calls are from people who don't intend to buy anything. Some need customer service, and some are cranks. (With a 1–800 number, you get a lot of crank calls or calls from children who think it's fun to play with the telephone.) If you get a lot of crank calls, or several unpleasant customers in a row, the telemarketer has to put it into perspective.

Our retraining reminds them how important it is to maintain a fresh attitude, to stay really focused, to treat each customer as an individual, and to not bring into this new conversation any bad feelings that may have been triggered by a previous call. The telemarketer must also learn to trust himself, and know that if he has done the right thing, treated his customer well, then, even if a sale did not result, just let it go. The customer might call back and buy later—or he may not. The important thing is to maintain a positive attitude, and go on to the next customer. If a salesperson can't learn these crucial lessons, he's not going to make it in this field.

HOW TO PREVENT BURNOUT

After handling several hundred calls a day, week in and week out, it is quite possible that your telemarketers will experience what is known as "burnout" at sometime during their careers.

One of the difficulties in being full-time telemarketers is that they must be "up" all of the time, or they will not be telemarketers for long. A telemarketer is not totally unlike a performer in the entertainment business: To show to the world an ebullient personality all of the time is just not a natural state for anyone. After doing several hours of entertaining, it is not uncommon for performers to return to the dressing room and to weep. . . for many reasons: physical and emotional exhaustion; a certain depression if things didn't go as well as expected; a feeling of phoniness if they said things that were not totally sincere; and, as stated, the need to always wear a smile.

It is absolutely essential that telemarketers should get away from the phone as much as is practical: frequent breaks, vacations, long weekends, and so forth. The idea is to reduce the exhaustion and anxiety that seem to be *de rigueur* for a telemarketer's job.

Don't allow a telemarketer to break down! It is up to you to work with them and to see to it that they get the rest and relaxation that are absolutely essential to their psychological good health. If you notice, through their call sheets, that certain of your telemarketers are not picking up as many calls as they usually do, or that they are not making as many sales, it is possible that they are experiencing burnout.

If they appear sad, anxious, angry, tense beyond reason, lethargic, or display any other negative feeling, it may be a sign of burnout.

If they are coming late every day or leaving early, or taking extended lunch hours, it may indicate that they are ready to burn out.

If they are working totally on commission, or on a salary/commission basis, it is possible that they are pushing themselves too much to increase their income.

Obviously, you want hard and committed workers, but there comes a time when too much is too much, and the telemarketer begins to focus entirely on his own detrimental feelings rather than on the consumer or the point of the sale.

Here are some additional ways that you can help your telemarketers cope with, and probably prevent, burnout:

1. Give encouragement to your telemarketers, especially during times when their daily or weekly sales totals are off. Let them know that everyone has a bad streak from time to time. Praise their past performances and try to get them back to that point. What are they are doing now that is different from when they were successful? Just showing concern on your part—not criticism—might pull them out of their doldrums.

2. Sit in with your salespeople (and *listen in*) as they receive a number of calls. The point is to continue your reassurance of their performance, and perhaps, *after* the call, to gently point out certain errors they might be making in their presentations. If you can help them boost their sales, it is possible that their spirits will be lifted, and it will alleviate their burnout problems.

3. Make sure that there is sufficient staffing to handle all of your inbound calls. If you are continually short-staffed, a telemarketer might feel overwhelmed or swamped by handling as many calls as he does, and this will invariably lead to burnout.

4. Assure the telemarketer that you have sufficient inventory to distribute and fulfill his orders. Nothing is as disheartening to salespeople as to have to tell the consumer that they are out of stock on an item. Often they lose the sale and become dispirited.

5. Suggest to your telemarketers that they experiment with the scripts or presentations just to add some variety to their work. It can become boring to recite the following a few hundred times a day:

SALESMAN: "Hello. ACB Novelties, John speaking. How may I help you?"

CUSTOMER: "I saw your commercial on television and I'd like to buy the wicker rocker."

SALESMAN: "Fine. Would you like the white or natural model?"

CUSTOMER: "The natural."

SALESMAN: "Fine. That will be $89.99, plus a $20 delivery fee. What credit card do you want it charged to?" and so on, and so on.

Suggest something a bit different, now and then, for example:

SALESMAN: "Hi. This is John speaking, from the ACB Novelty Company. What can I do for you today?"

CUSTOMER: "I saw your commercial on television and I'd like to buy the wicker rocker."

SALESMAN: "Great! Have your ever bought from us before? No, well ACB is known for its speedy delivery and low costs. The wicker rocker has a special value. It was

$129.99 and we've marked it down to $89.99. When do you want it delivered?" and so forth.

6. Include your salespeople in product development or quality control meetings and other meetings concerning the product or service that you provide. Make sure they feel proud and confident about your company and about your product or service. Sometimes burnout develops when there is loss of faith in the product or service, so it is essential that telemarketers are kept abreast of all the company's advances and all improvements in the product or service.

7. During slack times, perhaps because of an economic downturn or a short recession, but through no fault of the telemarketer, his sales might drop, and so his income will decrease. You might attempt to find him some other salaried work in the company, in order to add to the telemarketer's lowered income. Adding some extra income to a sagging salary check works wonders against burnout.

Not only will burnout affect the individual telemarketer's life and performance, it can have an adverse effect on everyone else in the company. Begin to recognize it and do everything you can to eradicate it. In addition to the solutions already discussed, consider the following: Make sure that your product or service matches your promises and prices. Encourage the telemarketer to talk about his problems; use up-to-date equipment and furniture; and attempt to make the telemarketer's work place pleasant and efficient, recognizing that the telemarketer's problem of burnout is just as much your problem, too.

HOW LONG IS TOO LONG?

No matter how convincing a sales pitch, or how attractive the product, there are some people who simply will not buy at a particular time. They may be just gathering information, or price comparing, or just passing the time of day. After a certain period of time (usually five to seven minutes), if the salesperson feels that he is not making any headway, he has to diplomatically end the conversation. Remember, the person he's talking to may not want to buy a mattress right now, but the calls that are waiting to be answered may contain a customer who does.

After several closing questions (three should be the limit), if the customer does not want to give a yes or a no answer, the salesperson should ask a direct question such as "Is there anything else I can tell you about this product?" or "How would you like to pay for the mattress?"—a variation on the closer. If the customer still responds in the negative, the telemarketer should regard him as a potential customer—for the future. Thank him politely and ask if you can get back to him, say you're sorry that things didn't work out and you look forward to speaking with him again. Then hang up and go to the next caller.

If the salesperson senses that the caller is reluctant to reveal his phone number, the salesperson might consider giving the caller *his* name and work number. If the caller takes it, there is a good chance the salesperson will receive a call back. At Dial-A-Mattress, a great number of our sales are callbacks directly to the *bedding consultant* (telemarketer) who initially talked to the customer.

Sales is a volume business, and while you have to take the time to develop a relationship with a customer, you cannot waste too much time in a relationship that is going nowhere. The higher the price of the item, the longer you may take with the caller. If you are selling a $40,000 automobile over the phone, it follows that you should be prepared to stay on the telephone for an hour or more, with several follow-up calls on your part. On the other hand, if you are selling a $6 newsletter subscription, you might time your call to not last more than a minute or two.

PROVIDE SUGGESTED SALES "SCRIPTS"

In addition to retraining classes and one-on-one advanced training, our sales department has introduced memos that are sent to the sales staff on an intermittent basis. Each memo deals with a specific topic, such as:

- The Advantage of Shopping by Phone Instead of Shopping in a Store
- How to Provide Information on Comparative Product Quality

The memos contain suggested dialogue that can be used in conversations with customers. This provides the telemarketing staff with a series of small "scripts" that can be interchanged as necessary, to fit the needs of each specific phone call. Here's an example:

MEMORANDUM

FROM: Jennifer Grassano
TO: All Bedding Consultants
SUBJECT: Handling Objection—The Advantage of Shopping by Phone Instead of Shopping in a Store

I can understand why you think you have to shop in a store.

Each manufacturer specializes in different features, which are designed for certain types of people. Being a trained consultant on all bedding, I am able to help you select the proper mattress to suit *your* needs and guarantee you the right support.

When you go into a store you are limited to trying only the mattress the store chooses to carry. You probably end up lying on each mattress all of about 10 seconds. Did you ever spend a week in a hotel and notice that the first couple of nights the mattress feels okay, but toward the middle of the week your lower back is sore and you are very uncomfortable? That happens to people all the time. That's why you never truly know how comfortable the mattress is until you sleep on it for many nights.

We eliminate that problem by spending time talking with you—finding out specifically what you need—then we suggest the right beds, and get you the delivery the same or next day. We also guarantee a 30-day exchange for comfort as well. Sleep on the bed for at least 20 nights. If it does not seem comfortable to you, call me back and I will personally exchange it for you at no cost to you at all! Fair enough?

I have the merchandise in stock. We can deliver as soon as this afternoon or tonight. What time of day is best for you?

Sometimes a customer will make a purchase right away. Sometime he isn't ready to buy now. He may need time to comparison shop, or ask someone else's opinion, or just think it over; so that phone call will not end with a sale. But if the telemarketer does his job properly, he will leave the customer with a good feeling—toward him, and toward the company. Actually, a good salesperson develops a rapport with the customer during the first two minutes of the phone call. And if he senses that the caller is not ready to buy, the salesperson can either ask for the customer's name and phone number to call him back; or, if the customer might be unwilling to give that information, the salesperson should give the customer *his* name, and a friendly invitation to call back. Many customers do. They have built a feeling of trust, so they ask for that same salesperson, and make the purchase during that second phone call.

Knowing that this happens, stress to your telemarketers the importance of giving the customer a positive feeling—to stay positive throughout every call, no matter how it ends. Leave the caller with a good feeling, so he will remember you. Leave an impression that he won't forget—and be sure to give him your name and encourage him to call back.

Remember, a telephone sale is interactive and when an objection is raised it can be dealt with instantly. You can also change your script at any time and test new approaches, prices, special offers, add-ons, upgrades and methods. This ability to change your policies is one of the great strengths of telemarketing.

HOW TO BUILD SATISFIED CUSTOMERS

The best way to gain customer satisfaction is to follow these two rules:

- Do what needs to be done. Don't procrastinate.
- Do the best you can the first time. But don't let the fear of not being perfect stop you from acting.

Dial-A-Mattress has conducted some research on how sales personnel should treat customers and what customers want from the sales transaction. These findings may be worth sharing with your sales personnel:

- *Listen* to what the customer is saying.
- *Understand* what the customer means.
- *Believe* in what you are selling.
- *Give* full attention to the customer.
- *Always* tell the customer the truth.
- *Mention* the benefits the customer is looking for.
- *Remember* that customers want speedy service, delivery at *their* convenience, good prices, and a courteous transaction.

Perhaps the most significant development shaping global communications this decade is a renewed focus on providing impeccable customer service. For companies ranging from Fortune 500 to niche-market startups, a vigorous commitment to customer service has become the cornerstone of strategic plans.

No longer viewed as programs designed simply to respond only to customer service complaints, customer service has evolved into a series of marketing strategies with the purpose of winning and retaining an increasingly cost-and-service-conscious customer base. Training centers all over corporate America stress this heavily to their personnel. To succeed in today's competitive market, companies must excel in providing an efficient, pleasant business environment. It is through your customer service, as much as because of your product, that you will attract and keep your customers.

4

HOW TO MARKET, ADVERTISE, AND PROMOTE YOUR PRODUCT OR SERVICE

The new challenge facing corporate marketing is in convincing customers about corporate and product credibility, quality, service, fairness, and customer satisfaction. The task of the virtual corporation is to develop relationships with customers to enable them to obtain the maximum value from the product they have purchased.

THE VIRTUAL CORPORATION
WILLIAM H. DAVIDOW AND
MICHAEL S. MALONE

During the years of my business career, I've met many people who have developed truly wonderful products or services but have given virtually no thought of how to market or advertise what they've produced, invented, or selected to retail. I can think of exquisitely decorated restaurants, with exceptional food and service, but whose proprietors refused to advertise or promote themselves. Eventually they go out of business, and sometimes they never know why.

Of course, on occasion restaurants do succeed without advertising. Through word of mouth and long-standing customer loyalty, they are filled to capacity every night, anyway. By spending money on advertising they would not increase their profits; they couldn't handle any additional customers, since they're limited as to how many dinners they can serve. For small businesses like these, with a limited capacity for sales, it may not pay to advertise. But those are rare exceptions. Normally, almost any business can profit by advertising: It propels the customer, either by telephone or in person, through the "front door" of your operation.

In telemarketing, the "front door" is your ringing telephone. It is then, of course, that the sales negotiation between the customer and salesperson begins. Your salespeople cannot sell to silent telephones. In a telemarketing operation, advertising is not just essential, it is vitally important, and the lifeblood of your prospects.

Some companies immediately cut back, or cut out, some or all of their advertising when business is poor. In an attempt to lessen expenses without letting people go, they diminish their advertising budget, forgetting that they may be at a crucial point in their business. This is precisely the time that advertising is most important, to get those phones ringing, to bring in income and activity. This is more important than cutting costs. In fact, some companies *must* advertise in order to survive.

Diametrically opposed to the marketing or nonmarketing philosophy of some stubbornly unenlightened businesses is the company that sells only the sizzle of its product or service, but not the steak. Such a company promotes itself constantly but really delivers inferior or shoddy merchandise, with no sensitivity to customer needs or wants.

I'm thinking of the retail electronics retailer Crazy Eddie, whose commercials were patently offensive (if you didn't buy at Crazy Eddie's, the ads blared, "YOU'RE INSANE!") and whose inventory was virtually nonexistent. They never had what you wanted, and their sales help were usually uninformed and standoffish. Crazy Eddie built traffic with its commercials and propelled people into their stores, but since they could rarely deliver what they advertised, at the price they were offering, eventually they went out of business.

Hard sell is one approach to advertising, but if you use that method, you have to learn to sell engagingly and memorably to compensate and hold on to potential customers. Actually, it's best to avoid callous methods of doing business. And remember that it's illegal to use "bait and switch" marketing—in which you advertise one product, then when customers respond to your ad, you try to pressure them into buying an inferior item. Always, always keep your business promises and fulfill your claims.

To have a successful telemarketing business, you must be as concerned with the *process* of *advertising* and *marketing* your product or service as you are with the product or service itself. Never neglect your sales methods, your employees, your product or service, your customer, *or* your advertising and you'll do all right. If you constantly approach and exercise these elements of your business, with an eye on nurturing them, they will become routine and will benefit your company on an ongoing basis.

As you have read, I was inspired to begin my telemarketing operation as a result of reading a small advertisement for Dial-A-Steak in the *New York Post*. Once I had decided to use the same method to sell mattresses, the next step was to create an advertisement for my product, and see whether it would generate sales.

I started by buying my first print ad, a small one for less than $50. It advertised an inexpensive mattress that could be purchased by phone. No sooner did the ad appear than our phone started ringing. At first, we were often so busy and understaffed in selling furniture in the traditional way—face to face, with the customer in our showroom—that we couldn't answer the telephone and process the mattress orders that were coming in as a result of our initial ads. But we quickly realized that our telephone sales were a profitable addition to our business. Eventually we bought two phones. Then we were forced to set up a telephone answering machine to handle all of our new "phone" customers. Our message was "Hello. This is Dial-A-Mattress. Unfortunately we cannot come to the phone just now, but if you leave your name and number, we will call you back as soon as possible."

As soon as one of us had a free moment from selling on the showroom floor, dealing with a "live" customer, we would literally dash to the telephone answering machine, collect whatever messages had come in, and call all of these prospective mattress buyers. We had relatively few hangups; almost everyone did leave their number, and our conversion rate of calls to sales was quite high.

Within a short time we learned that we had to create a word picture of what we were selling, since these consumers couldn't *see* any of our mattresses. When we mastered that technique, our sales-by-phone department really mushroomed.

However, I don't suggest that you try using an answering machine if you can avoid it because:

1. You *might* lose calls.
2. When calling people back, you may not reach them.
3. It suggests a "fly-by-night" operation if the customer cannot connect with a live sales consultant right away.
4. If the potential customer is really in a hurry to buy, he may purchase your product or service elsewhere and not wait for your return call.

I relate this experience only to prove to you that you can *start* a telemarketing business without sophisticated equipment and an enormous staff of salespeople to answer your phones. Despite this somewhat awkward method of marketing, which I quickly replaced with a fairly intricate call center to answer calls with well-trained bedding consultants, twenty years later I am still successfully selling by telephone and have become one of the largest mattress retailers in the world.

One of the major conduits to the success of Dial-A-Mattress was our recognition of advertising as a stimulus to inbound calls. We have used advertising, as you should, too, to increase sales. The primary objective, specifically, is to generate calls from interested buyers. There are also some additional uses for advertising, such as an attempt to build brand loyalty or to obtain dealer support.

Moreover, I am beginning to increasingly believe that every commercial I run on radio or television, every billboard I buy, every print ad I run, every truck I emblazon with my logo and number, not only directly sells one or more mattresses for me, but also helps to establish and clarify the image of Dial-A-Mattress as, quite simply, *the* place to buy a mattress.

So think of your advertising not only as a conduit to increase calls and, ultimately, sales, today or tomorrow, but in an institutional way for the future as well. In this way, the image of your business, or store, will merge with the product or service you're selling, and whenever anyone thinks of a mattress, or a machine part, or a motorcycle, or whatever, he'll think of your company as the natural one to call.

Your toll-free number is actually a commercial: the shortest and most effective advertisement for your company. It is not merely a telephone number. A toll-free number provides the potential consumer with significant pieces of information—especially if you're using a vanity number.

Here's what it tells your customer:

How does this company do business?
By telephone.

How much is it going to cost the customer to get to your "store"?
Nothing. A 1–800 number is a toll-free call.

What is your "address"?
Your 800 number.

What is your phone number?
Your 800 number.

What is your brand identification?
Your company will become known by its 800 number.

What product do you sell?
Our vanity number shows that we sell mattresses. Your vanity number can reveal your product or service.

What will the customer experience when he does business with your company?
Since the purchase and delivery can be arranged through a single phone call, the whole process will be easy, economical, convenient, fast, and pleasant.

If you are selling a product that has a brand name other than your own—say, you are selling mattresses and you specialize in Sealys, or you're selling watches and you specialize in Rolexes, or you're selling videotapes and you have a special sale on MGM classic films—include that brand name (if it's a good, desirable one) in your ads.

True, some potential customers who see your ads may not buy directly from you but might go to another retailer as a direct result of your advertisement or commercial. But most consumers will feel safer buying by phone if they know they're going to receive a trusted brand.

Including brand names in your advertisement or commercials can also have a very beneficial side effect. This doesn't only apply to merchandise. For instance, if you are an independent magazine agent, one of your ads might mention *Newsweek* magazine. If you're a travel agency, perhaps you might run an ad that mentions the Sahara Hotel in Las Vegas. The mention of his brand name will endear you to the manufacturer, establishment, publisher or supplier, since he will be selling more of his product and, in effect, you will be helping him do his job. And if you continually manage to promote the brand name, after a short time you will probably qualify for *cooperative advertising money*.

In a "co-op" ad, you and the manufacturer (or other company) agree to share the cost of an ad that promotes both of you. Department stores often run co-op ads with major vendors. If an ad tells you to come to Macy's to buy Ralph Lauren polo shirts, the ad was probably jointly paid for by both Macy's and Ralph Lauren.

Almost every manufacturer of brand-name products will reimburse you for a portion of your advertising costs, if you:

- Prominently mention or display their brand name and/or logo.
- Place the ad or commercial in media that they approve.
- Do not display their logo adjacent to a competitor's.
- Send them a copy of your ad or commercial to prove to them that it ran.

After you have complied with the requirements to receive co-op money, the manufacturer will either send you in dollars the agreed-upon percentage directly, or will deduct the amount, as an advertising allowance, from your bill, according to the arrangement that you have made with him.

Depending on the manufacturer and product, they will, on occasion, actually provide you with a complete copy of an advertisement or commercial—saving you the creative and production costs—and all you will need to do is to have the name of *your* company and your 1–800 number inserted in the proper position. The manufacturers are willing to do this so that they might have more control over how their product is going to appear to the public; and it saves you time, effort, and money.

This co-op arrangement should range from as low as 25 percent of your cost of the ad to 100 percent (if, for example, you are helping the manufacturer introduce a new product), with the average being a 50–50 split. As you can see, co-op advertising can markedly increase the dollar potential you have in your advertising budget.

Sometimes you may qualify for co-op money from more than one source. For example, if you are selling automobiles, Chrysler might have advertising co-op money for you, as well as the B.F. Goodrich Tire Co. that had provided its co-op money, in turn, to Chrysler. You might be able to really stretch your advertising budget by claiming all of these pass-along co-op dollars that are available to you.

If you are making a great deal of money for your manufacturer or supplier, don't be afraid to ask for even more support from them. Since you're going to promote and market *their* product, they should be part of every step. Where possible, bring them in during the creative process of developing or producing your ads. They should also support you with co-op money when you conduct a sale, and even pay a portion of the warehousing and administration as it concerns their product. I often ask my suppliers this question: *"What did you do to improve our marketing, selling and distribution last year, and what do you expect to do this year?"* If they cannot answer that question positively, should you consider securing another supplier?

If you are just starting out or are not dealing with brand-name manufacturers or suppliers, you will have to get along without co-op money at first. By all means, however, from the very beginning of your advertising schedule, attempt to secure as much co-op money as possible from the manufacturers or suppliers. I have been able to receive co-op money for years from the three major mattress manufacturers, Sealy, Simmons, and Serta, and the money they give me probably accounts for one-sixth of my total advertising budget, which is now into the millions.

PLANNING YOUR ADVERTISING CAMPAIGN

Before you spend a penny on advertising, you must understand who your potential customer is and realize that not all 280 million Americans, for example, are going to buy from you. So be careful to direct your advertising to *your* customer.

You could create a magnificent four-color magazine advertisement, or a truly attractive 60-second television commercial with high production values, trying to sell $1,000,000 yachts. But if you don't direct the ad or commercial to the correct market, to the few people in the country who 1) have enough money to buy a yacht, and 2) desire to do so, you'll just be wasting your money. You will not receive one legitimate phone inquiry and you will not sell one yacht.

On the other hand, it is possible to create an ad or commercial for a fairly modest cost, which communicates directly to the customer you want to reach, and it will produce hundreds or possibly thousands of responses and actual sales.

To clarify, if you are selling a special kind of golf club or tennis racket at a reasonable price, a small ad in a golfing or tennis magazine might be all you need, because golfers and tennis players already understand the value of such a club or racket. Look at a copy of *The New York Times,* for example. (See Figure 1.) Some of their ads, as small as one-inch-by-one-column, generate thousands, sometimes tens of thousands of dollars, in sales. The sellers understand that the average *New York Times* reader is *their* customer. Week after week, issue after issue, the majority of these ads have 1–800 (or the new 1–888) toll-free numbers.

WHO IS YOUR CUSTOMER?

Initially, there are dozens of pieces of information that you need to know about your potential customers before you write, create, or place your first advertisement.

Here are some things you should try to learn about targeted customers:

1. Why do they want to buy your product or service (as compared to someone else's)?
2. How much do they want to pay?
3. What goal, if any, does your product or service serve for the customers? (If you're selling an automobile: Is it a status symbol or "just transportation"?)
4. How old are they?
5. Gender?
6. Income?
7. What experience have they had in purchasing similar products or services?
8. Why do they want to buy now?

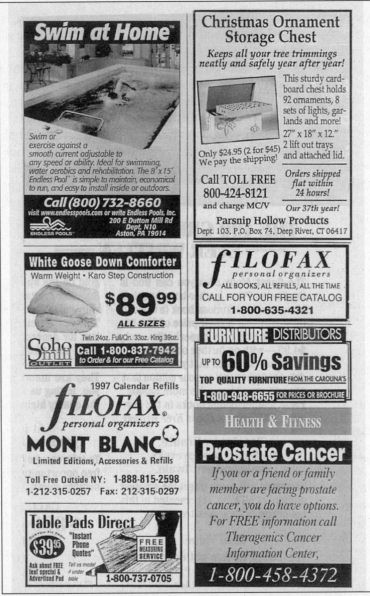

Figure 1. (Source: *The New York Times Magazine*, December 1996.)

9. What is the most important reason for their buying your product or service (price, quality, delivery, convenience, style, etc.)?
10. Where do they live?
11. What is the range of their occupations? (For example, it sounds like a good idea to advertise screwdrivers to mechanics, but not necessarily to brain surgeons.)
12. What is their marital or family status?
13. What is their lifestyle? (For example, frequent travelers would have more call for sturdy suitcases than stay-at-home couch potatoes.)
14. What are their media habits? (For example, most young people probably won't watch a Wagnerian opera on television, so to advertise Guess jeans during the commercial break between acts of such an opera would be fruitless.)
15. What is their education? (Advertising a volume of the complete plays of Shakespeare, for instance, to readers of the *National Enquirer*, who, demographically, are mainly high-school dropouts, would obviously not pay. Conversely, advertising a fast-food restaurant in *The New Yorker*, where most readers possess graduate degrees and eat in upscale restaurants would not pay either.)

In determining who your customer is, for advertising purposes, you must also attempt to analyze the absolute size of the market that you are going to address. If you are selling locomotives (real ones, not models), for example, there may be only a few railroad systems in the entire country, or possibly the world, that will be in the market for your product; therefore, there may be only one publication in which it would possibly make any sense to advertise.

But if, for instance, you are a general-purpose department store with tens of thousands of generic products, and where just about any consumer from the age of 10 to 100, male or female, might want to shop, you greatly increase the possibilities of where to advertise. Be sure to consider the price range of your merchandise to further determine your most effective arena. A high-end department store such as Lord & Taylor would probably not advertise in the same medium as, say, Sears Roebuck, a more bargain-oriented store.

So, before placing any advertising, learn to define the potentiality, peculiarities, and specifications of your market. What products are you going to include? At Dial-A-Mattress, in addition to selling mattresses, we sell complete beds, pillows, mattresses, covers, sheets, blankets, and a number of other products, but we usually choose, based on our experience, to advertise only our mattresses and leave the other products to additional sales efforts by our telemarketers when the customer calls in to buy a mattress.

The word most often used by customers (on the customer reply forms provided with each delivery) to describe Dial-A-Mattress' delivery service is *convenient*.

Create *customer reply forms* for your business, and distribute one to each customer, along with his purchase. The information that you receive on the customer reply forms can be invaluable, and you should always attempt not only to sell a product but to gather as many responses and reactions from your customers as possible.

Some possible questions you might include on a response form are:

- How did you hear of our company? (Advertising, word of mouth, etc.)
- Have you ever bought from us before?
- What was the single most important reason you purchased your bedding from Dial-A-Mattress?
- How do you rank the following on a scale of 1 to 10:
  - Price
  - Delivery
  - Convenience
  - Courtesy and efficiency of delivery
  - Satisfaction with product

- Would you buy from us again?
- Are there any ways that we can improve?
- Did you compare prices or quality of our product to any other company before buying?
- How did the sales consultant treat you? Any complaints?
- Was the experience of ordering the product satisfactory?
- What other products would you be interested in purchasing by telephone?

Generally, you may discover that consumers who purchase your product or service by telephone may be socioeconomically different from those who rely solely on going to a retail store and purchasing in the traditional way. Studies that we have made at Dial-A-Mattress have shown that telephone buyers often have relatively high incomes, white-collar professions, and more education than those who do not use the telephone to shop. For such customers, if you have a product or service that seems to be more geared toward a middle-class or upper-class clientele, you will be that much further ahead in your sales approach.

We usually include a business reply card along with the invoice that accompanies all of our deliveries. The card asks the consumer to tell us what was right or wrong about the sales transaction, and also asks for other information about the customer's reactions to our services.

This data is invaluable because, after analysis, we come to understand our customers needs and preferences better and better. I suggest that you survey your own customers in the same way, to gather as much information as possible. This will enable you to determine the ideal kind of advertising and marketing to sell your product or service, and in what media. Remember, in this age, the person with the most information wins.

Of the products that you have chosen to advertise and promote, have you selected the one that might have high sales potential? That is, will it be a popular item that your customers will buy in substantial quantities, and is it a product that gives you ample profit? It should be both.

What area is your advertising going to be directed to? The whole world? All 50 states? Or just your small town of Southeast Pleasantville, pop. 4,732? As you can see, where you are willing and capable of distributing your product may very well determine where you advertise. To illustrate, if you can only distribute to states east of the Mississippi and north of the Mason-Dixon line, then a commercial running on a local television station in Eugene, Oregon, will do you no good.

Is there a seasonality connected to your product or service? If so, not only where but *when* you should advertise becomes essential. Constructing a seasonal sales index, product-by-product, dollar-by-dollar, will give you a great deal of information *when* to place your ads or commercials. Cases in point are that air conditioners usually don't sell in the winter months; baseball tickets for the next summer's season do (or used to). Skis sell in late fall and all winter long; barbecue stoves sell only in the late spring or summer.

How can you learn more about your customer and more about the market in which you are operating, or hope to? To begin with, if you have been in business for virtually any length of time, you have *some* facts and figures, or even an innate sense, as to how many of a particular product of yours has sold, at what price, and to what kind of customer, and perhaps to what kind of addresses. If you normally sell to wealthy people living in the Gold Coast in Chicago or the Upper East Side in New York, the medium you select to advertise in must reach affluent, highly educated people. This seat-of-the-pants market research may give you enough information to begin reserved experimentation as to where to commence advertising for a telemarketing campaign.

If you are just starting out or launching a new product, you will need to gather, in any way that you can, the information that you need to target your customer, and to determine where and when to advertise.

Research data about potential customers can be secured from research companies. But I must warn you—and I speak from experience—that although they may be extremely helpful in determining who your customer is, or who he might be, the fees that are charged by these research companies are extremely high. Information is not inexpensive. At Dial-A-Mattress we had an extensive two-volume study conducted by the Western International Media Corporation to determine just exactly who our mattress customers are as to age, occupation, income, address, television and cultural preferences, as well as dozens of other essential pieces of information that we needed to piece together, to complete the puzzle called Our Consumer. We learned a great deal, which has enabled us to focus our energies and resources in the right direction and aim them toward our true market. If your business is doing extremely well, and you can afford an expenditure of $10,000 to $150,000 to collect the data you need, I say, "go for it." But if not, here are some less expensive ways to gather your own data:

- Consider hiring some engaging and intelligent college students, on a part-time, temporary basis, to poll, survey, and interview potential customers. This can be done either by phone (of course!), face to face if the customer is in your store, or even by surveying passersby on the street. Recently, I hired a young man to gather a piece of information I needed from the general public. Although I needed only a one-word answer to one question, I wanted a sampling of at least 1,000 people. Standing in the street, the young man was able to complete the task and retrieve the information that I needed, in about a day-and-a-half's work.
- Also, recently we did a telephone survey of 500 of our callers and learned a great deal of information that was extremely valuable to us. We asked six essential questions:

  1. Did you shop at a department or bedding store *before* you called Dial-A-Mattress? (If yes, what store?)
  2. Did you shop at a department or bedding store after you first called Dial-A-Mattress?

3. Did you buy from Dial-A-Mattress? (If no, did you have a problem that stopped you? If we could deal with that problem, would you buy from us?)
4. How much do you expect to pay for a good set of bedding?
5. How long do you think most people shop for bedding?
6. What convinced you it was time to get a new bed?

In essence, what we learned from this rapid but nevertheless salient survey was:

- Fifty-five percent of callers to Dial-A-Mattress have *not* shopped elsewhere before they called us. Fifty-eight percent didn't competitively shop after calling us. This confirms other data we've developed that indicates that our customers are generally new to direct response.
- Of the 45 percent who did shop around, either before or after they dialed 1–800–MATTRESS, Macy's was the store they checked out by a margin of 2–1 over second-ranked Sears.
- Half of all callers bought from us. The holdouts were overwhelmingly based on price objections. Surprisingly, when asked if we could solve their problem would they then buy from us, the answer was "No" by a 5–1 margin. Evidently when customers are presented with a price that's outside their comfort zone, they are gone and generally stay gone.
- Half of all callers expect to pay between $300 and $600 for a "good" set of bedding, though 21 percent of the people who called us have no idea how much a good bed should cost. Interestingly, 16 percent (almost one in five) thought a good set should run between $700 and $800 for a more high-quality mattress, though they haven't checked any prices in stores or advertisements to find out current price ranges.

- While half of all callers had no idea about how long it normally takes to shop around and select a new mattress, one third thought it fell between three days and two weeks.
- Evidently our message is stimulating demands for beds. 40 percent of callers said they needed to replace old or worn out bedding and that was the reason they came into the market. That's twice as many responses as the number two answer, moving, which was mentioned by 17 percent of the respondents. Surprisingly, marriage or divorce wasn't mentioned, though remodeling, the need for a child's first bed, and a bed for the extra room were mentioned a significant number of times.

In another telephone survey, shortly after that, we learned the following information:

- Roughly half of those we called made a purchase from Dial-A-Mattress.
- The number of customers claiming to call with a preference (51%), that is, calling and asking for a specific brand of mattress, is much greater than we previously thought, and almost everyone with a preference (94%) bought the brand they preferred.
- In spite of the greater-than-expected preference, 80 percent of buyers claim that their brand choice was influenced by our bedding consultants. Compare that to the 6 percent who claim that brand names influenced their choice!
- A surprisingly large number of customers (60%) have not made any direct-response purchases within the last 6 months. Those who have, primarily bought clothing, electronics, and household goods. This suggests that we are developing a market (for beds and for direct-response purchasing) as much as taking share from other retailers.

- Consider mailing a modest direct-mail survey of 1,000 to 2,000 pieces to a possible prospect list (if you are selling a new pharmaceutical product, as a case in point, you could write to a group of doctors and/or pharmacists), and see what kind of response you will get from your survey.
- Try circulating questionnaires in your store, if you have one.
- Include a questionnaire in the packing of the products that you sent to your already existing or new customers.
- Hold a contest with a valuable gift as first prize, for which all contestants must fill out a potential product survey.
- Talk on your own to direct or indirect competitors, or suppliers of similar products or services, and see if you can gain any information about the customer and/or the market. Bear in mind that most people are extremely competitive and are not eager to share their "wisdom" or information, but others might be quite willing to pontificate about their success, especially if you are not a direct "down the street" competitor.
- Survey your own employees, first as actual customers of the product or service involved, and then for whatever other information or insight they might have about your potential consumer. Many of your employees might have meaningful experience from other jobs and with customers of similar products and will be able to share their intelligence, knowledge, and experience with you.
- Request demographic information from your manufacturer or supplier. If you want to sell bicycles by telephone, as a case in point, the Schwinn Co. will probably be able to answer questions, such as: 1) What is the average age of a bicycle purchaser, 2) How much is the average retail price of a bicycle these days, 3) What kinds of styles of bicycles are most popular, and so on.
- Go to libraries, especially those with an extensive business section, and conduct some research on your product or the demographics of the group, or city, or area, or gender that you are trying to reach.

ADVERTISING AGENCY OR ON YOUR OWN?

We all like to think of ourselves as individualists; and if you are heading up your own operation, you probably are an independent spirit of sorts. This does not mean, however, that you should only rely on your own knowledge, talent, and expertise to complete every task necessary for a successful telemarketing operation. This is especially true in establishing advertising to produce inbound calls.

If you do have experience and knowledge in creating advertisements, selecting media, buying time and space, and all of the other elements that go into the advertising pursuit, then you probably *should* attempt to handle the advertising "in shop" rather than secure an advertising agency. But don't fool yourself: After much patient self-inspection and an honest appraisal of your abilities, you might realize that you do not have the time or expertise to write and/or produce a successful ad. Enter: The advertising agency.

Whether to secure an advertising agency (and how to secure one), depends on 1) as stated, your experience and ability; 2) the size of your business; 3) the amount of your advertising budget; and 4) what you hope to accomplish with your advertising.

There are some advertising agencies that will work with you even if you start out with an extremely limited budget. Perhaps you want to place one advertisement in your local newspaper, with your 1–800 number, advertising a janitorial service that you are promoting. You only want to spend $350 for your first ad just to see what kind of result you may have.

If you go to an advertising agency with your idea for the ad, they might write, design, and place it for you, using their specialized talent, in the hope that the ad *will* produce results and that you will not only continue to run it but perhaps, if successful, run it in other media, as well.

Advertising agencies work on commission paid by the media, usually 15% of the cost of the ad or commercial. In other words, for your $350 ad, the agency will be paid $52.50 by the newspaper as a discount or commission. You pay nothing to the agency except the $350 it cost to place the ad in the newspaper. If you need special services, such as having a photograph made, or artwork rendered, and so on, you will have to pay the agency on a cost-plus basis, the specific amounts to be negotiated.

Depending on your budget, the agency you select will be either large or small. I've known agencies who were happy to accept (and write) $50 ads; on the other hand, the average annual billing for individual clients for an advertising agency such as Bates Worldwide is over $1,000,000.

Large agencies usually set a minimum billing amount, unless they feel that your product or service is so exciting and brimming over with a possibility of success that they are willing to gamble with you in trying to promote it. Then the advertising agency almost becomes a silent partner of sorts.

In deciding what agency to choose, you should consider not only its size (because if your budget is small you might be overlooked as the agency spends more time with other, larger accounts), but what specialization, if any, the agency has.

Some agencies handle only direct-mail advertising, for example, and some concern themselves mainly with people like yourself who are attempting to bring in a substantial amount of inbound calls through 1–800 telemarketing. Other agencies narrow their activity to specific kinds of products or services such as financial or travel or pharmaceutical advertising. If you can find an agency that deals specifically with your product or service, you will be capitalizing on their experience with the line.

The most important criteria in selecting an agency are: 1) Are they willing to plug in their expertise, experience and talent to help your campaign become a success? and 2) What is their track record in promoting other clients?

If your advertising budget is somewhat substantial, you can ask the prospective agency for a speculative presentation. At Dial-A-Mattress, recently we asked for proposals from agencies because we were planning to spend $7–8 million a year in eight different markets. We wanted the agency that we selected to create new radio and television spots for us that would prompt more calls to our 1–800–MATTRESS number, reduce callers' initial skepticism, pre-sell the service, and attract buyers for higher-ticket goods.

We weren't looking for a Cindy Crawford as a spokesmodel, or a Michael Jordan to jump up and down on our mattresses, but we wanted an agency that could improve our already existing 30,000 calls a week, and we wanted the agency to prove they could do it before we went with them.

What kind of ad or commercial is best for your product or service? What media would best generate responses for your inbound calls? What did other ads or commercials that the agency created look like, and how did they pull?

If the prospective agency creates a speculative campaign for you, showing you mock ads and commercials, and presenting you with a list of media buys—where they recommend (and at what price) your ads and commercials should run—try to include as many of your executives or employees in the presentations as possible, so they can help you decide whether the agency's suggestions work with your specific product or service. If possible, have a few of your customers and manufacturers come to the presentation as well, so the entire assembly can act as a focus group.

Whatever advertising you do, don't just select the first agency that you go to. Shop around with at least four or five agencies and compare services, enthusiasm, performance, and general impressions.

DOING IT YOURSELF

There are other ways of handling your advertising, other than securing an advertising agency. There are media-buying services that will attempt to get you the best prices in the most responsive media, but who do not handle the actual creative work of producing ads or commercials. At Dial-A-Mattress, we use Western International Media, and they are extremely professional and have helped us a great deal.

You can do some or most of the creative and production work yourself, or secure the services you need—and perhaps lack—from freelancers. A company called New York Broadcast Services has created our commercials, for both radio and television, for years and has been instrumental in capturing the image that we have hoped to portray: a mattress company that is entrepreneurial, no-nonsense, competitively priced, designed for the customer.

Freelance advertising copywriters can be hired to create your print ads. Art directors, also freelance, can be secured to design them. Radio and television commercial writers and directors can be employed for a fee. You, or an associate, can check rates and frequencies and sizes of ads by going through library reference volumes, such as *Standard Rate and Data Service,* and make up your own media recommendations of where to run your ads. Call all the media that you are considering using (that is, each magazine, radio station, newspaper, and TV station where you might run your commercial or put your ad in), and have them send you a media kit, which usually contains sample copies of their periodicals, demographic information, circulation figures, deadlines, and prices.

In addition to considering the demographic profiles of readers of newspapers and magazines where you place ads, and the listeners of radio stations and viewers of television channels where you are going to run commercials, one of the most important elements of your media purchase lies in how much it costs to reach that audience in relationship to the number of readers, viewers, or listeners. This is usually referred to as Cost Per Thousand (CPM).

The formula for determining CPM is fairly simple and is usually computed as a point of comparison on the one-time rate for a black and white page:

$$\frac{\text{Cost per page x 1000}}{\text{Circulation}} = \text{CPM}$$

In order to calculate the cost per thousand for a commercial on radio or television, the formula works as follows:

$$\frac{\text{Cost of one unit of time (e.g., 10 second, 30 second or 60 second commercial)} \times 1{,}000}{\text{Number of households or individuals reached during a given program}} = \text{CPM}$$

Whether you are going to contract an advertising agency, do the advertising yourself, or, as we have done at Dial-A-Mattress, incorporate an amalgam of creative, production, and buying services, you should know what makes—and doesn't make—a strong advertisement or commercial in order to stimulate inbound calls.

Years ago, most direct-response advertising consisted of print ads with clip-out coupons, or advertising went to the home or business, often with a postage-paid reply card or envelope. It was believed that as a direct-response strategy, a clip-out coupon involved a deeper psychological resonance on the part of the consumer, because he must physically cut the coupon out, fill it in, find an envelope, address it, and place postage on it. This "investment" of time and effort on the part of the consumer, it was believed, indicated a seriousness concerning the product or service he or she was inquiring about.

Although a telephone response to a commercial or an advertisement might not display quite as much commitment of time and effort on the part of the responder, the ease of picking up the telephone and dialing a toll-free 1–800 number far outweighs virtually any other kind of consumer connection or interest in products or services. Most people find it much more convenient to make a fast phone call than to use the mail, and they are delighted that the call is free.

What you want to do with an advertisement or commercial is to create a message that is believable, brief, and that propels the reader or viewer to go to the telephone to call your 1–800 number.

Without becoming too technical or psychological, you might want to study Abraham Maslow's hierarchy of needs in an attempt to reach your potential customers. Maslow's theory of needs can be broken down into two major principles: 1) A satisfied need is not necessarily a motivator of behavior; and 2) a need at any level only becomes activated once a lower level has been satisfied. (See Figure 2.)

So when you are creating an ad, try to address avenues for individual needs and remove any obstacles blocking need satisfaction. For example, study the advertisement "Top Ten Reasons to Buy a Mattress from Dial-A-Mattress with your American Express® Card," on the following page, a Dial-A-Mattress approach that we ran successfully in a number of publications. (See Figure 3.)

What needs, according to Maslow, does that advertisement address? First, it touches upon one of the most basic needs: physiological. We all need sleep. . . and restful sleep at that. Buying a new mattress implies that the physiological need will be satisfied.

A second need that the ad confronts is safety, in that the customer is reassured that he can exchange the mattress within 30 days if it is not comfortable.

A third need reflected in the ad is esteem, since the $50 saving off regular prices, the delayed payment, and no interest if paid within 90 days gives the purchaser a personal sense of competency in buying our mattress, a mastery over one's own finances in recognizing—and acting upon—a bargain.

In creating your own ad or commercial, analyze what you are attempting to do: What are you selling; why would the customer want to buy it; and how can they either gain more information about it or actually order it without much further thought on their part? (See Figure 4.)

WHAT ARE YOU SELLING?

Make it clear that you are selling car washing, not cars; that you are selling food, not drink; that you are selling airline tickets, not hotel reservations.

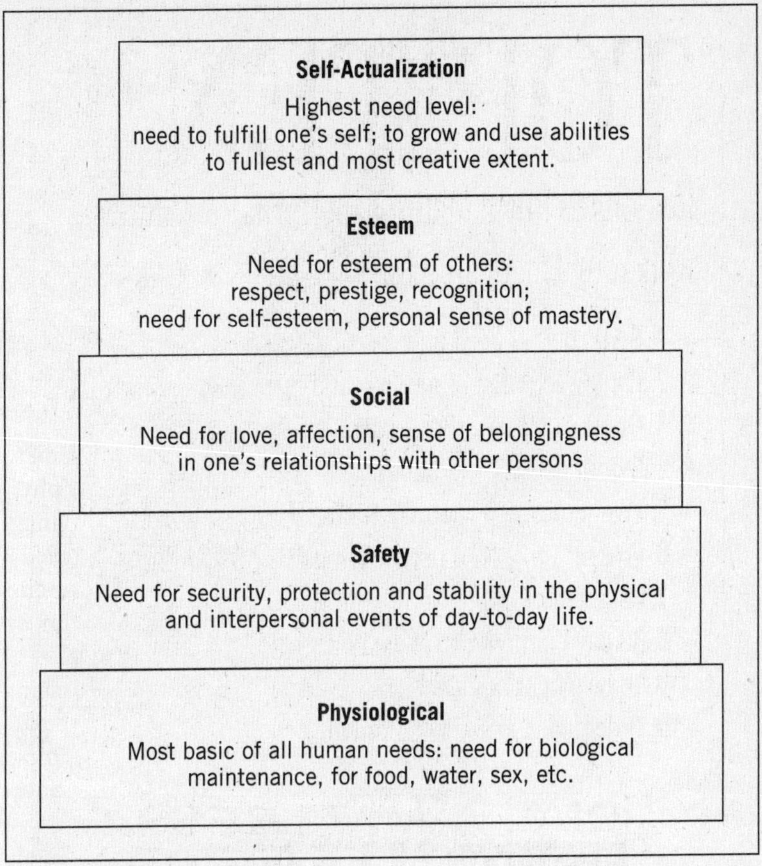

Figure 2. Maslow's Pyramid.

Have you ever read a travel ad that screams a low, low, low price at you, until you read the fine print below and discover all of the details, qualifications and restrictions that have no relationship to the headlined price? *These kinds of ads do not work!* They infuriate rather than convince; they repudiate rather than sell; they annoy rather than please.

Be honest and forthcoming in your advertising and convince the reader or viewer that you are sincere in your offers. Make

TOP TEN

Reasons to Buy a Mattress From Dial-A-Mattress with Your American Express® Card

1. **$50** coupon good till February 29th
2. Largest selection of name-brand mattresses in New York
3. Order 24 hours a day, 7 days a week
4. 2 hour delivery available
5. Free removal of your old mattress
6. Free set-up of your new bedding
7. Payment only after your approval
8. 30 day Comfort Exchange Policy
9. To help fight hunger
10. Order today, sleep better tonight

DIAL-A-MATTRESS
1-800-MATTRESS
LEAVE OFF THE LAST "S" FOR SAVINGS

Every time you make a purchase with the American Express® Card between November 1 and December 31, 1995, you'll help provide a meal for someone who is hungry.* Additionally, Dial-A-Mattress will match the American Express contribution to the Charge Against Hunger campaign for each Card purchase at Dial-A-Mattress.

*American Express will donate up to $5,000,000 to Share Our Strength based on 3 cents per Card purchase between 11/1/95 and 12/31/95. Donation is not tax deductible for Cardmembers.

Cards
Don't Leave Home Without It.®

$50 OFF ANY SET

DIAL-A-MATTRESS
1-800-MATTRESS
LEAVE OFF THE LAST "S" FOR SAVINGS

$25 MATTRESS ONLY

$50.00 off our already low prices on a premium Sealy Posturepedic,® Serta Perfect Sleeper,® Simmons® Beautyrest® or Dial-A-Pedic® mattress and box spring set ($25 for a mattress only). Payment must be made with the American Express® Card.

Coupon must be mentioned at time of order and presented to the driver at the time of delivery.

Cannot be combined with any other offer. Limit one coupon per order. Merchandise subject to availability. Some models excluded. May not be available in all areas. Void where prohibited. Expires: February 29, 1995. (NYM2/29)

Figure 3. (Reprinted courtesy of Mulryan/Nash.)

Who you sleep with is your business. How you sleep is ours.

1-800-MATTRES

Call Dial-A-Mattress anytime, 24 hours a day, 7 days a week. And leave off the last "S" for savings.
We feature Sealy Posturepedic, Serta Perfect Sleeper, Simmons Beautyrest and Dial-A-Pedic.

Figure 4. The advertisement above may seem to contradict some of the things I've been saying about trying to reach a general market. With this ad, however, we were attempting to reach a niche market, the gay populace. The ad was enormously successful. (Reprinted courtesy of Mulryan/Nash.)

sure they know by your message that what they see—or read—is what they'll get.

Why Should They Buy It?

In our ad, "Top Ten Reasons to Buy a Mattress from Dial-A-Mattress with your American Express® Card" (See Figure 3), we offer all kinds of incentives for a consumer to buy: price, convenience (delivery, set-up, and removal), and quality (we deal only with the best brands).

Search for the true value in what you are offering when you advertise your product or service, and then find a way to communicate that to the reader or viewer. This gives your potential customer confidence that he is not buying a pig in a poke. I'm reminded of the billboards in Moscow during the old Soviet regime that read: "BUY SOAP!" or "SMOKE CIGARETTES," without mentioning brand or rationale to buy. Is there any wonder that this unimaginative form of noncapitalist advertising failed to sell anything in the Soviet Union?

Your message should be directed *to* the consumers: How will your product or service help *them*, please *them*, entertain *them*? How will your product or service fulfill one or more of their Maslowian needs?

Offering Incentives

I'm a great believer in offering premiums or gifts in order to induce the sale. Over the years I have given away everything from free tickets to Broadway plays and movie theaters, to bestselling books and costume jewelry. My theory is that it really doesn't hurt to spend a little extra to get that sale, because once a customer comes into your "store" (by way of the telephone), you know that they may come back again, and also recommend your product or service to their friends.

Obviously you can't go overboard on giving away gift items if they cost more than you are going to make in profit. If I am only going to make $50 in profit on an inexpensively priced mattress, I certainly am not going to give away a pair of Broadway theater tickets that have a value greater than that.

So when Dial-A-Mattress decided to sponsor the appropriately named Broadway show *Once upon a Mattress*, we offered two tickets to everyone who bought an *ultra premium* mattress set. Now the show's ads promote us, and our ads promote the show. It also gave us the opportunity to use a great headline for our ads: DIAL-A-MATTRESS IS NOW DELIVERING ON BROADWAY. (See Figure 5.)

WHERE TO ADVERTISE

In starting my telemarketing business, I first advertised with tiny ads in the least expensive newspapers I could find. The idea of advertising on radio or television seemed to be totally out of my financial reach, an impossible dream. . . in my mind. Television was where such giants as Cadillac and Mercedes-Benz advertised, and where Burger King and Wendy's seemed always to be on the air. I didn't have that kind of money, I thought. Anyway, I was always hearing that a commercial aired during the Superbowl cost some incredible amount like $1 million *per second*, or that one 30-second commercial aired during prime time on a network cost almost a quarter of a million dollars.

I just didn't know that some commercials on television, depending on where and when they were broadcast, were quite reasonable. When I looked into the prices to air commercials, I discovered that you could buy spots on local stations, late at night, for about $30 per 60 seconds.

Aside from the relative reasonableness of cost, television commercials 1) had impact; 2) reached huge audiences; 3) could be more credible than print ads; and 4) were more memorable than newspaper ads. In the past few decades, people have spent more time with television than with any other medium; and remember, as long as the television set is on, your commercial message can

Figure 5. (Courtesy of D.K.B. and Partners, Inc.)

still be *heard* even when people aren't actually watching the screen.

I soon learned that television commercials closely paralleled personal selling. An enthusiastic, well-informed salesperson, on television, was not unlike my best and most effective salespeople in my showroom. If the walk-in potential customer was serious about buying, then my store salesman, if properly trained, informed, and motivated, would invariably make the sale. Why should it be any different with television?

And since all I was trying to accomplish was to get people to call my 1–800 number so that a *live* salesperson could talk to them and explain and sell the product, the commercial really didn't have to be all that complex.

Television has the ability of creating action, such as watching consumer-actors actually *use* your product or service. What other medium can show your product or service in use?

At first, my television commercials seemed to be somewhat rough-hewn—almost homemade—and were criticized in some quarters for their unprofessional look, being compared to those carrot-slicing machine commercials that one would see on a local station at 3 o'clock in the morning. On our first commercials, a salesman or saleswoman came on, spoke fairly rapidly, showed a few mattresses as though in a small showroom, and asked the viewer to call our 1–800 number.

Yet our no-nonsense approach, without scenery, image, jingles, actors, or props, made our commercials actually believable *and said what our consumers wanted to hear:* They could order a mattress over the phone; the price would be better than competitive; it was as easy as picking up the phone and ordering it; it would be delivered entirely at their convenience; and we would take their old mattress away.

The look, feel, and message of our commercials said that Dial-A-Mattress was inexpensive, speedy, convenient, and honest. In effect, we were selling a service, and we found it was a service that people wanted. The phones began to ring, and ring, and ring. . . .

This is the kind of television commercial that I suggest you consider producing: one that is straightforward in its message, void of expensive hi-tech techniques and superstars, and motivates your viewer to pick up the phone to call your 1–800 toll-free number. Make sure that your commercial, your announcer, or whoever is listing the benefits of your product or service:

- Mentions your toll-free number over and over again. (For a list of popular 1–800 numbers, see Chapter Two).
- Lists the name of your company (in case the potential customer copies the number incorrectly or forgets it).
- Mentions several benefits that the viewer will enjoy if he calls your 1–800 number.
- Uses short, familiar words.
- Gives the viewer a deadline ("Act now!") to receive a special benefit.

In addition to orally announcing the information mentioned above, you should also have it printed graphically on the television screen. Hearing your message and seeing it—and seeing the 1–800 number—will imprint it on the viewer's mind.

Make sure that your product or service, whether it is a mattress or a lawnmower, a set of dishes or a trip to Paris, is clearly visible early on in the commercial. You must also stress quality, reliability, and good taste. Later on in the commercial, you might consider introducing a few testimonials or recommendations of your product or service by several people.

Here is where I part company with the advertising experts—with some exceptions. I don't believe that it is necessary to secure famous people to sell your product or service. I am totally aware that if a Michael Jordan appears on the television screen, it will attract the viewer's attention, but does it truly make the viewer heed the advertising message?

Certainly, as examples of testimonials, you will be able to point to such figures as Ray Charles or Michael Jackson, who are both connected with Pepsi-Cola. Your argument would be that since these celebrities gain the attention of consumers, particularly young people who might identify them with the product or service, then sales will automatically rise.

But few companies can afford such superstars. You would have to sell a great many Big Macs, or whatever, to pay the $1,000,000-or-more fee that you would have to expend for their endorsements.

My suggestion is that you simply present brief interviews of people who will lend believability to the promise made in the advertising content of your commercial. These can be "real" satisfied customers, or actors who have the ability to project sincerity and give credibility to your product or service.

The exception that we have made with celebrity endorsement at Dial-A-Mattress is the use of radio talk-show hosts, such as Howard Stern, Bob Grant, or ex-Mayor Ed Koch. They depart from the prepared script and elaborate, in their own words, on the superiority of our service and the quality of our products. Although we may be paying as much as $1,000 a spot for one of these ad-lib attestations, they are cost-effective because they have been extremely successful for us in producing 1–800 inbound calls. The way that the talk-show hosts personalize their relationship to our product convinces the potential customer to call us.

Although it may be a cliché, nevertheless: It pays to advertise. Sometimes you never know who your message will reach, or how, or when. More than once, we have received telephone calls from people who found an old print advertisement of ours in a newspaper that they had used to line a cabinet drawer several years ago. When they removed the old newspaper to reline the drawer, they noticed our ad and called us to order a mattress. Other people have scribbled down our 1–800–MATTRESS number but did not have the time or opportunity to call us for a year or more. Then, when their old mattress became intolerable, they dug out the phone number and called us.

One of the more interesting sales adventures we had, occurred one Saturday afternoon. A customer was walking through the consumer electronics department of Macy's, where hundreds of television sets were displayed. The store had all of the sets tuned in to the same channel, so customers could see how clearly they played. One of our Dial-A-Mattress commercials was broadcast, and the customer stopped to watch it. She liked what she saw and heard ("two-hour delivery, discount prices, we remove your old mattress. . . "), asked the Macy's sales clerk to direct her to a public telephone, and phoned us from the department store to order a mattress.

As coincidence would have it, we had bought a substantial amount of air time on that TV station that day, and had scheduled several commercials to be played during a relatively short time period. Apparently the commercial was quite effective. Every time it was broadcast over that bank of television sets in Macy's, more and more people called us—sometimes directly from the store, and sometimes from a nearby phone just outside—to order one or more mattresses. Bear in mind that Macy's itself sells mattresses, as do most department stores. When our sales representatives asked why the customers called us, instead of buying directly from the store, they all said that they wanted to take advantage of our quick delivery service and better prices.

NOT JUST TELEVISION

Although television has been the best medium for Dial-A-Mattress in producing inbound calls, providers of certain products or services might find other media conduits more beneficial. I believe that the more narrowly defined the market is for your product or service, the less successful television will be as a device to bring inbound calls into your company.

If you are trying to sell to the general public, via television, an expensive chess set, for example, it could be that your target group—serious chess players—is too defined for a commercial to go into the mass medium. The thousands of dollars that you might spend on television commercials—producing them and buying time for them to be broadcast—might be wasted, whereas a small print advertisement in a small-circulation chess periodical might net you hundreds of calls.

In order for television to work for you in producing inbound calls, you must have a product or service that is relatively generic—such as a mattress, or dog food, or automobiles, or clothing—where almost all of the community that receives the broadcast are potential buyers.

Once your company is up and running and is fully operational, you should consider testing and experimenting with forms of advertising other than broadcast.

At Dial-A-Mattress, our weekly advertising schedule looks something like this:

Advertising Medium	% of Advertising Expenditures
Truck	1%
(In addition to trucks that deliver exclusively for Dial-A-Mattress, we have purchased advertising on other trucks, as well.)	
Radio	23%
Billboards	4%
Yellow Pages	4%
Television	50%
Bloomberg	2%
Internet	1%
Print	5%
(Newspapers and magazines)	
Direct mail	1%
Beach Fly-Over	less than 1%

It's extremely important to know that direct-response advertising sales by telephone usually entitles the advertiser to a 20 percent discount off the price of the general advertising rate card in most media.

In order to secure this relatively large discount, many of my commercials are run at off-peak times, which actually may be an advantage: At off-hours, the viewer might be not quite as engaged in or enthralled with the process of watching television, and is then more likely to pick up the phone and dial our number.

Also, for a mattress commercial, late-night advertising seems to be a natural. Twenty-four percent of all Americans watch television in bed, and if they have a less-than-comfortable mattress under them, then the connection between what they're experiencing and our commercial is irresistible. So, if you're selling cereal, advertise in the morning; pajamas, at night; toys for children, in the afternoons or Saturday mornings; and so on.

Rate card prices are not etched in stone, and whenever the economy is suffering, the possibilities for negotiating for larger discounts are greater. Whatever you do, as a direct-response advertiser, never, never, *never* pay the full rate card advertising price.

As you see, most of my advertising dollars, 50 percent, goes into television, but that does not mean that the other money is wasted, by any means.

I think that billboard advertising can be quite effective in building inbound calls. But be careful not to put too many details onto the billboard. *Remember, you are not consummating the sale as a result of the potential consumer seeing and reading your billboard.* The finality of the sale will come when the customer calls your number and speaks to your salesperson. Actually, you have only four or five seconds to get your message across as drivers speed down the highway or street. And you know what that message should be: your 1–800 toll-free telephone number!

If you use billboard advertising, it is essential that your 1–800 number be a vanity number. Consider the driver who sees your billboard ad for a Caribbean cruise, for example, and must remember a number, something like 1–800–922–8643, to reach you. Compare that to a number such as 1–800–FLY–CHEAP and you'll know how much easier it is to see and retain than a seven-digit phone number. Recall is low in any event; without a vanity number it could be nonexistent.

Before you create your first billboard ad, drive past a number of them and have someone time your reading of the message, and, if each billboard gives a phone number, determine whether you can recall it. Keep this in mind when you create your own billboard message.

Try to create a quick, clean, and understandable message, and attempt to restrict the ad to three or four elements at most: 1) a graphic of your product or service; 2) your logo; 3) the name of your company; and 4) your 1–800 toll-free number, displayed as large and as clearly as possible.

One of my current billboard campaigns contains only a graphic of a young lady speaking on a telephone, a delivery man holding a mattress, the words "Convenient & Fast," and my telephone number: 1–800-MATTRESS. (See Figure 8.)

In fact, one of the most successful billboard campaigns that I ever saw was on Queens Boulevard near my home in New York. It was for McDonald's. The billboard had the traditional golden arches, separated by the letters "M-M-M-M-M-M," one "M" between each arch. At the bottom of the arch, the address of the closest McDonald's was given. Simple, witty, effective.

All in all, billboard advertising serves principally to *remind* customers of what they already know something about. Your company, your product, your service, should already have been

Figure 8. (Courtesy of Modografics.)

I've even experimented with placing my advertisement in ball parks. Here, at Shea Stadium, our Dial-A-Mattress sign hangs behind home plate. In addition to the tens of thousands of baseball fans who see it "live" at the stadium, hundreds of thousands—and in some cases, millions—see it every time a batter comes to the plate. It's simple, uncrowded, and direct. . . and it works. (Photograph courtesy of the New York Mets.)

established in the consumer's mind. You should probably not use billboard advertising if you are just starting out, or introducing brand-new products or services. Also, you will only reach customers outside of their homes—perhaps one of the best places to advertise for a restaurant, for example, but one of the worst for medical supplies.

Similarly, despite the fact that I don't invest much of my advertising dollars in direct mail, if you have the right product or service and an up-to-date and specific mailing list that targets your potential customers, you could do quite well in producing inbound calls by using the mails.

To illustrate, if you were selling a resort honeymoon package and could secure a list of prospective soon-to-be-married couples, you could design a mailing directed to that audience and even personalize the letter and envelope that go along with your sales brochure. Under these circumstances, it is possible that you could have a return of 10 percent or higher (although a 3 percent return is considered excellent by most direct-mail companies) on your mailing, and you could achieve a successful campaign.

The disadvantages in using a direct-mail campaign might outweigh the advantages, however. Direct mail is expensive: roughly $300 for each 1,000 kits mailed. So, if you are selling a $100 product that cost you $50 to manufacture, buy, or ship, you would have to sell six of your items for each 1,000 kits that you mail out, just to break even. Depending on your market, this rate of return might not be possible.

Additionally, direct mail has the disadvantage of competition with large amounts of other advertising. If you need proof of that, just check your mail box tonight or tomorrow for the amount of "junk" mail that you normally receive. The throwaway rate can be extremely high. At the same time, probably the most interesting aspect of direct mail is the ability to measure performance against cost with comparative ease. You ship several thousand pieces, the calls come back immediately, and you can easily know whether it is working or not.

Remember that your goal is to build inbound calls, not necessarily complete the sale. To save money, you might consider the possibility of mailing specially printed postcards: The postage is less expensive, you save the cost of an envelope (not to mention expensive color brochures), and you are making it as easy as pie for the reader to pick up the phone and dial your 1–800 number. They don't even have to open an envelope.

In the summertime, I even spend a small amount of money on

...ached to airplanes that fly by crowded beaches. With
,-by banners, you have about the same amount of speedy
to address your potential customer as you do with a bill-
ard. The restriction, however, is that the banner, or streamer,
.s smaller than a billboard and is limited as to what the reader can
see. Suffice that you put on your name and 1–800 telephone
number.

I cannot overestimate the importance of your use of the Yellow
Pages—local and special toll-free editions—to advertise your
product or service. Yellow Pages reach consumers who are ready
to buy; they have high penetration, as they are found in almost
every household and business, and geographical targeting is relatively easy.

Another idea to consider, only if your costs permit, of course,
is to have a short videotape of your product made, which you can
mail or have delivered to your potential customer. Some real
estate companies handling very expensive properties are already
doing this. They provide tapes of houses for sale to prospective
home buyers.

Do not—I repeat, *do not*—try to make a promotional video of
your product or service by yourself, using your brother-in-law's
Sony mini-cam. Of course you would save money doing it yourself; and perhaps it would be fun to do. But unless you are a professional cinematographer or producer of TV commercials, the
result will look like a home movie, and your sales will suffer.

If you deal regularly with an advertising agency, they might be
able to produce the videotape for you, or else suggest a company
that can. The Business Yellow Pages lists hundreds of production
services that create corporate videos. Check out about ten of these
producers, do a price comparison, and ask to see samples of their
work. Call some of the companies that these producers have done
work for, and see if they were satisfied with the videotapes that
were made for them—and with the final cost. Then discuss what
you want the production house to do, and ask for their suggestions as to how they feel they can best show your product or service. After the tape has been produced and approved by you, keep

a master copy, and make only enough duplicate copies for one week's use. It takes very little time to duplicate a videotape, so you can replenish your stock of videos as the demand warrants.

Experienced production houses will have all kinds of special effects, graphics, and formats to suggest, which you would probably never have thought of yourself. Let them give you ideas on how they can create the most effective video for your purposes. Just make sure that the result is not too "hokey." Avoid blaring music, or an overly loud announcer, or sensational photographic gimmicks. It is better to be a bit conservative in showing your product or service, if you want to build confidence in the prospective buyer.

CUTTING COSTS

We've talked about co-op advertising money as a way to stretch advertising dollars. Some of the strategies that I am going to discuss, you may never have heard about, nor will you probably find them mentioned in primers or textbooks on advertising. But they do exist, and you should know about them if you want to streamline your budget.

The first thing you should know is that, as the man once said, "Everything's negotiable." You may receive a rate card from a newspaper that states that a full page costs $10,000, or one from a television network that lists a 30-second commercial as costing $5,000 per spot, but that may not necessarily be the price that the newspaper or television station is going to stick to if you begin to negotiate.

Remember that unsold air time, or unsold newspaper space, is gone forever once the publication appears, or the show is broadcast. If the medium thinks it might be left with any unsold space or time, it is in the medium's interest, *almost at any price,* to get you on the air or in the newspaper.

An essential rule that you should always incorporate into your business philosophy involving advertising space or time is: *Always ask for a discount.* Although it may seem crude to say, it is true: "If you don't ask, you don't get."

Only a few extremely traditional mediums refuse to budge on discounts. It works best, of course, if *you* are being pursued by the medium interested in having you spend some of your precious advertising dollars with them. If that is the case, then the basis for your giving them an insertion order to buy time or space is for them to give you a discount on their regularly published prices. No, it is not invariable, and, yes, it is often frequent.

Furthermore, you might consider convincing the medium to accept your print ad or commercial on what is known as the *per inquiry* basis. In "P.I." deals, you supply the ad (with a special code in a coupon) or the commercial (with a special telephone number), and for each inquiry that you receive, you pay an agreed-upon price back to the medium.

It works like this:

For example, suppose you submit your television commercial or advertisement to a station or newspaper to market a recording of Special Christmas Madrigals. You pay no money in advance. They air it or run it, and you (or they, if they prefer) receive the responses or phone calls. A record is kept as to how many responses have come in, and you pay the station or newspaper an agreed-upon amount for each response or inquiry. How much do you pay? Well, if a station or newspaper is willing to make such an arrangement with you (and many are not), they will try to predict the number of responses that each broadcast or each newspaper ad will produce. When one is dealing with new or untested products, or services, this is difficult to do, but the formula works like this:

Retail price of product or service	$100.00
Normal cost of time or space	$1,000.00
Predicted number of inquiries or responses	500
Cost per inquiry/response charged by the medium	$ 2.00

What happens if the ad "drops dead" and only brings in 25 or 30 inquiries or responses? In that case, you still pay your $2.00 for each inquiry, and the station or newspaper loses money.

You might be interested in knowing why the media would take such a gamble as to run "free" advertising for you, to be paid only on the strength of the response. Here's why:

- If they are a new or untried medium, they might be desperate for advertising and willing to take a gamble just to fill their pages or commercial time.
- They might be gambling on the commercial or ad pulling even better than your own prediction. If, referring to the example above, the ad pulls better than 500 responses, they will be making a larger profit than if they had charged you their normal rate card price.
- They might believe in the ultimate potential of your product or service and feel that they are getting in on the ground floor with your company. If they ingratiate themselves now, on a per-inquiry basis, you might advertise with them later, they believe, when you are more successful and can pay the regular rate card fees.

An equally important method of saving money on your advertising is the system called "remnant" or "stand-by" space or time. Certain entrepreneurs—media salespeople, really—buy up blocks of space and time from the media at severely discounted prices. For example, one of these media-buying services will purchase five full pages per week in a daily newspaper, and guarantee to buy five pages per week for an entire year.

Let's say the normal price is $10,000 per page for this space, but because they *guarantee* the purchase of hundreds of pages over the course of a year, they are given the price of, say, $2,500 per page. Usually, with these arrangements, the media service is forced to pay cash in advance.

Then with these pages "spoken for," it is up to the media service to sell them to advertisers. Since sophisticated advertisers know what the rate-card price is (in this case $10,000), any break in the price will be advantageous for the advertiser. The negotiation, therefore, will be (in this example) somewhere between the $2,500 paid by the media service and the $10,000 regular rate card price charged by the medium; it will be your job to get as much discount from the regular rate as possible. The difficulty is that you will not know, nor will the media service tell you, how much less they paid per page. Just bear in mind that it is not unlikely that they have paid as little as, and sometimes less than, 75 percent off the regular rate-card price.

Stand-by ads and commercials can often be bought directly from the medium itself. A full-page ad in *The New York Times* could cost you as much as $45,000, as indicated by the rate card. As a stand-by ad, you might get it for much less.

There are a few difficulties in buying remnant space or time. Often, you are given very little advance notice regarding available insertions, which does not allow you much time to decide whether to accept. After you have made contact with one of the services or directly with the media and confirmed your willingness to do business with them, you may receive a call on a Thursday or Friday, for example, stating that they can give you a full-page ad in that Sunday's *Detroit Free Press,* or 20 spots on a local television station in San Francisco that Sunday, at 50 percent to 60 percent less than the full rate-card price.

Of course, you must have your advertisement ready to print or your commercial ready to air. You must also have your extra personnel ready to field the additional telephone calls that will come in as a result of the advertising, and your inventory must be up to par, in order to service your new customers.

Another problem with remnant or stand-by space or time is that you have little control over the position of your ad in a newspaper (you may be "buried" somewhere deep within the innards of the paper), or over the time when your commercial may air (4 o'clock in the morning). If this is a problem, you may choose not to buy remnant or stand-by time or space until you can be assured of the position of your ad or the timing of your commercials.

ADVERTISING WITH NO CASH

If you have a new product or service and your company is cash poor, it is possible to "buy" advertising (aside from per-inquiry advertising), without laying out *any* cash, and without going to a bank to borrow the necessary funds to start or continue your advertising campaign. In effect, the media becomes your bank.

You can approach a selected group of newspapers, television and radio stations, or wherever else you want to advertise and display or present your product or service, and ask for a minimum amount of credit. This will take a great amount of persuasion and persistence on your part, not to mention all of the tact, charm and intelligence that you can summon.

In order to secure time or space on credit, you will have to sign a contract promising to pay in the future, and sometimes you must put up something for collateral (such as your car, house, etc.), but the media have been known to help struggling new businesses in issuing advertising credit. You must prove that your business is reputable and that you *will* pay, and if *you* believe that you can pay sometime in the future, you might try to secure advertising in this way,

Should you be accommodated and given advertising on credit, don't overdo it! You could find yourself in well over your head, with bills in the hundreds of thousands and no real way to pay it back. It could force you into corporate and/or personal bankruptcy.

I actually know a businessman who started publishing a national magazine in this way. *He had no money to begin with.* He convinced an art director to design a two-page advertisement for him, the type was set on credit (using the A.D.'s contacts), and

the erstwhile publisher visited a number of noncompetitive magazines and asked them to take the double-page spread on credit.

Almost everyone refused, but one accepted. In a matter of
weeks, he pulled in over 1,000 subscriptions from that one ad,
paid back his advertising bill to the magazine, started placing the
ad elsewhere, and, before long, had enough cash to launch his
periodical.

Precarious? Of course. But the publisher believed in his magazine and the strength of his advertisement, and the rest came
fairly naturally.

PUBLICITY AND PROMOTION

There are some new companies that are so undercapitalized, and
others that are so strapped for cash, that they simply *cannot*
advertise, even on credit. In that event, how can they promote
their 1–800 toll-free number to the public? And how can you
promote your company and your 1–800 number without
expending large amounts of advertising dollars. The answer is:
publicity.

Publicity is the term that refers to the publication of news
about a product or a service—or a person connected with that
business—for which time or space was *not* purchased. If you *pay*
for a mention of your product or service, it is *advertising*. If the
media mention it for *free*, it is *publicity*.

In many ways, free publicity is more powerful than paid advertising. If a subscriber to a newspaper reads a story about your
company, or a viewer sees a story about you or your product or
service on television, in a way you are receiving what amounts
almost to a third-party endorsement from the station or the
newspaper. A story is more believable than an advertisement.
People are more inclined to read stories than advertisements; you
yourself have also probably "tuned out" of watching commercials
on television sometimes, or have even muted the sound of certain
commercials with your remote control so that you couldn't hear

their messages. This credibility factor makes publicity essential to your financial health.

I've always been impressed with the following story: An old-line publishing house, whose origins went back to the 1870s, had the curious policy of not sending review copies of their books to book reviewers or editors. Although they would advertise their books, they felt, incorrectly as the case may be, that good reviews did not sell books and that bad reviews had a negative effect on sales. Also, they had trouble measuring the response to a review, so they just abandoned their publicity department and let the chips fall where they may.

One day, unbeknownst to the management, a secretary mailed a copy of one of their latest titles to *The Tonight Show,* specifically addressed to Johnny Carson. The book was titled *Presidential Tidbits and Trivia* and contained such arcane, but humorous, information as the fact that Lincoln gave seances in the White House, and George Washington had wooden false teeth.

Carson liked the book and, within a few days, incorporated it into one of his skits, reading from it aloud, cracking up, and making mention of the book, prominently holding it up so that the tens of millions of Americans who were watching that night could see it.

The next morning, the phones began ringing off the hook at the publishing house. Bookstores all over America wanted copies. Individual readers wanted to buy it. Magazines wanted to purchase syndication rights. Other television shows wanted to interview the author.

You get the idea. For the cost of one free copy of the book, a Jiffy bag, and a postage stamp (perhaps at a total of about $1.50), the book sold several thousand copies over and above what was expected, opened new bookstore markets and publicity conduits for the publisher, and generally proved to them that free publicity was, if not better, at least *as* good as their paid advertising attempts to sell books.

No matter what your product or service, even if it's screws for machine parts, you can gain free publicity to generate inbound

calls. Some of the publicity, such as the launching of a new product, or the announcement of a new CEO, will go, of course, into
trade or business publications, such as *Crain's, Advertising Age,
Railroad Age,* or *The Wall Street Journal.* But even these trade-
oriented stories can produce business and actual dollars for you.

Because of the innovative nature of Dial-A-Mattress, as the
leading telemarketer of mattresses in the world, we seem to be a
natural source of stories for the trade press. We also seem to
attract the attention of the general press, as well. Although it is
difficult to measure, I would say that, as a result of every story
that appears about us, whether in print or broadcast over the air,
we sell more than ten times the number of mattresses than we
sell through our normal advertising channels.

In other words, we may run a 30-second spot on a local television station and end up selling four mattresses; by comparison, if
a 30-second story about us appears on the news, we can expect
to sell 40 mattresses as a result.

To think of just a few publicity "stunts," we have had Phil
Donahue and David Letterman test our two-hour delivery claim
and actually film us, on live television, delivering a mattress.

Letterman called us on his car phone and broadcast the actual
call on his TV show that night. A camera mounted on another
vehicle recorded the transaction.

The talk-show host told Dial-A-Mattress' salesperson that he
wanted a mattress delivered to his *car* so that he could drive it
home. The surprised voice of the salesman—he did not know
that Letterman was the caller—repeated the request in a quiet,
slightly skeptical but polite tone:

"To your car. . . "

"Yup," said Letterman.

"Well, how are we going to recognize it?" questions the salesman.

"I'm in a red Dodge," Letterman replied unhelpfully.

At that point, the location (right outside of the TV studios)
was provided, and Letterman insisted on our famous two-hour
delivery.

Within the two-hour window, the camera recorded a Dial-A-Mattress truck drive up behind Letterman's red sports car, and the driver was instructed to put the large mattress on top of the small car. So he did, and Letterman drove away with it.

By the way, there was no old mattress to remove.

Howard Stern had one of our mattresses delivered for one of his promotions, and when movie star Hugh Grant was in hot water with his girlfriend because of his highly publicized infidelity, the press cited Dial-A-Mattress as proof that the couple was getting back together again, after she ordered a new king-size bed from us. The phones continued to ring constantly, as a result, and our sales shot up. Believe me, you cannot *buy* that kind of publicity.

In the early weeks of January 1993, when President Clinton and First Lady Hillary Rodham Clinton first occupied the White House, Dial-A-Mattress received a call to deliver a queen-size mattress to 1600 Pennsylvania Ave. When we asked whether we could announce that the First Couple was now resting on one of our mattresses, we were told that we could not release the story to the papers.

We complied with the request, but after six months of a bureaucratic snafu, and we were still not paid for our mattress— I'm certain that Bill and Hillary knew nothing of the late bill—it was leaked to the press all over the nation that Dial-A-Mattress had sold a mattress to the White House. (We *were* paid eventually, by the way.)

As a result of that free publicity, our sales in Washington soared, and not only the general public but Senators and Congressmen also began to buy. Representative Sonny Bono bought four mattresses from Dial-A-Mattress: a king-size for the master bedroom, a full-size for the guest room, and twin mattresses for his and his wife's children's bunk beds.

Over the years, a number of celebrities have purchased our mattresses. Here are just some of the celebrities whom we have had in our beds:

Cher
Christie Brinkley
Tony Guida
Storm Field
Chuck Scarborough
Don Henley
Bruce Springsteen
Donald Trump
Kevin Bacon
Maureen O'Boyle
Wayne Gretsky
Eileen Ford, Ford Models
Frank Gifford and
    Kathy Lee
Howard Stern
Sylvester Stallone
Ralph Kiner
Tuesday Weld
Rita Moreno
Heavy "D"
Steven Segal
Peter Jennings

Carly Simon
Eric Baldwin
Robert Shapiro
Tony Danza
Alexander Haig
Bob Grant
Danny Bonnaducci
Geraldine Ferraro
Rosie Perez
Sam Champion
Bob Guccione
Leslie West
Marla Maples
Dwight Myer Wilkins
John Zagarro
Michael Jackson
Dominique Wilkins
Mats Wilander
Sasha Danilovic
Kurt Thomas
Kareem Abdul-Jabbar
Adam Baldwin

Of course we thank them all, as we do all of our customers. Selling to famous people sometimes involves unusual situations. When Hollywood director Paul Mazursky was on location shooting the film *Faithful*, with Ryan O'Neal and Cher, he suddenly realized that he needed a mattress for a crucial love scene. The film could not continue without it. He called us, and within two hours we delivered the mattress he needed directly to the set. The story of this little adventure made most of the New York papers, and, again, we could feel our sales increase.

You might consider hiring a public relations agency to help you publicize your product or service. I use Howard Rubenstein Associates, one of the finest in the world. If you feel you cannot afford the retainer necessary to engage a PR agency, consider the possibility of hiring a full-time PR person, who engages in nothing but publicizing your product or service.

Failing that, assign someone already in your company—or do it for yourself—the job of handling publicity. Just remember that publicity should not be considered any less important than any other function of your business. It could actually be the key to whether you succeed or fail.

Here are some suggestions on what to publicize:

1. Any new product or service that you are going to introduce
2. Promotions or hiring of key personnel
3. A change in pricing or company philosophy
4. New locations for stores or offices
5. Free resources or benefits for buyers or consumers of your product or service
6. The use of your product or service to the benefit of the community
7. News of mergers, franchises, or acquisitions
8. Any public testing of your product or service
9. Results or surveys that you may have taken of your customers, especially if the tabulations can be tied into a sociological comment ("60 percent of the customers of the Acme Garage are women. They claim that Acme is the only garage where they invariably can leave their cars during the day for repairs, while working at the Oxford plant, and pick them up after work without fail.")
10. Any contests that you may run
11. Donations to nonprofit organizations or community service rendered by your employees
12. Corporate sponsorship of worthwhile events (such as a walk to benefit charity)
13. Any individual accomplishment that one of your employees might have achieved (such as earning his doctorate, or becoming a licensed pilot)
14. Any research—long term or short—you might be engaged in

15. Any industry, governmental, and civic awards that you, your employees, or your company might have achieved
16. The news of any seminars or classes that you might conduct on your premises for the help of your employees, or for the general public at large
17. Results of industry or corporate tests that would indicate the strength or worthiness of your product or service (such as appears in *Consumer Reports* or *Money Magazine*)

The press release is one of the most essential items in publicity, and you or your designated public relations person should know how to write it. Keep these rough guidelines in mind, concerning your press release:

- Try to keep it to one page, two at most, typed double-space.
- Keep the information direct and factual.
- Send it to the appropriate medium. (Sending a press release about your lowering the price of dinners at your restaurant to a trade magazine for engineers does not make sense.)
- Don't lie. . . about anything. First, it's dishonest. Second, you'll be caught.
- Always try to localize your news.
- Make sure there is a contact name and telephone number, including a home number, on your release so that the newspaper or station can get in touch at any time.
- Verify the facts in the release over and over again.
- Use basic newswriting style, especially in your lead sentences:
  - Who?
  - What?
  - When?
  - Where?
  - Why or How? (The most important factor in your news item.)
- If possible, include a black-and-white, 8"×10", professionally done photograph along with your press release.

Although what I am going to say may sound arbitrary, I believe it to be true. Virtually all publicity, even negative stories, can help your business. It is amazing how many people retain the name of the product or service without remembering the negative connotations.

This theory has been proven over and over again with book and movie reviews, some of which—although savage—propel people to the bookstores or movie theaters and keep the cash registers ringing. (People remember that they read about a specific movie, although they can't remember what the reviewer said.)

Of course, certain negative publicity can hurt: The sale of Tylenol plunged when it was discovered that someone was spiking bottles with poison; but in the long run, the sales of Tylenol went right back up there.

Given the opportunity, certainly you should avoid negative publicity. I've had a small share of it over the years, and it has hurt me personally, but honestly, I don't think my business ever suffered the loss of one penny as a result.

WHAT IT'S ALL ABOUT

To summarize, there are so many reasons why you *should* advertise (wisely!) and engage in publicity for your business or service. I could write a book just on that.

In the telemarketing business, however, the main reasons to advertise and to promote are the following:

1. To increase the number of inbound calls
2. Ultimately, to increase the number of units purchased ("buy three for the price of two")
3. To introduce new products or services
4. To keep up with and, perhaps, surpass your competition
5. To increase your sales during slack or off-season periods, or generally when business trails off

6. To imprint on the potential customers' minds the name of
your company and your 1–800 number, so when they want
to buy a canoe or kayak, for example, or an aardvark or
accordion, anytime in the future, they will eventually think
of your company

As important as advertising is, you can go overboard on expendi-
tures. Depending on the cost of your product and your overhead,
allocating something like 10 percent of your sales to pay for your
advertising budget would not be inappropriate. (It's what I spend.)

Periodically, try mixing and matching media with your advertising dollars. If your business is relatively small and you are just
starting out, you probably don't need such heavy saturation as,
say, a company that has been doing business for years and has,
perhaps, already reached many of its customers. My suggestion is
that you try:

- Mostly television
- Some radio
- A small amount of print

There are many, many other ways to approach the advertising
and promotion of your product, which we just don't have space
enough to elaborate upon, but briefly:

1. Put leaflets describing your product or services into co-op
advertising packets (usually carrying dozens of other products or services) that are mailed by the millions. Consider
also inserting your leaflets into local newspapers.
2. Hand out leaflets advertising your product or service in
crowded downtown areas.
3. Consider getting together with noncompetitive, but closely
allied businesses and jointly advertising with them. (For
example, if you are on the same block or are in the same
mall, or if you are a theater, you could cosponsor an ad with
a nearby restaurant.)

4. Be willing to consider "trade-out" advertising. Trade-out deals are arranged as follows: A medium, such as a television station or a newspaper, will run your ad or commercial at the agreed-upon price, except that no money changes hands. If the ad costs, say, $1,000, you must give them the same amount of your product, *in trade*. Trades are often made with TV or radio stations, for example, and restaurants or airlines. Whenever someone from the station has to conduct an expensive lunch, he goes to the tradeout restaurant and his bill is charged against whatever is "owed" by the restaurant to the station. If you were in the rug business, for instance, you might give the station an equivalent of the cost of your rugs for their commercial time.

I've heard of tradeouts of dentists and television stations; radio shows and steam baths; cleaning services and newspapers; and so forth. Yes, it is totally legal.

Tradeouts are just one of the creative methods you can use to advertise and promote your product or service. The object of all of these methods is to bring your company to the consumers' awareness, and to give them enough interest or incentive to inspire them to telephone your company. The rest is up to your sales staff.

THE DIAL-A-MATTRESS GALLERIES

Although I believe that anything can be bought by phone, as I've said many times in this book, there are a hard-core group of potential customers who simply feel that they *must* see what they're buying, *must* kick the tires and honk the horn, *must* sip the wine or poke their finger in the whipped cream to taste it, before they sign on the dotted line. It's for this reason that Dial-A-Mattress has started a group of galleries—hundreds of them—all over the world. You might consider doing the same thing with your product or service: opening a "gallery" in the appropriate venue.

This is how it works: We contact furniture and bedding retail outlets and make arrangements to provide them with several of our standard mattresses for their showrooms. Additionally, we provide them with a neon sign, with our logo, which they can place in their windows, or in some designated spot in the store. Three merchandising possibilities then occur: If any of our telephone customers, calling us at our 1–800–MATTRESS number, insists on seeing the mattress before they buy it, we simply give them the name of the nearest Dial-A-Mattress gallery and suggest that they pay that store a visit to "try on" the mattress. If they end up buying the mattress from the store, we receive a commission from the store for the referral.

Additionally, if a customer spots our sign in the store and makes an inquiry of the salesperson, and the store does not carry the specific mattress that is wanted, the salesperson can offer the customer the option of calling Dial-A-Mattress directly, right there, from the store. At that point, one of our Bedding Consultants will complete the sale, delivery will be arranged, the customer will have the mattress he wants in a few hours, and the store will receive a commission from us for the referral. Everybody wins, and the sale endures.

Think of comparable gallery possibilities and venues for your product or service.

If you sell a home improvement product, perhaps a Home Depot will allow you to set up a gallery in all of their stores. If you sell sporting goods, perhaps your local stadium will allow you to set up a gallery there. If you sell a special kind of clothing, perhaps a department store in your area will encourage you to establish a gallery on one of their floors.

Obviously, you need incorporate a gallery program into your telemarketing business only if you have a product that really needs to be seen, examined, or analyzed before the sale is made. And you must be generous enough with your commissions to the participating store that they will be interested in giving you the space that you need to attractively display your product.

5

HOW TO DELIVER THE GOODS, AND TACTICS FOR HANDLING YOUR INVENTORY

> Above all, the intensity itself, stemming from strongly held beliefs, marks these successful American companies. During our first round of interviews, we could "feel it." The language used in talking about people was different. The expectation of regular contributions was different. The love of the product and customer was palpable. And we felt different ourselves, walking around the Hewlett-Packard or 3M facility, watching groups at work and play, from the way we had in most of the more bureaucratic institutions we have had experience with.
>
> *In Search of Excelleance*
> Thomas J. Peters and
> Robert H. Waterman Jr.

Although you may be in the business of selling a *product*, with telemarketing you are really providing a *service*. That's why an effective delivery system is essential to your company's success. I try to make buying a mattress, even those that cost several thousand dollars, as effortless as ordering a pizza. And we have succeeded. A June 1996 nationwide survey by Fred Wiersema asked more than 100 senior managers to rank the customer service of

U.S. companies, both large and small. Nordstrom, MCI Communications Corp., The Home Depot Inc., and Domino's Pizza Inc. were voted the top four "Most Customer Sensitive." AT&T, Sears, Roebuck and Co., True Value, and Dial-A-Mattress were rated "Most Improved Customer Service," because of the ways they have adapted to competition and change. The survey demonstrated that good customer service is extremely important to American consumers, and companies that provide excellent service can increase their productivity and revenue.

Like the other corporations in this select group of 22 leaders, Dial-A-Mattress implements and executes the philosophy of customer service into our corporate management practice. We continually look for ways to improve our service, to meet changing customer needs. Fast, reliable delivery is, of course, of paramount importance to our customers. Providing this service is one of the keys to our success. Every month, we deliver more than 10,000 orders, using a fleet of trucks and distributors we contract with to make deliveries nationally, often within hours of a customer's call.

Not too long ago, a potential customer called us from somewhere over the Atlantic Ocean, from an airplane flying from Europe to New York. He lived on Long Island and ordered a mattress to be delivered to his house as soon as possible. We completed the sale over the telephone as he was flying, he landed shortly after at JFK airport, and as he drove into his driveway 45 minutes later, the Dial-A-Mattress truck had just arrived. This customer was so impressed with the service we provided that I truly believe he will buy from us for the rest of his life, and recommend our company to other people.

I believe that it is imperative to provide this service even if a particular delivery might seem to cost more than it's worth. My son, Luis Barragan, Assistant General Manager of Dial-A-Mattress, feels this as strongly as I do. "If you look at each sale in terms of how profitable it is for the company," Luis cautions, "there are many situations where it does not pay to deliver a mattress, because that delivery might be so costly that the sale becomes unprofitable for you. You might be tempted to refuse such an order. Don't! Take the point of view that every customer you satisfy—which you do if you treat the customer right—gives you the potential for ten more customers by referral. Right now, 30 percent of our sales come from referral by other customers. So we're not all that concerned if a number of mattress sales are unprofitable. The emphasis is not on hitting the jugular with each and every sale. Everything prepares us for something else. It's all part of the company's overall momentum, and that momentum makes the business a success."

To create an efficient delivery system, realize that the clock starts to tick the moment your sales consultant hits the Enter key on his or her computer. That gets the whole mechanism going. Once the sale has been made, the telemarketer must check the computer to find an available delivery time that is convenient for the customer. Then the order is sent down to Dispatching, and then, on the appropriate day, to the Distribution Center, which pulls the merchandise. Then it goes to the driver, who loads it and goes out to complete the delivery. Later on in this chapter, I'll go over in detail how we handle each facet of the delivery process and how you can adapt our methods to your own needs.

Regardless of the size of your company, appoint someone to be responsible for getting the products delivered on time. If your operation is small, one person might be able to handle this. If you have a large company, you might need a delivery department. This is a complex, multifaceted procedure, and someone needs to coordinate all the steps to make sure the proper merchandise gets to each customer when promised.

It seems almost parochial to say, but you can't take the delivery process for granted. Explore and investigate every different way of delivering your product. You may find that one and only one method is ideal for you, or you may decide to use different methods for different purposes. Consider all possibilities of delivery when you start your company, and then remember to *re*consider these factors as your company grows and your needs change.

Consider *shipping* some or all of your merchandise. Consider using *messengers*. Check out the price and reputation for reliability of all methods of delivery within each type of delivery system. For example, would it be best for you to use the U.S. mail, UPS, Federal Express, or some other delivery service? Remember that almost every service nowadays will pick up the package at your location, so you don't need to send an employee to their depot to get your product delivered.

If you sell large items, such as furniture, look into using established trucking firms to make your deliveries. But also consider hiring a driver who has only one truck. Which size firm do you need to deliver your product? Which would give you better delivery availability, or better prices? The answer will vary according to factors such as the number of deliveries you make within a geographical area, and the size and weight of your product. Consider how cost effective it would be for you to use large trucks, small trucks, or vans. Consider starting your own fleet or a part-time fleet.

If the product that you're selling is small or lightweight, such as a book, a part for a machine, or a box of cigars, and if you are selling mainly in one defined geographical area, you might consider employing a messenger service to distribute for you. Often, for less than $10, a messenger can deliver your product to anywhere in your city, within a few hours. Look into the financial feasibility of establishing your own messenger service, staffed possibly by young people (perhaps college students) who have automobiles or bicycles.

Remember that the cost of delivery is only one factor. Don't just take the most inexpensive way to deliver your product. Each function in the delivery process represents a time allotment. The narrower you make those windows, the faster the whole operation becomes, and the quicker the bed or the burger or the balloon gets to the customer. In the long run, *speed, reliability, and flexible delivery days and hours* are probably much more important to the financial success of your business than cost.

A DELIVERY SERVICE BETTER THAN THE COMPETITORS'

Dial-A-Mattress, which is intent upon exploring ways to improve service to its customers, now offers around-the-clock delivery in the New York metropolitan area. New York is the "city that never sleeps," but when our customers decide they *do* want to sleep, they can call us and we'll deliver—any time of the day or night. We offer this service option in addition to our existing two-hour express delivery and standard same-day delivery (in which the delivery is scheduled at the customer's convenience, within a two-hour window). We're concerned not only with the needs of the customers but also with those of their neighbors. We have added soundproofing to our trucks and equipment to ensure that nighttime deliveries do not disturb the neighborhood.

We also deliver bedding to our convenience-oriented customers across the country. We have satellite warehouses in Chicago, franchises in Boston, Maryland, and Miami, and trusted retailers across the country who handle deliveries within their areas. That's the core of our company today, though we'll soon open additional locations in key cities throughout the rest of the United States. In the meantime, if an order comes from somewhere in the United States where we don't yet have an arrangement with a trucking company, we'll send the merchandise by Federal Express. It's an expensive way to ship such a heavy object, but the customer still comes first.

At this point, people are beginning to order mattresses from us from all over the world. Delivering to other countries, of course, creates its own set of challenges. We're developing a system to handle worldwide sales and deliveries. It's explained later in this book, in the chapter called The Future of Telemarketing.

What else sets our delivery system apart from the competition? Ask employees of Macy's and Bloomingdale's who, much to the chagrin of their employers, regularly purchase mattresses from

Dial-A-Mattress. Even though these employees could save money by purchasing where they work, and taking advantage of their employee discounts, they don't want to wait several weeks for their department store to deliver a mattress. So they buy from us, instead. "I phoned, you helped, I ordered, you delivered, I slept," wrote one satisfied customer, who worked at a well-known Manhattan department store. In fact, the word most often used by customers (on the customer reply forms provided with each delivery) to describe Dial-A-Mattress' delivery service is *convenient*.

The key strengths of our operation are price and efficiency. A bedding transaction can be completed in seven minutes—and we're able to get the bed to the customer quite rapidly. But as Luis notes, "Our delivery system may well be the best in the country, but that doesn't mean it satisfies us."

There's always room for improvement. Our system is continually being refined. Technology is improving it. Our plans to upgrade our entire computer system will help. There are advances in inventory maintenance through bar-coding that we do not yet use to our advantage. The bedding industry is light years behind other industries when it comes to technology. That's due in large part to the fact that there's not nearly the same amount of money streaming into the bedding industry as there is in, say, the beer industry. The average person buys a bed once every ten years. The total number of beds in America, in terms of U.S. dollars (at an average ticket price of $450) would be $5.5 billion, which, when you think about it, is not that much.

In your telemarketing operation, try to keep up with all of the continual changes in computer technology. Don't rest on your computer laurels just because things seem to be going smoothly. Have the computer specialists and hardware and software manufacturers suggest ways you can improve your system. Go to trade shows and read journals on the new technology. Keep up!

HERE'S HOW WE DO IT

In essence, Dial-A-Mattress became a success in the telemarketing business by streamlining our advertising, promotion, selling, and distribution. And to make it all work, we have evolved a comprehensive system for maintaining inventory, running our warehouse, and organizing our deliveries so that everything runs efficiently. Here's how we do it. You can adopt many of our techniques for your own company.

DISTRIBUTION CENTER: LOCATION AND LAYOUT

Locate your *Distribution Center* close to a major thoroughfare if at all possible. You'll minimize a lot of traffic delays if your trucks can get onto a major highway as quickly as possible.

Once you've established your center, the first thing you'll need is a physical setup that lets you shift your merchandise as needed. You will need several separate areas, which should be set up specifically for the type of products your business carries.

Create a *Storage Area* for your merchandise, and organize it using whatever kind of shelving or bins or dividers are appropriate to keep your inventory neatly in place and easy to locate and access.

Then create a separate *Dispatch Area,* to be used for preparing merchandise to be delivered. When an order comes in, the different pieces of merchandise a customer buys must be selected, taken out of your inventory, and placed together in the Dispatch Area so that they can be recognized as one specific order, which will be loaded onto a truck and delivered to the customer.

Set up a series of in-and-out paper trays within your Dispatch Area. At Dial-A-Mattress, we have several trays; each one holds the orders for one of the counties in our market area that we deliver to most frequently. Then we divide each of these areas into A.M. and P.M. sections, to distinguish between early and late delivery times.

When you're laying out the floor plan of your Distribution Center, also establish an adequate amount of space for offices for Inventory Control and Dispatching. This area should be strategically placed to maximize productivity and diminish the likelihood of theft, or "shrinkage," as it is politely called. Equip all exits and entrances with alarms to alert key warehouse personnel in case of robbery.

Equip your Distribution Center with appropriately sized loading docks or bays that will be adequate to receive and ship your merchandise. This will give you easy access, so your merchandise can be moved into and out of the building easily. At the very least, you will need room to roll merchandise in and out. At best, it would be good to have enough room for a truck to back in for ease of loading and unloading. Determine how large your loading docks should be by considering the size of the largest boxes you send or receive, or the size of the trucks you use for your receiving and shipping.

For our purposes, Dial-A-Mattress requires that our distribution centers have a minimum of two loading docks. One is used for receiving, and the other for distribution.

QUALITY CONTROL

Set up a small area at each entrance, to be used for *Quality Control* assurance. Assign personnel to inspect both incoming and outgoing merchandise.

When you are preparing an order for delivery to your customer, your Quality Control personnel should look carefully for any damaged or defective pieces. You may want to have your merchandise double-checked for damage or defects. In fact, it's a very good practice to require people from several different departments—such as the driver, the person who takes merchandise out of your Inventory, and your Quality Control group—to check each item. Dial-A-Mattress has established contracts with several trucking companies to deliver our merchandise. Our written *agreement* clearly states that the owner or operator of each truck must inspect each product before he loads it, and thereafter assumes responsibility for it. (If you establish such relationships, make sure your legal agreement includes this.) If you set up a different system in your company, just be sure that the last person to inspect the merchandise—usually the warehouse supervisor—must take the responsibility for final sign-off that the product is good enough to send to a customer.

Never release any order unless all of the merchandise is in perfect condition. Your company's reputation depends on this. In addition, since you will then be sure the products were in good condition before shipping them out, if you get complaints from a customer that the goods are damaged, you can be certain that the problem originated either with the driver or with the customer.

However, breakage does occur. Allow for this, and establish a *return policy*. If one of our customers complains that newly delivered merchandise is damaged or defective, we have it inspected as quickly as possible. If the driver verifies the problem, or if the *inspection report* states that the product is defective, we offer the customer two choices: He may accept the damaged item at a discounted price, if the damage is only cosmetic (it just affects its appearance) and is not structural. Or if the customer prefers, we will replace the damaged piece with a new one.

If the inspection report states that the product is okay, we telephone the customer and explain that the coloration or shape or other characteristic that has worried the customer is a normal and natural occurrence, such as the tiny bumps and color variations that exist in silk fabric. We explain that this is not a manufacturing defect. If the customer insists on replacement, we refer the call to the manufacturer.

We also stress that we provide delivery on approval. (All our products carry a 30-day guarantee for comfort.) So we suggest that the customer keep the product and try it out for several weeks to see if it is satisfactory.

RECEIVING

Establish a specific area of your warehouse to be your *Staging Area*, the section where all new merchandise will be inspected as soon as you receive it. Have merchandise unloaded onto forklifts or carts, and move it immediately to the Staging Area. Every order arriving from a manufacturer or a vendor must be checked to make sure it is correct: that you have received the proper quantities and the products you actually ordered. Also determine whether any of the pieces are defective. Each order should be inspected as it is counted. Finding problems now, before you accept the delivery from your supplier, will maintain your credibility with the vendor, and save you a lot of aggravation later on.

Assign one designated individual to be responsible for the inspection and the accurate count of each shipment, as it is unloaded. Instruct the personnel in your Receiving Department to sign for merchandise that is actually received. If there are any errors in an order—too many items, or too few—that should be written on the manufacturer's or vendor's *shipping order*. And if any merchandise arrives damaged, this too should be noted on the shipping order.

Within your Quality Control area, assign a small section to be used for damaged merchandise that will be returned to the vendor. We do not accept merchandise from manufacturers that is less than perfect. Damaged pieces are returned to the manufacturer right away, and the *bill of lading* indicates the exact number of pieces we have accepted. The manufacturer's *invoice*—the bill he will send you—will be based on this number, so it is important for your Receiving personnel to inspect incoming merchandise carefully.

If you need to return merchandise, for any reason, to your manufacturer or distributor, create a *merchandise return form*, which should list the manufacturer or vendor's name, the *invoice number* or *purchase order number*, and date (referring to your original ordering of the item), the *SKU number* of the piece of merchandise, and an explanation for the reason you are returning it. Then arrange to have the damaged merchandise promptly returned to your vendor, and have someone in your bookkeeping department make sure you are given proper credit for it.

Tag each defective piece carefully, so the vendor will understand what is wrong, and so you can both refer to it by invoice number. We created our own *return authorization tag* for this purpose. Customize a similar tag for your merchandise.

STORAGE PRINCIPLES

The traditional approach to *Storage* is to group merchandise by vendor, size, and model. In addition, we created a section for our fastest-moving items. These are positioned closest to the shipping doors, also sorted by vendor, size, and model. Since some of our products are very large, unwieldy items, such as king-size and queen-size mattresses and box springs, we store those near the shipping area, too, to minimize work for our warehouse crew. Follow these concepts, and apply them to the size and type of merchandise you sell.

When you decide on the type of shelving or bins that are best to hold your products, be sure that the lowest shelf is at least three inches above the floor. This should protect your merchandise from water damage and condensation.

INVENTORY AND PURCHASING AFFECT YOUR SPACE REQUIREMENTS

If you already have a company, you have probably created your own system for dealing with inventory. If you're not yet established in business, set up an inventory system as one of your first priorities. An efficient distribution center and inventory system has two goals:

1. To enable you to move your merchandise out to your customers as rapidly as possible, so you can get paid!

2. To cost you as little as possible during the time the merchandise is sitting in your distribution center. In effect, you are paying "rent" for the space your undelivered merchandise takes up in your building. Yes, this is true even if you own the distribution center. The "rent" is the cost of the building itself, the real estate taxes you pay for the building every year, and all costs of maintaining it.

Clearly, then, your primary objectives should be to develop a system that enables you to ship out:

- As much merchandise as possible
- As rapidly as possible
- From a building that is as small as possible

When you are considering inventory procedures, use the following four functions as guidelines to ensure proper inventory levels. Be sure to take them into account:

1. Space requirements, or limitations of existing space
2. Purchasing
3. Receiving
4. Inventory control

First, take a physical inventory, a count of all the merchandise on your shelves, to know what you're starting with. Then set up a computer program that keeps an ongoing tally of your inventory, differentiating items by size, color, and any other factors that are specific to your merchandise.

The last thing that you should do each night, or first thing each morning (but *before* your company begins writing new orders for the day), is to update your inventory screen on the computer.

Always check the computerized inventory against your physical inventory, and update it daily. Bear in mind that special products have their own space needs—for example, hazardous and perishable materials have specific storage requirements.

PURCHASING

Establish and maintain an *adequate* amount of stock. This is imperative for the success of your company. Too much and you'll waste money on excess warehouse space and over-investment of your money. But too little is just as bad! You need to maintain enough inventory to cover your normal daily orders, plus some extra merchandise for those days when you get more orders than usual. Running out of stock means delivery delays, and that invariably means annoyed customers—and sometimes canceled sales! A large part of your success will depend on your *reliability* in making deliveries when you promise them.

How can you figure out what your optimum stock level should be? It depends on the following factors:

- Your company's sales history for each type of merchandise (obtained by analyzing your sales records to determine "product movement")
- Trends in your product market
- Sales held by your competitors
- Forecasts set forth by sales and marketing management

Since your company's sales records will provide you with the most readily available and reliable information, this will be the most useful gauge to determine your stock needs. One simple formula is to take the previous month's total "movement" of a specific SKU, or "stock keeping unit." (A SKU—pronounced *skyu*—can be defined as any model of a product, in one specific size and classification. For example, a blue short-sleeve woolen sweater in size 10 is one SKU; a blue short-sleeve woolen sweater in size 12 is another SKU; a red short-sleeve woolen sweater in size 12 is a third SKU; a red long-sleeve woolen sweater in size

12 is a fourth SKU. Each different item in your stock has its own individual SKU.)

The total "movement" of a specific SKU means how many of that particular item you sold and shipped or delivered to your customers.

How to Compute How Much New Inventory to Reorder

1. Look at last month's orders (or the number of deliveries you made) for each SKU (a particular piece of merchandise).

2. If you want to order enough merchandise for the entire following month, use that full amount—it is the total required for 30 days. Assume that there may be a 5 percent to 10 percent margin of error, and factor in your company's growth; also allow for any projected loss. To account for these factors, order 5 percent to 10 percent more than you sold last month.

3. If you want to order only merchandise that will last you for 15 days (perhaps because of warehouse space limitations), divide last month's total deliveries by two.

4. Take into account how quickly each vendor can resupply you with that item. For example, suppose you determine that you sold and delivered 500 of a certain item last month, but your distribution center doesn't have room to hold 500 of these all at once. If your vendor can deliver that item to you once a week (that is, four times a month), then divide 500 by four and you'll get 125. Now, as I said, add between 5 percent and 10 percent to that 125. (To make this example easy, I added 10, which is an 8 percent increase.) You now have a total of 135 per week. So, to meet your current sales of this item, you'll need four deliveries per month, with 135 items per delivery. Of course, if your vendor cannot assure you of a delivery every week, you'll have to have fewer shipments per month, with a larger number of products within each order.

5. Your *reorder* calculations will be based on the activity of each piece of merchandise over the last calendar month, as well as what sales were made prior to the last date you placed a reorder. Again, this makes it extremely important that you check the computerized inventory against the physical inventory daily.

6. Be sure each reorder is correctly dated! Your computer will take that date and apply it to the screen your sales consultants see when they want to find the date the merchandise will be available for delivery.

INVENTORY CONTROL

Keep careful track of your inventory, and make sure your sales department receives daily information about the stock on hand and about every order for new merchandise. Your sales department must know current, accurate inventory counts. This is vital.

To keep an accurate inventory count, add all incoming merchandise received throughout the day, from vendors and delivery personnel. Then subtract all outgoing merchandise from the count. This will give you an "on hand" inventory count, which can be spot-checked during the day.

If you are using a manual system, give the telemarketing supervisor a hard copy of each *purchase order.* If you are using an integrated computer system, the revised inventory will automatically appear on the screen. The point is, be sure your salespeople know just how many pieces of each type of stock are available for sale. Sometimes, they may see that there won't be enough merchandise on your shelves to take a new order, but enough additional merchandise is due to be delivered by your vendor or manufacturer. In that case, your salespeople can "sell off the truck"—take orders for merchandise you don't actually have in your warehouse but is due to be delivered to you in time for you to get it to your customer.

At the risk of repeating myself, let me emphasize a key point: If you frequently ship or deliver a lot of merchandise, as we do, reconcile the physical inventory with your manual or computerized inventory count *daily*.

DISTRIBUTION AFFECTS INVENTORY

As Dial-A-Mattress grew, and we received an increasing number of orders per day, we needed to expand our inventory to have sufficient merchandise on hand. Since one of the hallmarks of Dial-A-Mattress is our rapid delivery, we can't allow ourselves to run out of merchandise and have to wait for the manufacturers to replenish it.

To maintain larger reserves of our stocks required more and more space in our distribution center. That is the key reason we moved to our current location—to give ourselves more affordable space. Our New York center is the company's major distribution point for the New York metropolitan area. It accounts for 80 percent of our business. From there, we ship mattresses all the way out to Montauk, the easternmost point of Long Island, and to most of New Jersey and the quasi-urban parts of Connecticut, as well as to the five boroughs of New York City.

When we moved into our current building in 1990, the distribution center seemed huge! It's 45,000 square feet. Yet now it's already too small. But we have found that by using the manufacturers' resources better, and increasing our efficiency, we can make do with relatively less space. Now they ship us new merchandise much more frequently. We order five days a week, and they deliver merchandise to us six days a week. We get each shipment two days after we order it. Then we verify it and route it very quickly, so our inventory "turnaround" is much more rapid than it used to be. Our total inventory is now replaced by new merchandise at least once a week. We purchase the quantity we need to replenish what we sell.

The manufacturers are cooperating with us, because it benefits them to help us increase our business by selling more of their products. For example, we first started carrying Serta mattresses in 1991, and that year we sold about a quarter of a million dollars worth of their products. Now we sell more than $10 million in Serta, alone. Obviously, the more we sell, the happier Serta will be. So they've been developing a system to provide us faster service, filling our orders within hours, instead of weeks. This gives us the availability of a much larger group of mattresses, without any need to increase the space in our distribution center.

In 1990, our inventory was about 7,000 pieces (mattresses and box springs), and we made about 100 deliveries per day. Today we make more than 500 deliveries each day, yet we keep the same amount of stock. We now send out 10,000 pieces in seven days by having our manufacturers deliver merchandise to us much more rapidly. So our cost for maintaining an item in stock is lower, and we can minimize the cost of expensive real estate and of stock on hand.

The distribution center also handles the returns. When merchandise is returned to us, most of the time it isn't because of a canceled sale; it's due to some other reason, perhaps damaged items. We guarantee our merchandise, and permit a generous 30-day return policy, so our distribution center has to be ready to receive the returns that do occur. Rather than have the drivers stand around and delay the process, we set up a "return ticket." When a driver brings back a piece of merchandise, he takes a number, waits his turn until it is called, and then completes his transaction.

SPACE REQUIREMENTS FOR YOUR DISTRIBUTION CENTER

Let me summarize: To determine how much space *you* require for your merchandise, you need to know two things: the volume levels established for your market, and more importantly, the delivery terms you have established with your vendor or vendors. The faster your vendor agrees to deliver new merchandise to replenish your stock, the smaller the amount of products you'll need to keep in your inventory. If it's going to take a long time to get new products from your supplier, you'll have to keep a large amount of merchandise on hand, so you'll have enough products to sell. That means you'll need a larger amount of space to store the merchandise, and it will sit in your warehouse for longer periods of time. Also bear in mind that it is always necessary to maintain a certain amount of stock above and beyond what you expect you'll need to fulfill your daily orders. Some days (or weeks, or seasons), you'll get more business than usual. Be sure you have enough merchandise in your inventory to cover you at those times, so you can fulfill your normal delivery schedule and keep your customers happy.

THE DELIVERY OPERATION

Although people see Dial-A-Mattress trucks all over the tri-state area, we don't actually own any trucks. Our drivers are independent contractors who work for hire. As independent contractors, liability insurance for their vehicles and workman's compensation insurance are the responsibility of the person who owns and operates each truck, or of the owner of each group of trucks. Most have come to the company by referral. They usually come extensively trained in the industry. They are well-versed on how to do home deliveries. Of course, they must meet with all state and federal regulations.

Last year, the average driver earned $70,000–75,000 per vehicle. The payment schedule is based on the distance from the center warehouse to the location of where the mattress is to be delivered, with additional amounts paid according to the size of the mattress. A driver can deliver as many as twenty mattresses in a single day. Drivers are trained to take cash, check, and credit card payments. We have a cash control department that has very clear criteria to be followed for each form of payment. Credit card transactions simply follow the guidelines set by the credit card companies.

Many of the drivers deliver exclusively for Dial-A-Mattress and have the Dial-A-Mattress logo and telephone number painted on the side of their trucks. This is additional "free" advertising, and I suggest that you do it with your deliveries as well.

All data pertinent to delivery is put into the computer by a salesperson (a telemarketer) at the time of the customer's telephone order. The driver is given a copy of the invoice, bearing the necessary delivery information: address, time, date, amount of sale, item description, and form of payment. Once a mattress is ordered, regular delivery takes approximately six hours, at a cost to the customer of $30–$40, depending on the area to which it is delivered. The optional two-hour delivery costs an additional $100. At the time of delivery, the driver sets up the new bedding and frame (if ordered), takes down the old bedding set, and removes all plastic and boxes from the customer's new purchase. Old mattresses are delivered to the central warehouse and disposed of from there.

Whatever you're selling, always have an option for the customer to have the product delivered as fast as he wants it or when he wants it. Some people want or need to have delivery immediately, for whatever reason, and they are willing to pay for it. Don't deny them.

We not only encourage the drivers to make their deliveries on time: It is a requirement! The on-time percentage is measured on a daily basis and that information is culled together weekly, then monthly. It's generally over 90 percent, but we want it to be 100 percent. Obviously, we will talk to a driver who is not delivering on time to try to determine the root of his problem, and then we will work with him to solve it.

One strong suggestion: When you first begin your delivery system, go along in the truck, van, or whatever, for several deliveries, so you will better understand the problems of the deliverer.

If you are attempting to develop a delivery system, I suggest that you secure the services of an expert on distribution: someone who's not afraid to travel. The people you hire to deliver your merchandise have to be smart, hard working, and good at what they do. Choose them well, because they are the people who can make or break your business.

Remember that people *have to be motivated,* even truck drivers. Encouragement is always a way to build positive reactions. It must be on a personal level. Thank people personally when they do a good job, and give them a tough but sincerely respectful reminder when they make a mistake or do something that is negative. I tell my people to beat themselves to death over the mistake—at first. Then, *get over it, and don't do it again.* If an employee makes the same mistakes repeatedly, he is not only hurting you but is sabotaging himself. *He has the problem,* and you cannot afford to continue your business relationship with him. Tell him good-bye and good luck in whatever he might choose to do in the future.

To get the best performance from your delivery staff, they need to know specifically what you require of them. When you hire new delivery personnel, give them a brief training session to discuss the different components of their job and to highlight its importance to the company. Then hold occasional meetings with the staff to remind them of these guidelines.

Here are some topics to discuss with the drivers:

1. Do I try to deliver service to customers as a number one priority?
2. Do I do this even if my efforts appear to go unnoticed by management?
3. Do I understand and know the performance standards for my job?
4. Do I have a job description or know what my job description is?
5. Do I fully participate in the performance appraisal and obtain maximum benefit from it?
6. Do I make it as easy as possible for my supervisor or manager to help me with a customer problem?
7. Do I accept both praise and constructive criticism from my supervisor or manager?

Always remember, however, that your front-line delivery service can only be as good as their backup. Your telemarketers must be sure to write each order correctly so that the proper merchandise will be put on the truck. They need to record the correct and *complete* address and location, be sure the customer understands and agrees to the time of delivery, and include all of this information on the order form. Then the staff of your distribution center must keep careful track of all orders and all stock to be sure they will have the merchandise on hand the day it will be needed, and to be sure they schedule each order to be delivered as promised.

Establishing Costs and Charges

Decide what delivery services you intend to provide, find out how much it will cost you to do this, and then establish what you will charge your customers. It's a good idea to see what your competitors are providing, and how much they're charging, so that you can be competitive. To give you some ideas of service possibilities, here is what Dial-A-Mattress provides:

- Two-, three-, and four-hour time frames. For example, we can schedule an appointment to ensure that a customer's merchandise will arrive within a two-hour time period, such as between 8 A.M. and 10 A.M. (Since it is often inefficient to make such short delivery-time guarantees, they will cost you more money to provide. Decide whether you need to pass this additional cost on to your customer.)
- Deliveries available from 6 A.M. to 12 midnight
- Deliveries available seven days a week
- Set-up of delivered products
- Removal of old products the new merchandise is replacing

We also provide drivers who not only have the knowledge and ability to set up our products, and remove old products, but can also collect various forms of payment—checks, cash, or charge card.

If you expect to have your own delivery staff deliver your merchandise, provide training and reinforcement to be sure they can carry out all of these duties.

The distance of a customer from your warehouse also affects how much it will cost you to make a delivery. Consider how far from your warehouse you are willing to deliver or ship your merchandise, and establish a *delivery zone* for your company. This will show the area you are willing to deliver to. Then, working with a regular map, assign a dollar value to each grid point, escalating in price as you move farther from the point of distribution.

DELIVERY DO'S AND DON'TS

Set up an efficient, well-run *delivery system* to ensure that your products will be delivered correctly and on schedule. The larger your company becomes, the more imperative this will be. With a good system, your deliveries will go smoothly. With a poorly arranged system, your company will not be able to provide the service today's customers demand.

Dial-A-Mattress has become famous for its prompt and courteous delivery. This is one of the key reasons for its success, and it didn't occur by accident. I realized early on that delivery is the most essential service to the customer, and one of the most important ways to influence the customer's opinion of our company. Why do we care what they think of us? It's good business! Satisfied customers will buy from us again, the next time they need our product. And they will recommend us to their friends, neighbors, and business associates.

Make sure your company's delivery service is equally good. Here are some dos and don'ts that will make the difference. If you are providing your own deliveries, have each member of your delivery staff learn and understand these rules. If you are looking for an outside delivery service, ask the trucking company or independent contractor to adhere to them. If they think these guidelines are too much trouble, look around for a different trucker.

It's never too much trouble to do things the right way, especially when your delivery people are the ones who will be interacting with your customers.

DRIVERS' OPERATOR

The delivery process itself begins in your warehouse, with good preparation. The *drivers' operator* acts as a liaison, a link between the drivers, the customers, and the sales department. He or she plays an integral role in the dispatching and delivery process. After the *dispatcher* has set up the day's delivery schedule, the drivers' operator is the person who ensures that the *driver* gets to the appropriate delivery site. If customers call in with questions about the order, the *driver's liaison* is the one who will help answer those questions.

Prior to each delivery, the drivers' operator should look at any special instructions the customer provided, which your telephone salesperson should have written clearly on the invoice. (For example, "Ring the back bell" or "Use Main Street instead of Center Street, because Center Street is being repaired.") After that, and after the truck has been loaded, the people primarily responsible for making sure deliveries are carried out smoothly are, of course, your drivers (or the trucking company who does this work for you). Even though each driver is essentially alone, he must always have access to backup by your company, whenever he needs to contact you. His key support person will be the drivers' operator.

The drivers' operator must also record when every delivery is completed, on the *driver's daily log.* It is the driver's responsibility to contact his operator as soon as he is finished with each job. You will need these records to monitor deliveries, so you can keep track of where each driver is and whether he's on schedule. The information will also enable you to provide accurate delivery time estimates to customers, who often call on the day of delivery to ask what time their merchandise will arrive.

If a customer telephones to ask information about a scheduled delivery, and the drivers' operator does not have this information available, he or she should contact the dispatcher and/or the driver immediately to obtain the information and relay it back to the customer. One of the best ways to maintain a good relationship with your customers is to ensure that your employees are always willing to speak with them cheerfully, and provide whatever information they need. Even if a delivery is going to be late, it's far better to notify the customer, apologize, and give the new, realistic estimated time of arrival than to try to avoid the angry customer's phone call. Providing accurate information is part of providing good service.

DRIVERS OPERATIONS LOG

Create a *log* for your company that includes the information you will need to keep track of each day's deliveries. (See next page for an example.) The drivers' operator is the one who records all data on this log, as soon as he or she receives new information. Start a new log every day. The log should include items such as these:

- *Time of Call:* The time the driver called in after completing a particular delivery.
- *Scheduled Time:* The time period in which the delivery was scheduled (for example 2–4 P.M., 10 A.M.–Noon).
- *Invoice Number:* The applicable invoice number for that merchandise order.
- *Reason:* The driver might call in for such reasons as:
    To report his location
    Because of a credit card problem
    Because of traffic problems
    Because the customer is not home to accept delivery
- *Driver Number:* The company's or owner-operator's number, as generated by the computer.

Drivers Operations Log

Name: Christine

Date: 7/27/96

Time of Call	Scheduled Time	Invoice Number	Reason	Driver Number
10:36	M(8-12)	763297	Mastercard approval # 131111	19
11:07	M(8-12)	762143	Stop completed	19
6:19	E(4-9)	763802	No one home	148
9:40	E(7-10)	764603	New total $501.96/ Ok Juan/-$25 Coupon	148

UNEXPECTED PAYMENT BY CREDIT CARD

When the telemarketers make each sale, they will find out how the customer intends to pay for the merchandise: by check (certified check, if your company requires it), cash, or credit card. This information will be listed on the invoice that the driver takes along with the merchandise.

In some cases, at the time of delivery the customer will decide to pay by credit card, even though that was not the initially agreed-upon form of payment. The credit card must be checked with the card company to obtain approval before it can be used for payment. This is the responsibility of the drivers' operator. Both the driver and the drivers' operator need to take specific actions in such a case.

To Accept a Credit Card for Payment

The driver should get the credit card information from the customer, including:

- The customer's name as written on the card
- The name of the credit card company
- The expiration date of the card
- The full amount of the purchase

Then the driver should call the drivers' operator, explain the situation and give the operator this data.

The drivers' operator should:

- Call the credit card company for approval.
- Verify that the customer's credit rating is sufficient for the amount of the purchase. The credit card company will provide an *approval number,* if it's okay to accept the card.
- Call the driver back and give him the approval number.
- Note the approval number on the drivers' operator's daily log.

The driver should write the approval number on his copy of the invoice.

If No One Is Home to Accept Delivery

As soon as the driver calls in to report this problem, the drivers' operator should:

- Look up the phone number from the *dispatching report.* (See next page for an example.) A dispatching report is a summary report of the daily activities by drivers or owner-operators. For example, it lists deliveries scheduled for morning, afternoon, and evening. It is prepared by the dispatcher, and is used as a reference tool whenever needed by the dispatcher and the drivers' operator departments.

Dispatching Report

| | Dial-A-Mattress | Route Manifest | 12-281996 | Page: 1 (of 1) |

					CHECK:	0.00
		TOTAL STOPS:	11		CASH:	699.57
First Stop Time: A12-4		TOTAL PICKUPS:	0		MC or VISA:	13,590.99
		TOTAL TAKEAWAYS:	2		AMEX:	2,337.26
Last Stop Time: A3-7		TOTAL DELIVER:	34		OTHER:	3,095.99

STOP NBR	DELV TIME	INVOICE NBR	CUSTOMER--------NAME HOME-TEL--------BUS-TEL	ADDRESS-------- CITY/COUNTY	CROSS ST. APT.#	PAY CODE AMOUNT	TOTAL UNITS	PICK UPS	TAKE AWAY
01	A12-4	828097	Doe, John	88 Salka Ct	28St/Bantha Rd	MC	1	0	N
	SALE		H:310-000-0000 B:310-111-1111	Braithwaite, NJ	PH	634.94			
02	M10-2	827165	Doe, Jane	95 Duffwood Lane	Rt19	Cash	2	0	N
	SALE		H:212-000-0000 B:212-111-1111	Brunswick, PA	PVT	699.57			
03	M11-3	828111	Brute, Sizolo	555 Washington Avenue	Rt4/Rt17	Amex	2	0	N
	SALE		H: 908-000-0000 B: 908-111-1111	Old Barrens, NY	76	1112.98			
04	A2-6	838056	Radiccio, Jane	29 Canterbury Lane	3rd Ave/53 Street	V	2	1	Y
	SALE		H:213-000-0000 B:213-111-1111	New York City, NY	2B	839.17			

- Call the number and try to reach the customer.
- Check with the *sales supervisor* for any special numbers or instructions the customer may have left.
- Have the driver leave a message for the customer on a company form or card, saying that no one was home to accept the delivery, and asking the customer to call your company when he or she gets home.
- The drivers' operator should record on his daily log that no one was home, and the reason, if it is known. This record will be given to the driver at the end of the shift, to verify that he attempted to make the delivery; this allows him to be paid for this attempted delivery. (Since your company obviously loses money on such delivery attempts, it is to your advantage to make your arrangements with the customer as definite as possible before each delivery is made.)

- Have the driver describe the type of house, or if it is an apartment, the color of the door or some distinguishing feature. This will be used to prove to the customer that the driver brought the merchandise to the proper location.

PROBLEM WITH SIZE OR TYPE OF MERCHANDISE DELIVERED

If the driver phones to say that the customer claims some or all of the merchandise is incorrect, the drivers' operator should:

1. Look up the invoice.
2. If the merchandise is incorrect—wrong product(s), wrong size(s)—have the driver find out from the customer what the correct merchandise is, and then relay this information to the sales supervisor. In our case, the Customer Service staff handle such problems.
3. If the merchandise is too large to fit through a doorway or a staircase, etc., the drivers' operator should get the pertinent information from the driver, write it down on the *drivers operations log,* and then relay this information to the sales supervisor.

LATE DELIVERY

Whenever there are late deliveries, it is imperative to document them on a daily basis. You will need accurate records of all late deliveries to be able to gauge the reliability of your drivers, drivers' operators, and dispatchers, as well as the performance of any delivery company you have contracted with. The drivers' operator is the person responsible for keeping a careful record of every late delivery. There are four things to look for:

- The driver
- The invoice

- Exactly how late the delivery arrived past the appointed time window. For example, if your company promised a delivery between 2 P.M. and 4 P.M., did the delivery truck arrive one hour late, at 5 P.M.? Or two hours late, at 6 P.M.?
- The reason for the lateness (for example, the driver's instructions were routed poorly, there was heavy traffic, the driver was delayed by the previous stop, there was wrong information on the invoice, and so forth).

SCHEDULING DELIVERIES

When you schedule your drivers to report to work, keep in mind the times that your customers prefer to receive their deliveries. If many of your customers are businesses, they may prefer delivery between 9 and 5. Some companies often prefer their deliveries to be made before they open for business, or after they've closed at the end of the day. If your customers are individuals who want their deliveries made to their homes, most will prefer deliveries in the evenings or on the weekends.

We negotiated with the truckers who handle our deliveries so that they will provide their services during our busiest delivery hours. If your deliveries will be handled by your employees, schedule your drivers accordingly. In addition, have other drivers (or teams of drivers, if your products are large or heavy) available at other times, to provide delivery availability whenever it is requested. If your company, like mine, intends to promise delivery whenever a customer wants it, have separate driver teams that start their workdays at different times: 8 A.M., or noon, or 3 P.M., or 6 P.M. This gives maximum coverage to meet customers' demands.

DELIVERY ROUTES

Use detailed maps of your delivery areas to be sure your dispatchers will be able to establish proper routes for each delivery. The maps should show zip codes, local streets, which streets are one-way and which are two-way, and features such as bridges and tunnels.

To assist the driver in plotting a route:

- Purchase regional maps that indicate street addresses.
- For each delivery, make a copy of the map and highlight a route from a major thoroughfare.
- Obtain a list of all the fire stations in the area. When the customer is not sure of where they live, and if their address is not on the map, call the fire department. They have very detailed maps, and are usually willing to give instruction.

Have your dispatcher establish each day's routes for your drivers within geographic areas, according to the concentration of orders. If you have numerous deliveries that must all go to a relatively small area next Tuesday, you may be able to schedule one truck to take care of this entire batch of orders. If there are several delivery sites, arrange the driver's schedule so that after he drops off an order, he will then go to the next nearest location. This will not only minimize unnecessary driving, it will— even more importantly—cut down on wasted time, and keep your delivery schedule efficient. We use such a schedule as a guideline but permit our truckers—or the owner-operators of the trucking companies—to replot their routes at their discretion, as long as they will satisfy the delivery window promised to each customer.

Obviously, delivery distances within a route should be realistic. It makes much more sense to schedule a driver's daily deliveries within a reasonable geographic area rather than send him from one side of your market territory to the other. Sometimes, however, optimum routes are not available. In those cases, your dispatcher should try to use good judgment to deal with the situation—perhaps give a driver a lighter schedule to allow for the greater driving time that might be necessary. (If your drivers are paid by the number of deliveries they make each day, you will have to provide a different basis for compensation on such occasions, perhaps including mileage into the computation so that the driver will not be shortchanged on days that require an excessive amount of driving and fewer deliveries.)

On or before the day an order is to be delivered, your Dispatch Department should generate a *picking slip*, listing all of the merchandise that is going to be in a particular truck. This list should be given to the driver. The driver and the dispatcher should inspect the merchandise thoroughly, and the driver should be required to sign off that he received the correct merchandise in good condition.

Our new automated system allows information about each day's delivery schedule to be available to everyone who might need it, including the sales department. As each sale is completed, the computer tells the telemarketer what soonest delivery times are available within the customer's geographic area. The computer is also constantly updated with data concerning everything that might affect delivery routing and scheduling, such as a parade that might interfere with the trucks, or a hurricane or snowstorm. In such cases, our normal two-hour window may become a four-hour window.

THE DRIVER'S PRIMARY DUTIES

We give our drivers the following instructions and responsibilities. They may work for you, too:

- The driver should read the specific directions written on the invoice by the salesperson. Then he should locate the street names on maps before leaving the warehouse.
- The truck should not leave the warehouse until the driver has checked to be sure he has:
  - The correct merchandise to fill each order
  - The invoice and *receipt* for each order
  - A credit card machine, and sufficient credit slips
  - Any equipment, tools, and supplies that might be needed to deliver the merchandise and complete each sale

- As soon as the driver reaches the location, he should contact and greet the customer. It is important that the driver introduces himself, and makes sure the customer is ready to take possession of the merchandise. *The driver is your company's representative*, whether he works directly for you or is from an independent trucking company. So it is mandatory that he be polite and friendly.
- Always make sure the customer has the proper payment. If there are any problems, the driver should contact the drivers' operator for assistance or further information.
- Instruct your drivers to be careful and considerate. For example, before walking into the customer's home or place of business, they should wipe their feet. That's obvious. Less obvious, but extremely important, it's necessary for every driver, on each and every delivery, to check out the area they will be going into, and clear the path of anything that looks like it might be in the way or that may be broken. Tell them to look at any fixtures and wallpaper that could be damaged when they carry or wheel the merchandise into the room, and to point out such items to the customer before they begin to carry in the merchandise.
- If the customer has old merchandise that your driver is supposed to remove, have him take it out of the building before he brings the new merchandise in. (For example, Dial-A-Mattress picks up and removes our customers' old mattresses when we deliver new ones to them.) If the item needs to be taken apart or packed into a box, the driver is responsible for doing this before he removes the old merchandise.
- If the driver discovers that he is going to fall behind schedule because of this disassembly and removal, he should ask permission to use the customer's telephone to call his drivers' operator. Then the drivers' operator should notify the next customer on the route that there has been a slight delay, and when the delivery truck will be there. We find that keeping our customers informed, even if it means

telling them about a slight delay, is far better than not con-
tacting them when a delivery is going to be late.

- The driver is now ready to bring the merchandise into the customer's house or workplace. Educate each driver (or trucking company owner or representative) to bring the new merchandise into the customer's home or office in a logical sequence. If more than one large box or item is to be delivered, and if one product is going to go on top of the other—as a mattress goes on top of a box spring, or an open hutch goes on top of a closed cabinet—the driver should bring in the "bottom" item first, and set it up in the proper place. Then he should bring in the "top" item, and put it on the bottom one.

- The same process should be followed if a piece of furniture is to be delivered, as well as something that's going to be placed inside it, such as a TV cabinet and a large television set. Have the driver bring in the TV cabinet first, set it in place, then bring in the television set and put it inside the cabinet.

- If the customer asks the driver to do any installation that is not part of the normal delivery service, he should first see if it can be done without damaging the new merchandise. If there is the slightest danger that something might break, the driver must tell the customer of the danger, and explain that he is not responsible if it is damaged. The customer must sign a *release form* before the driver takes any further steps. If the customer is upset or confused, or if there are any problems with this matter, instruct the driver to phone his drivers' operator. Most importantly, he should *never argue with a customer*.

- The customer needs to learn how to work the new merchandise, and how to take care of it. The driver should briefly explain this, and if necessary, demonstrate what to do. The "lesson" should be short, but clear and courteous, and he should be sure the customer understands and can do what is necessary, before he leaves the premises. This not only protects the new merchandise, but makes the customer happy that he can use his new purchase properly.

- Have the customer inspect the new merchandise, and sign the invoice or release that it is okay. If the customer does not or cannot inspect it before the driver leaves, that should be written on the invoice, and initialed by the customer. If the customer does not want the merchandise installed or set up, the driver should write this explanation on the form, state that he left the merchandise wherever the customer wanted it, and then have the customer sign the invoice.

- In some instances, the driver is responsible for collecting the payment for the merchandise. He should check the invoice, when he first arrives at each delivery site, to see if the merchandise has been fully paid for. If the driver is supposed to collect the payment, he should do so according to your company's policies regarding cash, certified check, or credit card, and then give the customer a receipt for the payment.

- As your representative, the driver should thank the customer for doing business with your company, and then show him his *guarantee* or *warranty*, or explain where the manufacturer attached or packed it.

- Your company's copy of the inventory, receipt, release form, payment, and any other paperwork relating to each delivery must be brought back for your records. The driver is responsible for collecting these papers when he leaves the customer's home or office. Have him keep all of the papers in one place or envelope, then bring them back to the company and hand them over to the drivers' operator.

If a driver has a complaint about a customer—and some customers are less than pleasant—insist that the driver not argue with the customer. Instruct him to politely leave the premises, then have him call your office and let the drivers' operator know what happened. Every customer is precious to a company. They are your lifeblood. The driver is the only person who will meet our customers in person. The impression he leaves them with will be the impression they will remember about the company. This impression will determine whether or not the customer will recommend you to other potential consumers, and whether this customer will buy merchandise from you again.

EQUIPMENT AND SUPPLIES

Every driver should carry whatever tools and equipment will be needed to deliver and set up whatever merchandise you carry. He should never ask the customer to lend him even the most basic items, such as a hammer or a pair of scissors. You can help, by planning ahead to determine every possible piece of equipment or any supplies that a driver might need; then create a complete package of equipment and supplies for every driver. Provide a check-off sheet, also, that lists all of these components. Each driver should go over that list before every trip to be sure he takes whatever materials he might need along with him. This is his responsibility.

If you accept credit card payments, ask the credit card companies to provide you with enough card "swiping" machines so that you can provide one to each driver or owner-operator. You can then issue them blank credit card slips or, ideally, have a credit card section imprinted right onto your invoice. Here, too, it will be the driver's responsibility to be sure he has enough slips with him each day.

Supply the driver with a multiple-part invoice and/or a receipt for the merchandise. At the end of every delivery, the customer should sign this form, keep one copy, and return the other copy to the driver, who will bring it back to his drivers' operator.

Finally, if your drivers will ever have to install or assemble your merchandise for the customers, provide the drivers with a release form. This has no bearing on normal installation or assembly. It is to be used whenever a customer asks for *extra* service—for example, attaching your bookcase to their wall—that might conceivably damage either the new merchandise, or the customer's premises or property.

As I've already explained, Dial-A-Mattress does not have drivers on our *staff*. Instead, we use the services of trucking companies. No matter which system you use, be careful to explain to the delivery people how important it is for them to be polite and considerate to every customer.

LOADING PROCEDURES

Set up a procedure for how your merchandise will be loaded onto the trucks. Be certain that this procedure is followed, by your own drivers and by any outside company you contract with. The following procedures are basic, and should be adhered to no matter what kind of products you sell:

- The driver should park his truck securely at the loading platform, before anyone begins to load or unload merchandise.
- The dispatcher should give a list of merchandise for each specific order to the appropriate person, who will pull that merchandise from stock.
- The driver and the appropriate warehouse personnel should inspect the merchandise for defects and/or damage, prior to having it loaded onto the truck.

  If you are using a trucking company or independent contractor to make your deliveries, notify them in writing that *they* will be held financially responsible for any damage to merchandise, after they have accepted it in good condition from your warehouse. This should be in your contract with that delivery company.
- The driver, trucking company, or independent contractor should make certain that they receive all merchandise listed on the delivery tickets. They are responsible for checking model numbers, sizes, product names, or any stipulations, and must make sure all merchandise for a particular order has been gathered and loaded onto the truck.
- The truck should be loaded in reverse order of delivery. That is, the merchandise that is to be delivered first should

be loaded last, so it's nearest the door of the truck. The merchandise that is to be delivered last should be loaded first, so it's against the far wall of the truck, not blocking any other items that must be removed first.

USING AN OUTSIDE DELIVERY SERVICE

If you prefer not to establish your own delivery department, there are delivery services you can hire to provide these services. Get cost estimates from at least three of these independent contractors, and determine which company can provide the best service at the best price. Then decide what works best for you: establishing and maintaining your own delivery department, or contracting with an outside concern. (You might also elect to have your own delivery department for your main distribution center, and hire outside delivery services to handle other parts of the country.) Remember to reassess your delivery needs as your company grows and changes.

Even if you hire an independent contractor, *you* will be ultimately responsible for making sure your merchandise reaches your customers on time and without damage. To protect yourself, be sure that the delivery service is in complete compliance with all federal and state regulations.

We will only use the services of delivery companies that provide delivery personnel who are well groomed. The delivery men provide our company's contact with our customers. Since sales are made over the phone, our consumers don't *see* our salespeople. So the unofficial representatives of our company are our delivery people. And since customers don't know or care whether these people work directly for us or are employed by an outside delivery service, it is imperative that the delivery men are clean and well groomed. We also request that they be polite and friendly, and as helpful as they can be to our customers.

Your dispatcher will become your company's expert on all aspects of delivery. One of the responsibilities of the dispatcher is to determine whether or not each outside delivery company is appropriate.

Confirmation of Orders

People change their minds. People make mistakes. Since these things happen in all areas of life, they can certainly happen concerning the ordering of merchandise. And they do! If you prepare for such problems, though, you can minimize the inconvenience or cost that they otherwise might cause your company.

The solution is simple: *Before you dispatch every delivery, call the customer and confirm the order.* This confirmation has several purposes:

- It lets you make sure the customer still wants the merchandise. It also reveals whether an order is fraudulent, perhaps placed by someone other than the customer.
- It lets you verify pertinent information such as the address, the size, and the style of the merchandise ordered, the form of payment, and any special instructions your driver will need.
- It lets you be sure the customer understands when the merchandise will arrive, how much it will cost, and so on. This phone call is a simple but invaluable way to prevent costly mistaken deliveries, and to minimize snags and delays in your delivery process. It will save you both money and aggravation.

Assign a person to make your confirmation calls as a regular part of his or her duties. In our company, this task is done by the same person who is doing the dispatching, since he or she already has all of the data on that particular order. Using your dispatcher to do your confirmation calls works very well, until your company gets large enough to require a full-time confirmation person.

Before calling to confirm the order:

- Check your inventory to make sure the merchandise is available.
- Check your *delivery dispatching zone sheet* to make sure that the delivery time is accurate.
- Clearly highlight all special instructions, or attach a separate note, to be sure your driver sees this important information.
- Assume that all the information on your invoice is *inaccurate*. If your confirmation person starts with this assumption, it will ensure that he will thoroughly check every detail to correct any errors that may be on the invoice.

Now that your company has done everything possible at your end to make sure the order is correct, it's time to telephone the customer to verify the following information:

- Name
- Address (have the customer *tell you* his or her address to be certain you have it correctly)
- Day and evening telephone number
- Form of payment
- Time and date of delivery
- Size and style of merchandise ordered
- Price, including tax, delivery, and additional charges
- Driving directions to the location, and cross streets
- Special instructions or requests by the customer. These should be noted on the invoice.
- The identity of the person confirming the order. This, too, should be noted on the invoice.
- Whether payment is to be made by credit card. If this is the case, the Confirmation Department should complete a credit card slip before delivery. The driver should take this slip on the delivery, have the customer sign it, and bring it back to the company at the end of the day.

- Make sure the merchandise ordered will fit into the customer's building, and that it will fit into the room for which it was ordered. (This usually applies to very large items, such as king-size mattresses or large pieces of furniture. Obviously if a single large box won't fit through a door, but the products themselves are small enough fit separately, then that order should be packed in more than one small box.)
- Make sure the area through which the driver will carry the merchandise has no fragile or cumbersome objects that might get in the way, or be damaged or broken by accident.

Once these points have been verbally confirmed, and any necessary additional information obtained and noted, the order is ready to be given to the dispatcher.

When confirming orders for the next day, have your dispatcher (or whoever is making your confirmations) start phoning early in the afternoon. It may take several attempts to reach certain customers, and it can take hours to phone a number of people. It also takes time to correct any necessary information, and to prepare the paperwork for the deliveries. Remember that after each order is confirmed, you still need to have time for your warehouse personnel to pull the appropriate stock, and have the order checked for accuracy and for damaged merchandise.

If a customer cannot be reached, the dispatcher should note this on the invoice, with the times that confirmation was attempted. When possible, leave a message requesting that the customer call the Confirmation Department. We write "LM" (left message) or "NA" (no answer) on the invoice, if we can't get through, to help us keep track of the status of each confirmation. If we can't contact a customer, we cancel the scheduled delivery, and reschedule it as soon as we do confirm the order with the customer.

If the order is canceled or postponed, if no merchandise is available, or if the customer sounds doubtful about the purchase, have the dispatcher contact the sales manager or a supervisor immediately to have one of them contact the customer and re-establish the sale, if possible.

If the customer calls the Confirmation Department to confirm when delivery will take place, it is important to validate that the call is, indeed, coming from the customer. Thus the dispatcher should make a follow-up call to the customer to be sure everything is in order.

TROUBLESHOOTING

In any business, problems will arise. Telemarketing is no exception. Expect difficulty from the constantly emerging facets of your business and learn from them, realizing that their prevention and early recognition are keys to the success of any operation.

In the delivery process, certain problems come up regularly: The driver was late; the driver was rude; he brought the wrong size, etc. In such cases, apologize to the customer with a phone call or a letter. When a complaint is registered by a Dial-A-Mattress customer, it's usually because of damage done to the paint on the wall in a home during the installation of the new mattress or the removal of the old one. In this case, a representative will telephone to apologize and the company will pay the cost of repairs, or send out a sheet set as a gift.

When you sell merchandise, the variety of complaints can be virtually endless: The flowers you delivered were slightly wilted; the jacket was not the advertised color; the shoes don't fit; the chest of drawers has no knobs; "I don't want it anyway"; "My wife doesn't like it"; the steaks weren't fresh enough; the shape of the lampshade doesn't fit the decor; you took too long to deliver it; the toy doesn't work; it cost too much; and so on and so on.

Don't try to browbeat the customer into keeping the merchandise if they don't want it. A courteous response, with the offer to take the merchandise back or possibly even pick it up, will do your business much greater good than harm in future sales and referrals.

The biggest problem occurs when a customer accuses a driver of theft. It becomes a question of one person's word against another's, so you must ask the customer to file a police report.

Each complaint must be dealt with on an individual basis. Sometimes it *is* the driver, and sometimes it's the customer who is merely a crank. If you know the driver and know that this is not typical of him, you should tell him about the complaint and leave it at that. Obviously, if complaints about a particular driver occur frequently, you have to take further measures, perhaps even replacing him. These are routine problems facing the operation of any delivery system. But there are unexpected problems of a more serious nature that will challenge your system from time to time.

For example, one Saturday morning we were hit by a strike from the drivers. We had never been struck before. The trucks are our lifeline to our customers, and we sell so many mattresses that it is impossible for us to deliver them ourselves without our regular drivers. My son Luis approached the line of striking drivers and Teamsters to personally ask some of them if they would do the deliveries. They said that they would not do the deliveries. He didn't know the organizers very well (which is a lesson: *get to know everyone*), but there were people in that line with whom he had a personal relationship and he felt they were being somewhat disloyal. They must have felt the same way, because afterwards he realized that he only saw those men on the strike line *one day*, while the strike lasted the entire weekend. On that first day, they got caught up in the excitement. But when it came down to a personal level, they had as much difficulty with the strike as we, the management, did.

That's another reason why personal relationships are good—and good for business. These drivers had to think about it—the damage to the business and to their wallets—and they kept on thinking about it on the way home and at home. They lost sleep over it, especially the specific drivers who were asked to deliver. "That's going to remain as an imprint on their minds and on mine. I know I will never forget it," said Luis.

During the strike, we had to hire some outside drivers to make the deliveries. Our record for deliveries in a single day is 701. Believe it or not, we were competing with that number the

Saturday of the strike. We made 650 deliveries, and we hadn't done a 600-plus day for months. This is an important exercise to incorporate into your business: Learn to use problems as lessons, examples, testimonials of corporate philosophies, and work ethics that otherwise might fall by the wayside. Turn these fissures of your work stoppage or slow-downs to your advantage if you can. To the extent that you can succeed in delivering your goods under adverse circumstances or conditions, by turning the situation around, your self-respect and that of others in the company will rise.

Learn to love the different, the blemished, the broken, and learn to deal with it. In the difficult dynamics of life are positive forces that can forge the mettle of any company.

6

BUILD EXCELLENT COMMUNICATIONS— INSIDE AND OUTSIDE YOUR COMPANY

The source of the communication—his or her perceived honesty and objectivity—has an enormous influence on whether or not the communication is accepted by the receiver. If the source is well-respected and highly thought of by the intended audience, the message is much more likely to be believed. Conversely, messages from a source considered unreliable or untrustworthy will be received with skepticism and ultimately rejected.

Consumer Behavior
Leon G. Schiffman and
Leslie Lazar Kanuk

As soon as you begin your telemarketing operation, no matter how small the staff, you should have regular meetings. They can serve two kinds of purposes. Some meetings are to share information, so everyone in your company, or specific people in your company, are kept up to date regarding new developments, problems, successes, or whatever else they need to know. Our daily *Directors' Meetings* fall into this category.

Other meetings are rather like "classes" where you instruct your staff, and sometimes learn from your staff, about all aspects of the business, not only those directed to increasing sales.

MEETINGS TO SHARE INFORMATION THROUGHOUT THE COMPANY

We hold a *Directors' Meeting* every day. As its name implies, the attendees are directors of each department, or a designated representative. We go around the group, and the director or his surrogate presents two sets of "numbers"—what happened yesterday and what they expect to happen today. For example, the Sales Department will report on how many telephone calls were received, how many of those were translated into sales, the average price of each purchase, and how many calls and sales they expect to have today, and so on. The Delivery Department will report on how many deliveries were scheduled to each area, how many were made, and how closely they adhered to their schedule. The Marketing and Publicity Department will announce when advertisements and commercials will run, and will play new radio or TV spots, so everyone else can be aware of them.

As each department gives its quick run-down on what is going on in its section, the other participants record the information on charts we have created for this purpose. Why does Delivery have to know about what's going on in Promotion? We have learned that everything connects. If we run an ad or a commercial, all departments need to be ready for a sudden influx of calls from potential customers, and the rush of new orders that must then be delivered.

As we listen to the "numbers," we pay particular attention to anything that seems out of the ordinary, which might signal a problem that is beginning. We also discuss any emergencies that have arisen since the previous day.

After this meeting, the directors will return to their departments and each will hold a small meeting with his or her staff to provide them with the information that has been shared. Then each department will continue to do its own work, but with an awareness of what is happening in other parts of the company. Sometimes this awareness results in important changes, as one department discovers how it can be of assistance to another.

MEETINGS TO EXPLORE IDEAS

We hold these "class" meetings at irregular times, but as frequently as feasible. As I said, they are to help the staff learn how to improve various aspects of the business.

Here are some of the questions you might explore at these "class" meetings:

- How do you create customer feedback?
- How do you improve the quality of the product or the service?
- How do you define the mission of your company?
- How do you develop low-level personnel into managerial staff?
- What other businesses should you start?
- Are you in the right business?
- What long-term or short-term problems do you face?
- How can you successfully warehouse and inventory enough stock?
- How can you begin to diversify?
- How can you expand to other markets throughout the country and overseas?
- How can you distribute your product or service successfully and economically?
- How can you use the Internet to sell?

At a recent meeting, I distributed the following questionnaire, in part because I truly wanted to know the answers myself, but also because I wanted everyone to think these issues through themselves so that they would get to know their own jobs better. Some people gave me extended answers, and some members of the same department teamed up to provide joint answers. It became a two-way education.

QUESTIONNAIRE

1. With Dial-A-Mattress's new outbound call program, won't there be a high degree of burnout by bedding consultants (our telephone sales-people), and will it not take more sophisticated sales techniques? How will this special training, if any, be provided?
2. In general, how is burnout prevented?
3. Should a telemarketing company have a variety of scripts for its sales consultants? Does Dial-A-Mattress have this variety? How is the script that gives the highest close ratio measured?
4. At present, how is Dial-A-Mattress maintaining quality control? How should a new telemarketer establish and maintain quality control guidelines?
5. Should field calls be considered a viable adjunct to telephone sales (obviously, if the ticket is large enough)? So, if a customer fails to buy a $3,000 mattress, should a personal visit be made to his home, business or wherever to provide further assistance in selecting a mattress?
6. Does on-time delivery cut down on returns? Do we have any statistics or information to back this up?
7. What percentage of gross sales should go into:
   • Training?
   • Further education of employees?
   • Quality control?
     Why?
8. What is the difference, if any, in selling a service (such as legal advice) over the telephone as opposed to selling a product? Advantages and disadvantages?
9. Which would a potential customer purchase more readily, a product or a service?
10. How can a person know whether his service or product will be tele-marketable?
11. How many actual dollars should be invested in advertising to determine whether a product or service is going to succeed?
12. What if the new telemarketer has no reputation or brand-name recognition? How does he overcome this?

13. The U.S. Office of Consumer Affairs states that half of all complainants will buy from that company again. Does Dial-A-Mattress have any statistics that bear this out? In other words, is Dial converting their complaints into new sales?

14. How important are follow-up calls ("Are you happy with your bed?")? Does Dial-A-Mattress do this invariably? Should other telemarketers do this? Does it ever backfire?

15. In general, is customer pick-up a feasible alternative to most products? Should it be encouraged?

16. In a national (or even regional) campaign, how are differences in consumer income handled?

17. How important are giveaways and premiums in boosting sales?

18. Should toll-free numbers be tied into faxes? (So that customers can fax their orders in?) Is this done at Dial-A-Mattress? What products or services should this be applied to?

19. How important are toll-free *vanity numbers*? Do they ever work against the sale? (Reader: A vanity number is a telephone number that spells your company's name or slogan, such as our 1–800–MATTRESS number.)

20. Should celebrity endorsements be used in the advertising of a telemarketer? Why or why not?

21. How important are titles such as "Bedding Consultant"? (Reader: This is what we call our telephone salespeople, or telemarketers.) To the consultant himself? To the consumer?

22. What relationship do titles have to performance?

23. In establishing all of the new businesses, such as Dial-A-Box, financial services, etc., why doesn't Dial-A-Mattress stick closer to its experience with products such as furniture and other household goods?

24. How does Dial-A-Mattress keep abreast of competition? How should other telemarketing operations keep abreast?

25. How important is it to sales to be listed in the 1–800 Yellow Pages and by 1–800 Information Services? Can this be quantified?

26. How should sales compensation be determined? Why?
   • Straight commission?
   • Straight salary?
   • Combination of salary and commission?

27. What percentage of gross sales should be devoted to advertising?

28. Traditionally, the law of demand states that more goods will be sold at lower prices. What is Dial-A-Mattress's experience with this?

29. Some bedding consultants have said that they never tell the caller to go to Macy's or wherever to try out the bed for fear of losing the sale. Other BC's say they have had a good experience with this strategy. What is recommended?

30. What are the advantages and disadvantages of a home agent telemarketing program?

31. How can one measure the effectiveness of advertising (or any single medium), as to cost per call, if you are using many different outlets?

32. Has a two-tiered approach, combining direct mail and outbound calling, ever been tried by Dial-A-Mattress? (That is, sending a catalog or flyer to hot prospects such as new home buyers, apartment renters, purchasers of home furnishings, etc., followed by outbound calling.) Is this method recommended for other products or services?

33. How much up-selling should the sales consultant attempt? (Or should he stick to the price that is originally mentioned by the caller?)

34. What are the dynamics of catalog telemarketing compared to the straight inbound approach of Dial-A-Mattress?

35. How much should a sales consultant "schmooze" with a customer? Obviously, the more talk, the slower the sale. But doesn't it pay off in the long run in cementing the sale?

36. What kind of advice can we give to people such as Henry Medina, with his emergency evacuation chair, who spent $1 million in developing his product and virtually nothing in selling or distributing it? Is marketing more important than product development?

37. Should high potential sales (say, customers who have already purchased beds in excess of $1,000) be contacted on a predetermined scheduled with outbound calling? (At the fifth anniversary of the sale, perhaps, and then every year afterward?) Is this system recommended for other products or services?

Obviously you won't have a formal questionnaire to distribute or to discuss at every meeting. Do have one or more topics to discuss, though—and be open to topics, suggestions, and comments by your staff members.

Consider the possibility of having invited speakers at your weekly meetings; discuss the competition; show films of commercials, or copies of ads if applicable; make certain that significant articles or even books are required reading before each meeting takes place; and have someone from your personnel department present reports about conferences or industry-wide shows that they may have attended.

Try to include as many people from your company as possible, and have such a meeting at least once a week. Some of your staff might resent such theoretical meetings, claiming that it is taking them away from what they feel is the "important" part of their specific job: making sales, creating product, whatever. But I can assure you that these meetings are essential for growth. Don't be afraid to actually give quizzes or ask people to make oral presentations, just as though they were in a class. Teaching is a great learning experience, so you—and those who make presentations—may end up gaining as much, if not more, than your employees. Everyone profits from learning new concepts, and from sharing their perceptions and ideas.

After a short time, once your people know their presence is not only demanded but truly needed and that some of their ideas will be implemented, they will begin to prepare for each meeting and look forward to it in anticipation. You might announce, in advance, the topic of the next meeting, and request that your staff do some advance thinking or actual preparation for it. Be as concrete as possible. For example, you might have everyone submit, in writing, five ideas each week on how sales can be increased, or expenses decreased, or any other element of the business that is pertinent.

Try to keep your meetings to no more than an hour, always at the same day of the week, perhaps one hour earlier than normal starting time so that they do not interfere with "regular" business. Serve breakfast, or at least coffee and doughnuts. Try to keep each meeting serious, but with a touch of festivity about it. Mondays are often good days to have these "think-tank" meetings. It sets an optimistic tone for the week. Prepare questions, take attendance, distribute an agenda, keep minutes (and distribute copies shortly afterwards).

If your operation is too large or bulky to have all employees attend, consider conducting these meetings divisionally, or by department, with minutes from each division being shared with everyone else. Essential: Try to include *everyone* in your operation, from security personnel to porters, and from accountants to lawyers. Every cog in the wheel of your operation is important. Without exception, after a few of these meetings *all* of your personnel will treat the business with a sense of benign proprietorship. Everyone in the company must feel personally responsible for the success of the business, and through the interaction that I am suggesting, they will feel more of a part of that formula.

They will also come to understand one another's responsibilities and problems. This helps individuals, and departments, take steps to work together better. At one of our meetings, someone from the delivery department explained that incorrect or insufficient addresses resulted in delays that annoyed both the customers and the drivers. So we worked out a more specific way of recording the customer's address, even including the nearest avenue, and listing what streets the house is between. Our telephone sales staff now ask for this information, a follow-up call confirms or clarifies it (as well as confirming the order and delivery date), and deliveries are now faster and more efficient. This constructive solution to a problem came about because people from different departments, who normally have little or no chance to talk, were given an opportunity to meet and discuss their respective sides of issues that affect the whole company.

At Dial-A-Mattress we have experimented with all kinds of meetings, of all different frequencies and durations and with different strategies and agendas. But the underlying rationale has always been to educate everyone in the company to understand what the customer wants and how to satisfy that want or need. Everyone in your company, from that most junior entry-level employee to the most senior CEO or CFO, should embrace not only the philosophy of the company, as to its concepts and issues, but also understand fully the methods of operation.

Everyone at Dial-A-Mattress is also trained to understand everything possible there is to know about our product—bedding. Train your employees so that they know not only the smallest details of the product or service that you are offering, but they also truly understand the deeper implications of your business. I consider all of my employees as assets, not liabilities. *They* are the ones who will make or break the business, and they, like your customers, should be afforded total respect.

At Dial-A-Mattress, we have a slogan hanging prominently in

our training room: "The one with the most information wins." Development of employees through the kind of education that I've been outlining should be at the top of your strategic priority list.

Johnson & Johnson, the health-care products company with over 89,000 employees, has a particularly enlightened view, not only toward its customers but to their employees as well. Upon hiring, each employee is given the credo, below, which presents the set of values and principles by which the company conducts business.

OUR CREDO

We believe our first responsibility is to the doctors, nurses and patients, to mothers and fathers and all others who use our products and services. In meeting their needs everything we do must be of high quality. We must constantly strive to reduce our costs in order to maintain reasonable prices. Customers' orders must be serviced promptly and accurately. Our suppliers and distributors must have an opportunity to make a fair profit

We are responsible to our employees, the men and women who work with us throughout the world. Everyone must be considered as an individual. We must respect their dignity and recognize their merit. They must have a sense of security in their jobs. Compensation must be fair and adequate, and working conditions clean, orderly and safe. We must be mindful of ways to help our employees fulfill their family responsibilities. Employees must feel free to make suggestions and complaints. There must be equal opportunity for employment, development and advancement for those qualified. We must provide competent management, and their actions must be just and ethical.

We are responsible to the communities in which we work and to the world community as well. We must be good citizens— support good works and charities and bear our fair share of taxes. We must encourage civic improvements and better health and education. We must maintain in good order the property we are privileged to use, protecting the environment and natural resources.

Our final responsibility is to our stockholders. Business must make a sound profit. We must experiment with new ideas. Research must be carried on, innovative programs developed and mistakes paid for. New equipment must be purchased, new facilities provided and new products launched. Reserves must be created to provide for adverse times. When we operate according to these principles, the stockholders should realize a fair return.

Johnson & Johnson

THE PAGER: THE KEY FOR KEEPING UP TO DATE

Management systems are based on communication, and in my opinion one of the most important tools is the pager. You probably think of pagers as "beepers" to contact someone when they're not reachable by phone. For some companies, that's only a small part of their function. These small but increasingly powerful electronic devices are primarily compact storehouses of information, which can constantly update you with the information that you need to run your business.

Pagers can keep you continually informed about changes in critical data concerning several aspects of your company, including sales, inventory, the average price sale, deliveries completed, problems, orders, daily totals, and so on. Pagers can serve as the heart of the company's internal communications network.

You can use a pager in the following way: Each department gathers its own data. Every two hours, this data can be fed to a separate department in charge of collecting it and inserting it into the data system. Then this updated information can be sent out over the pagers. Staff members with pagers thus receive updated information regardless of where they are—in a meeting, at their desks, in their cars, at home. They will then know how many sales calls or inquiries the company has received within the last two hours. They will know how many of those calls resulted in sales, the gross total income from those sales, and the average price of each sale. They will also know how many deliveries were made during that two-hour period, and how many more deliveries have been scheduled for the rest of the day.

My General Manager, Joe Vicens, calls these facts the pulse of our business. To continue to grow, my key staff—my directors, supervisors, and managers—must keep their fingers on that pulse 24 hours a day, seven days a week. (Dial-A-Mattress never closes.) We're not physicians. Neither are you. You don't need stethoscopes to hear the patient's heart. But you may need pagers, to track the life of your company.

Here is a suggested list of fifteen key points of operational data that you might consider programming into your pager:

1. Call volume
2. Abandoned calls
3. Total dollars
4. Total orders
5. Closing ratios
6. Same-day deliveries
7. Total deliveries
8. Orders dispatched
9. Late deliveries
10. Total personnel
11. Agents on phone
12. Average calls per rep
13. Dollars per call
14. Customer service calls
15. Average ticket

The pager is thus a device for continuously measuring, monitoring, and managing your company's performance. If you find that a key figure is lower than it should be, it means you have to do something—sometimes quickly! Suppose the number of sales calls is substantially lower than tradition or your past experience has led you to expect. That means you have a problem—something that needs attention immediately, before the sales continue to fall. You may know, for example, that one of your television commercials, when run on a particular station during a specified time, usually results in approximately 200 inquiries, from which you make 20 actual sales. If your pager indicates that you have received only 14 calls during that time period, and only one sale, you know something is radically wrong. You should immediately check with your advertising department to determine whether all of your scheduled commercials have actually aired, or all of your print advertisements have actually been published. Or perhaps you are running a new commercial, which apparently is not as successful as the old one. Whatever the cause, you know something is radically wrong. . . and you can then do what is necessary to rectify it immediately.

Here's another example: Suppose the number of deliveries slips below your norm. The people in charge of related departments should immediately check to find out why. Was it an odd blip of time during which few people *wanted* to have their orders delivered? Or was something wrong? The manager of your Distribution Center should check to see if there is a problem in his area. The manager of Drivers' Operations should find out if there is something wrong regarding any of the trucking companies who service you. The manager of Traffic and Dispatching should see if there's some snafu in getting merchandise out of inventory. And, because you probably depend so much on a constant resupply of merchandise from your manufacturers and vendors, the managers of Inventory, Merchandising, and Purchasing should all jump in to make sure you're receiving new products on schedule.

Once the source of the problem has been discovered—or if the reason for the problem can't be determined quickly—there should probably be an emergency meeting between the director of the area in question and the managers involved. They should deal with the issues and find ways to resolve them before much more time goes by.

The pager also lets you know when things are going well— sometimes unexpectedly well. If you run a new commercial and it results in an unusually high number of customer calls, that sounds like a delightful surprise. But it could quickly turn into a nightmare, if you can't handle the additional business. The pager would alert your executives that they had better put on additional staff—quickly! It might also indicate that you need to adjust your delivery schedules, and possibly your advertising schedules.

For senior management, the pager identifies trends. It even can produce a rough P & L statement, which you can use as a guide in helping you to make decisions about every area of the company. The availability of all of this critical data, and your decision to update it every two hours, will increase your ability to catch small problems before they become big ones, and to take care of problems very quickly. It's the "stitch in time" concept. Things go wrong in business, as in the rest of life. That's a given, and you should expect it. The point is to institute a system—a process—that enables your company to deal with new situations as they arise. The pager can be your tool for doing this. Some bureaucratic corporations take days or weeks to rectify certain problems, in large part because they take what I consider to be unnecessary time compiling their data, scheduling a meeting to discuss it, and then deciding on a strategy to resolve the situation. With the pager system, I truly believe that you can save *weeks* of time, and probably save literally millions of dollars each year. Don't wait for regularly scheduled meetings if the pager shows that something is beginning to go wrong. Deal with the small problem, before it becomes a big one.

There is one problem with the pager that I must share with you. Since all of your most vital day-to-day information can be processed into a pager, such data could become extremely valuable to your competitors, should they become privy to it. For example, supposing you test one of your radio commercials on a new show being hosted by a popular celebrity, and the result is a huge increase in sales for you. Should your competitor learn of the direct success of your commercial by gaining access to the information displayed by your pager, he might broadcast his own commercial on that show the next day, thereby cutting into your sales. How likely is this scenario to happen? It all depends on the business you are in, how quickly your competitors can act, and whether you have any disgruntled employees who are eager to ingratiate themselves with your competitors. A word of warning: Distribute your pagers carefully, tighten your security, and make sure that the information on your pager does not fall into the wrong hands.

THE OPEN DOOR POLICY

As you can see, theoretically and practically I firmly believe in sharing information with my employees. It works the other way around, too: Often they have information that *I* need to know. I've found that the best way to ensure this sharing of ideas, facts, or problems is to establish a very open line of communication between us. And so, I've instituted an "open door policy."

The meaning is quite literal. Unless I'm in a private meeting, the door of my office is always open—and that's most of the time. Employees can walk in and talk to me, and they do, whether they be salespeople, security guards, or directors of departments.

When meetings are small enough, we hold them in my office, which contains a conference table and chairs. There are still more chairs around the perimeter of the room, to fit in as many people as possible. Often I don't conduct these meetings. We take turns allowing every member of my executive staff, as well as my directors and my managers, to have a chance to conduct our meetings, following a prearranged agenda. This experience not only builds leadership, but it also helps everyone become acquainted with the personnel and the problems of departments other than their own, and sharpens their awareness of all facets of the company.

As long as a meeting is going well, I rarely interfere. In fact, often I sit in one of the chairs along the wall. The chairman of the meeting sits at the head of the conference table. Other employees sit wherever they wish, sometimes on top of my desk. That's okay. They're in the room to participate in an important meeting concerning the company they work for, which just happens to be the company I own. Their contributions are critical to its success, and I want them to know that my company cannot succeed without them.

A variation of the Open Door Policy also extends to companies with which Dial-A-Mattress works very closely. I call these companies my *Partners in Business*, and I have much closer relationships with them than most companies have with their suppliers and other support businesses. For instance, we work extremely closely with IBM and AT&T. It isn't only that we buy their equipment and services; we also share ideas and expertise with them, and much of the technology we have developed stems from their ideas and information about telecommunications. A while ago, it became clear that representatives of these two companies spend so much time at Dial-A-Mattress that this is sort of their office-away-from-home. So we gave them official office space here.

Establishing good communications with other companies also provides us with needed information. I don't believe in reinventing the wheel. Whenever we come upon a new problem or situation, we look around to see if someone else has already solved it. Then we ask them how they did it. When we started to think about updating the procedures in our distribution center, we needed information about bar coding. A little research told us that Federal Express had the most sophisticated bar coding system, so we contacted them and asked their advice. They were kind enough to give it. As a result, we not only increased the efficiency of our inventory and other warehouse systems, but we deepened our relationship with Federal Express, which delivers some of our merchandise. I firmly believe that a company can only become successful if it develops a network of alliances with related companies: its partners in business.

HOW TO GET COOPERATION FROM MANUFACTURERS AND DISTRIBUTORS

At first, when we were just starting our telemarketing business, some blue-chip mattress companies refused to sell to us. It took us years to gain their cooperation, and to get them to do business with us. In the interim, I developed my negotiating skills. First, I learned that I had to understand their reasoning, to see the situation from *their* point of view. These manufacturers were afraid that if they sold their merchandise to us, they might antagonize the traditional retailers who were already established marketers of their products. The manufacturers feared that those stores might stop doing business with them if they allowed us to sell their mattresses through our nontraditional approach. Their concern about antagonizing traditional merchants seemed to be more important than the possible income we could offer to the manufacturers.

It took me years to convince manufacturers to sell to us, and my most persuasive argument was to *demonstrate* that Dial-A-Mattress could sell large quantities of their products. As I've mentioned, I first bought these nationally known mattresses surreptitiously, from small retail stores or distributors. Eventually, when Dial-A-Mattress was already selling significant numbers of name-brand mattresses, their manufacturers finally realized that my company was not a fluke; it represents a new way of doing business. And then things became easier for me. If you have trouble acquiring merchandise directly from a manufacturer, be creative. Find different sources from which to purchase it, or consider marketing different brands. In time, as you become successful, more companies will be willing to do business with you.

A company is best known for the competition it creates; as soon as your telemarketing business begins to thrive, you will have many others following suit. Remember this when you begin your telemarketing operation, should you, perhaps, experience the same obstacles that I did at the start in trying to get suppliers to sell to me. Surprisingly, for the most part you will not be taking customers away from the established companies. Instead, you will be bringing in a new kind of customer, and if you are willing to share the information and knowledge that you gain from telemarketing with other businesses, they can only gain, too.

The best way to gain cooperation from a manufacturer or a distributor is to explain that you will give them what they are seeking: higher profits. Obviously, the more their product sells, the more profit they will earn. And for several important reasons, telemarketing will substantially increase product sales. Point out to the distributor that because of the ease and uniqueness of telemarketing and the speed and efficiency of delivery you will incorporate into your business, his product will gain in reputation and prestige.

If you can sell and deliver a new Buick or a Brooks Brothers suit or a pair of Reebok running shoes, with the speed and exceptional service available through telemarketing, then your customers will buy these products, perhaps again and again, and this will increase the sales of the brand-name's manufacturer or distributor. As the customer becomes pleased with the convenience of ordering over the phone and your speed of delivery, the margin of satisfaction will ultimately lead to future sales of this product or service.

Obviously, your negotiating power with a manufacturer or distributor increases in direct proportion to your alternatives (as to quantity, price, models, styles, countries you're selling in, and such). If you are forced by circumstances to buy from only one supplier, who may be dominating the product or service that you are dealing with, your strategy to convince him to sell to you may be diminished. If this is the case, optimize your position by pointing out all of the relevant factors of your case.

If you excel in providing good service, you will own the customer, which is far more important than owning a brand name. Get this message to your manufacturers and suppliers. It will give them strong reason to support your company.

I don't think I'm exaggerating when I say that to manage a

business successfully, with all of the negotiations that are necessary on a daily, sometimes hourly, basis, requires as much courage as that possessed by the soldier who goes to war. Negotiation, with suppliers, the media, employees, customers, debtors, banks, franchisees, or interested investors, takes up the better part of my day—and sometimes it takes a mental and moral resolve that is greatly taxing. If you can ever develop a system that makes negotiation less stressful, please pass it along to me. I will be forever in your debt.

Generally, my philosophy is to give in on the little points, and eventually get to the key issue and put all of my energy into that. I try to be as forthright and honest as prudence will allow, but on the other hand I will often not let the other side know how important a particular point is to me. Otherwise the person I'm dealing with will understand the true value of what I am trying to accomplish, and my negotiating power might be undermined.

Usually, my automatic response is to refuse the first offer. Let the person you're negotiating with work a bit. Perhaps he was just testing you with some ridiculous trial balloon. If, in the final analysis, you accept that original offer, then the person will feel as though they have won, and you will be thought of as a generous person.

Another strategy is to request something extra after the negotiations end—perhaps a request that had been rejected earlier. But remember, a crucial time occurs *after* the negotiations end, when the other side begins to ask *you* for small, last-minute concessions, which can, on some occasions, totally skewer the deal.

Explain that your company strives toward excellence. Therefore, there will be several dramatic aspects for the manufacturer who agrees to do business with you:

1. You will increase customer loyalty and positive identification of his brand name (especially if you use the brand name in your advertising).
2. He will experience larger sales volume (and additional profit).

3. Because the results of telemarketing are fairly predictable and measurable, the manufacturer or supplier will be able to determine month-to-month and season-to-season production quotas quite easily from your orders.
4. Selling to a telemarketer will help the manufacturer to define markets and create new outlets.

One of the major factors in helping you sell the concept of telemarketing to prospective suppliers is to indicate the strength and growth of this relatively new medium. What you, as a telemarketing retailer of a product or service, are actually selling is not merely that product or service itself—not just the tangible entity—but the *concept* of offering exceptional service, of allowing consumers to buy what they want, when they want it, and to have it delivered when they want it. He profits most who serves best.

But it's much more than just convenience. What you want to do is show an integrity, a thoughtfulness, a reliability, and an efficiency that will make your customer not only come back again and again for repeat sales, but also—by word of mouth—end up being an unpaid promoter of your product or service. At Dial-A-Mattress, a great percentage of our sales come from referrals by satisfied customers.

You have undoubtedly heard of—or even experienced yourself—both the dreams and the nightmares of retail consumer stories. One of the most famous retailing "happy dreams" is that of L.L. Bean, which took back a sweater ten years after it was purchased because there was a slight defect in the sleeve. The company then cordially offered the customer a replacement, a credit or a cash refund. In comparison, there's another true story—but this one was a nightmare. A customer walked out of a housewares store with a magazine rack he had just purchased. As he put it into the trunk of his car, the bottom of the rack fell out. When he went back to the store, just minutes after purchasing the product, it refused to take the defective magazine rack back or to issue any refund or credit, and were even incredulous at what it thought was the presumptuous behavior of the customer in demanding satisfaction.

Here's another happy dream experience: The fortunate consumer was a Chicago-area father. The Pleasant Co., a Wisconsin-based manufacturer of historical dolls and books, saved the spirit of Christmas for his little girl. "All she wanted for Christmas was one of our dolls," said Jean Dollar Dunham, a supervisor in order processing. "She wrote a letter to Santa but didn't tell anyone because she was afraid her wish wouldn't come true." Her dad found out just two days before Christmas. It was too late to have the doll sent, but he called the company's 1–800 order number anyway.

"We were closing down for the holidays, but we told him we'd keep the distribution center in Madison open if he could come pick up the doll," Dunham said. "It was a four-hour drive and the roads were bad, but he came—and that little girl got her Christmas wish."

Then there's the story of one Lands' End customer who used the company's 1–800 number to do some truly last-minute shopping. "He called from the hospital birthing room to order a diaper bag," said Mike Gillispie, Lands' End director of customer services. "His wife's contractions were less than two minutes apart. They were having trouble deciding whether to have the bag monogrammed."

Or what about the dream offer, admittedly clever and profitable, made by the supersuccessful Wal-Mart: "Buy all the film you need for vacation; return what you can't use." They made many of their customers quite happy, and they increased their film sales by over ten times.

Dial-A-Mattress also tries to give our customers only happy dreams, on or off our mattresses. We deliver the bedding to the customer, remove his old mattress if he so desires, and let him sleep on the new one for thirty days. If he is uncomfortable sleeping on his mattress, we will pick it up and bring him a new one, *with no questions asked*.

Just imagine it: Some friends, a husband and wife, call unexpectedly at 9 A.M. from Washington to announce that they're going to pay an overnight visit to someone in New York whom they've known for years. They'll arrive sometime around 5 P.M. The newly designated hostess is embarrassed and frantic, because the double bed she has in the guest room, rarely used, has a lumpy mattress, is some 20 years old, sagging on one side with a few springs sticking out in spots.

She remembers the Dial-A-Mattress commercial she saw on television, easily recalls the vanity number 1–800–MATTRESS ("Leave off the last 'S' for Savings"), and dials. Two hours later, not only does she receive a new, clean, and firm mattress, but a new set of sheets and pillowcases to go with it. Her old wreck of a mattress is discreetly and conveniently removed and whisked away to some unknown dumping place by the delivery men.

When the friends arrive, they're shown to their room, and that night they experience a restful sleep in the Big Apple. The hostess is a heroine to herself, and through our telemarketing operation we've helped her to achieve that status. Believe me, she will not soon forget the service she received from us. This is the kind of customer help and respect that you need to incorporate into your operation, whatever your product or service.

This commitment to please the customer has made billions for Wal-Mart and millions for me. It can do the same for you. Obviously if you want to establish a reputation for efficient and helpful service, with speed and convenience of transaction, where the customer is *always* right, you must follow the dream scenario rather than the nightmare sequence. But don't be bashful about this commitment. Announce, loudly and clearly, not only to your customer but to your somewhat skeptical supplier, that the type of telemarketing operation you intend to run will be one of friendship and professionalism.

At Dial-A-Mattress, the customer always, always, *always* comes first, and although, of course, we prefer not to lose money on a sale, we will invariably go out of our way to accommodate the customer's wishes, even if it means we must occasionally break even on a particular item. Obviously, if we have done something wrong, or inadvertently sold something defective, we *will* take the loss if the situation demands it.

I have always admired the customer service guidelines of the Graebel Van Lines Company. You might consider applying some or all of these policies to your own business, and give a copy to your prospective supplier to indicate your intentions:

- We will meet the needs of our customers.
- We will meet every commitment we make.
- We will communicate well.
- We will do it right the first time—every time.
- We will treat every customer with courtesy and respect.
- We will treat every article as if it belonged to our mother.
- Our services will be on-time, efficient, effective, and dependable.
- Our customers' needs vary; we will adapt our services to meet them.
- We will follow up, measure our efforts, and encourage feedback.
- Policies and procedures will guide us and not rule us.
- Slogans, buzz words, and a list of guidelines do not make superior customer service happen—our professionalism, dedication, and commitment do!

Point out that over one third of all the sales made by the giant conglomerate IBM are through telemarketing, and that other blue-chip companies such as Chrysler, General Motors, General Electric Company, Delta Air Lines, Fingerhut, and Wal-Mart have all greatly increased their telemarketing operations, for the reasons already discussed. They have also come to realize that telemarketing is an effective technique for:

- Qualification of prospects (potential customers)
- Use of a less expensive method of marketing
- Alternative methods of handling inquiries

When distributors fear for their already existing customers and are making life difficult for you, show them how you will share the information and knowledge that you are gaining or will gain in telemarketing—that *everyone's* business is actually going to grow if you succeed. Invite them to sit in on some of your daily or weekly meetings so that they will be able to see for themselves how your organization is developing.

You might consider the possibility of establishing relationships with other telemarketing companies that can sell your product or service. For example, try to get your product or service listed in catalogs and with special buying services. Some of these buying services such as CUC International garner tens of millions of calls each year and have over 1,000 operators answering their phones, 24 hours a day, 365 days a year. A listing with such a buying service could greatly increase your sales volume.

As you can see in this book, I have no fear of sharing the details of my operation with others, and I do so frequently. In the long run, for every piece of advice or information I give, I receive at least that same value in return: in the form of a business contact, an eventual partner in business, or some form of positive relationship.

If you can assure the supplier that you will conduct your business along the lines that I've been discussing, and that not only the customer but he, too, will be satisfied with the relationship, I would venture to say that you will almost invariably be accommodated. The supplier will recognize your sincerity and commitment and understand that telemarketing is the wave not only of the future, but of the present as well.

7

THE FUTURE OF TELEMARKETING

The most immediately accessible of the new markets involves communication and information. Demand for telephone service in Third World countries and the countries of the former Soviet bloc is practically insatiable.

PETER DRUCKER, 1995

Sometime in the very near future, the conventional way of doing business is going to have difficulty surviving. There does not seem to be any fixed or immutable laws concerning business *except* change. It was Napoleon I, for whom I was named, who said that one must change one's tactics every ten years if one is to maintain one's superiority. I think that with such rapid technological advances in society today, and with people's values and ideas constantly in a state of flux, two or three years for every major change in business tactics and strategy is more like it.

The way of doing business really changes *very* rapidly, regardless of how big or small a company. Just remember what happened to:

1. Small video stores when Blockbuster entered the market
2. Small stationery stores when Staples entered the market

3. Small drugstores when Rite-Aid entered the market
4. Small hardware stores when Home Depot entered the market.

We must keep alert to safeguard our businesses and constantly explore how products, new methods, new venues, new markets, and new strategies continually mutate and modify themselves.

In recent studies of consumer behavior, a whopping 62 percent of people surveyed stated that at least once within the past six months, after deciding to buy something in a store, they left without making the purchase because sales clerks were simply not available to give them the information about a product that they needed, or were not even to be seen on the sales floor to ring up the purchase, or that the lines were so long to simply pay for the items that they wanted to buy that they left the store without spending any money. These retailing horror stories are true: The scenario is that there are legions of frustrated, non-buying customers, perhaps never to buy from that store again. Think about it.

Many consumers complain that when they are in a store and ask a retail sales clerk a question about sizes, or care of the product once purchased, or how to use or operate an appliance, or whatever question they may have—profound or trivial—they are often told that the clerk has no knowledge or no answer, and doesn't know how to obtain it.

Often the response the customer receives from a sales clerk is not only slipshod or dense, but also insulting and rude. A case in point: Recently, when a customer gently inquired about the lack of steamed vegetables and carbonated sodas at a Kenny Rogers' barbecued chicken and ribs grill, he was peremptorily chastised by the manager, who shouted: "That's not my problem. The machinery broke down. What do you want me to do about it?!"

Modern consumers will no longer tolerate such impolite, unknowledgeable answers to their queries and requests. Average citizens work too hard for those dollars, money is in short supply, and their lifestyles do not permit them the luxury of waiting on long lines to eventually leave the store or the establishment without the merchandise or service that they came to purchase, whether it be a pair of pants or a hamburger, a Xerox copy, or a new lamp.

More importantly, the customer must always, *always*, be treated with respect. In the long run in business, manners are more important than money. That is, if you lose a customer because you have insulted him, you will probably never get him back, whereas if you lose some money on any specific sale, you can always make another sale another day.

We have all probably experienced driving or traveling by public transportation downtown or to the mall, fighting the traffic to arrive there, finding it difficult, if not totally impossible to locate a parking space, and after this time-consuming struggle, entering the store, only to discover that the product that we were interested in purchasing is either out of stock, off the shelf, no longer on sale, or not available in the color, size, shape, or price that we wanted.

Telemarketing can ease the customer's frustrations and save countless hours for him or her. To exemplify, at Dial-A-Mattress, we're open 24 hours a day, seven days a week, 365 days a year. The customers shop when they want to shop, whether it be 9 o'clock in the morning or 12 midnight, a Sunday afternoon or a Tuesday morning, Christmas Day or Passover.

They can determine whether the product they want is available, how much it will cost, and *precisely* when it will be delivered. Furthermore, they can accomplish all of this in the comfort of their own homes, sitting in their own easy chairs, in a matter of minutes!

As an example of how excellence of *service* can produce an impact upon a customer, I am reminded of the story of a Canadian movie actor who recently moved to Chicago. On his first evening in his new apartment, he called Dial-A-Mattress because, although he had a wood-frame bed, he had abandoned his old mattress in Canada and needed a mattress to sleep on that night.

After he ordered his mattress from us, he called a local Chinese restaurant and ordered a rack of spareribs for dinner. You guessed it. He had his new Dial-A-Mattress delivered and set up in his apartment *within about 30 minutes, before his ribs arrived from the restaurant located two blocks from where he lived.*

The actor was so impressed with our exceptionally speedy delivery that he reported the story to a local newspaper, and it was ultimately published all over the country.

This is why it is important for you and for your business to consider securing, or to begin using more effectively, a toll-free telephone number, and joining the hundreds of thousands of businesses all over the world that are integrating telemarketing into their operations. Telemarketing will make your potential or already existing customer feel special—by keeping him in truly close contact—and it will help you to reach your customers (and them to reach you) efficiently and economically.

By way of further illustration, I'm reminded of the story that I heard recently of the man who, for the first time, ordered all of the Christmas presents that he needed to purchase for friends and relatives—some 60 items, reflecting a variety of prices and sizes and different kinds of gifts, from the traditional Christmas tie, to small electronic appliances, to pajamas for growing nephews—over the telephone, from a group of catalogs, in less than two hours.

He claimed that he was totally satisfied with the merchandise he received and that only one item had to be exchanged because it was not exactly the color displayed in the catalog. But more importantly, he noted, the annual Christmas shopping that he usually did in a number of stores would often take the better part of four or five complete Saturdays prior to Christmas, sometimes forcing him to traipse about in inclement weather and making him pay what he felt were exorbitant parking fees. He feels that by using the telephone he saved about forty to fifty hours out of his hectic and intense schedule, and perhaps of equal importance, he also received better service and comparable prices and merchandise.

As more and more people have such experiences, or hear about them from friends and colleagues, they become increasingly more willing to shop by phone. Accordingly, if you are interested in creating customer satisfaction and future sales-generating opportunities that will truly accommodate the new customer of the present and of the future, a toll-free number might very well be the answer for you.

It works even if you're selling a service. To cite an example, in a study of the banking industry done in 1995 by Jay Marwaha, senior vice-president of Technical Assistance Research Programs, it was determined that after initiating a toll-free number to a number of branches, those banks reported a 30 percent increase in overall satisfaction *by the customer* and an increase of 30 percent in sales in that specific branch.

Although it is not an original thought of mine, I have always believed that nothing succeeds as much as success itself. A company that I know and do business with, Select Comfort of Minneapolis, started selling air mattresses in the 1980s and had worked up its gross sales to $700,000 in 1991.

Most people thought that air mattresses really couldn't compete with traditionally made mattresses, but through belief in their product, innovative marketing, patience, aggressive promotion and, mainly, through the use of a 1–800 number, practically overnight Select Comfort shot up to doing $7 million in sales, and then to $70 million in sales in its air mattresses in 1995.

If the owners of Select Comfort had believed the naysayers of its product, it would never be in the position it is today: one of the leading manufacturers of mattresses in the U.S. Theories and guesses about what will succeed are extremely thin; only experience is tangible.

Take a moment to ask yourself: What are *your* gross sales? Now, what will happen to that figure if you use a toll-free number and incorporate a sound telemarketing campaign into your operation? I can't guarantee that your sales will jump as high as 30 percent (of course, it is possible that they may jump even higher), but I *will* guarantee you that they will increase substantially.

Perhaps you might care to begin gingerly and test only one or two of your products with an abbreviated telemarketing campaign, or else give your product or service a test run of six to eight weeks tied into a more prudent or conservative telemarketing effort. Or you might want to consider earmarking only a certain amount of money, which you subsequently place in a special account for a telemarketing experiment, and then parlay whatever net income you realize into the further promotion and fulfillment of your product or service.

As I indicated elsewhere in this book, I started Dial-A-Mattress with an investment of less than $50 for a small classified ad in a weekly newspaper. As the income came in, I continued to invest the profits into larger and larger print ads, and then finally to television commercials, and that is how the business grew.

However ambitiously or modestly you begin, keep scrupulous and accurate records as to how many calls you receive, how many actual sales you make, how many upgrades or add-ons you've introduced, the cost of your advertising, your cost-per-sale, your cost of shipping or delivery, customer complaints and suggestions, and any other scraps of information that you can possibly compile. For example, below is a list of key topics that we are constantly exploring and compiling data about.

DAILY DATA SUMMARY

1. Total advertising dollars
2. Total advertising dollars (special projects)
3. Total ad $ as % of sales
4. Cost per lead
5. Total customer calls
6. Number of local calls
7. Uncontrolled nat'l customer calls
8. Abandoned %
9. Revised abandoned W%
10. Incomplete calls
11. Customer service calls
12. Customer service retrieval calls abandoned %
13. Customer service retrieval revised abandoned %
14. NY sales dollars

15. NY sales dollars as % of total sales
16. Sales dollars outside New York
17. Percent of business outside New York
18. New York closing ratio
19. Avg call per bedding consultant
20. Number of showroom sales
21. Total showroom dollars
22. Number of clearance sales
23. Total clearance dollars
24. Recovered by outbound calling
25. Total dollars recovered as % of sales
26. Total pieces in (inventory)
27. Total pieces out (inventory)
28. Number of invoices with no merchandise
29. Deliveries dispatched
30. Late deliveries
31. Deliveries returned
32. Employees scheduled
33. Employees absent
34. Employees trained
35. Month to date mdse shipments
36. Net profit % month to date
37. Daily deposit
38. Money collected (mdse) month to date

Without such product, customer and service data, you will really not know whether your idea is viable enough to continue. Furthermore, without fail, always remember to retain the names, addresses, and telephone numbers not only of the customers who buy, but of potential customers—people who merely inquire about your product or service. *Never* discard those names! A sales effort to them in the future could spell the difference between success or failure.

Obviously, although you know your business better than I, I'd like to suggest that if you are dealing with a fairly high-priced item, consider the possibility of renting it to your consumer rather than selling it

The rental business is absolutely booming, from power tools to high-priced jewels, from television sets to luxurious yachts, from fur coats to table settings. If you are insured properly (to make sure that if your product is damaged, you'll receive its full worth from the insurance company), it is extremely possible that through numerous rentals you will realize much more profit than if you sold the product outright.

If you are unsure about what I am suggesting, check with any automobile dealer to determine their profit ratio since the boom of "lease rather than buy" practices came in during the 1970s.

WHAT CONSUMERS WANT. . . AND NEED

Society is in such a state of flux that the entire syndrome of human wants and needs are constantly changing. I remember the time, not even 15 years ago, that most small businesses did not even have one computer. Now, most companies have sophisticated computer operations, and seek instruction, new applications, new hardware, new software, and more memory.

Entire businesses, such as Dial-A-Mattress, now virtually revolve around the use of the computer. Not only the wants and needs of corporations, but the wants and needs of consumers regarding the computer, have spawned one of the largest businesses in the world.

The same thing can be said of the videotape business, which in the early 1980s, accounted for only a tiny percentage of the entertainment industry, with Mom and Pop stores selling a relatively small amount of films. Now, virtually every motion picture becomes available on videotape within a short time after its release to the theaters. Consumers flock to national chains such as Blockbuster that carry an almost unlimited variety of whatever movies they might want to see, and the income derived—*in the billions*—is helping to finance the production of new major and minor motion pictures. Twenty years ago no one would have thought that such an increase in video sales was possible, or that consumers would want as many millions of them as they are now buying and renting.

When I first started—even talking about—selling mattresses by phone, people thought I was insane. . . literally. Now, hundreds of millions of dollars of sales later I can only point to my early opinions and predictions as simply a variation of my proof that this whole new way of marketing can be successful. Closed-minded people do not listen to either proof or opinions, so my advice to you is not to worry too much if people tell you your ideas won't work. Remember, it's very possible that they don't understand what you're planning, so they can't see the idea's potential. Don't exhaust yourself trying to prove your point before the fact. Just go ahead and take a chance. As the man once said: chances don't come every day.

The point that I am trying to make is that you must stay attuned to the changing needs and wants of your customers and consumers in general. Automobile manufacturers, suppliers of bathroom fixtures, clothing designers, and all sorts of other product and service suppliers must recognize how the consumer in general relates to products and services (and specifically to *your* product or service), and how the consumer is changing. We must always remember that needs and wants are never completely satisfied, and that new products and services—or restructuring, redesigning, and repricing old ones—must take place in order to satisfy, even temporarily, an individual consumer's desires.

I believe that because of the relative ease and economy of using telemarketing, both for consumers and businesses, by the year 2000, fully one third of all retail purchases *of all products* will be transacted over the telephone and that this figure will rise to 50 percent of all retail purchases by the year 2015. These figures, although admittedly my own subjective guesses, may be *conservative*. If you need further proof of the explosion of telemarketing, check out the AT&T Yellow Pages for 1–800 numbers and you'll see that well over 100,000 companies listed there are doing their primary business by telephone.

It could be that one day soon, virtually all purchases—including such things as food, clothing, automobiles, homes, *all* necessities, and luxuries—will be purchased by telephone. A great part of this growth, I predict, will be the growth of global telemarketing and the ability, and actual *necessity* (because of the inevitable realignment of marketing and economic boundaries), of selling your product or service all over the world. Dial-A-Mattress has begun to sell by telephone on every continent, and I would like to share my philosophy, my rationale, and my experiences on how and why we're doing this with you.

GLOBAL TELEMARKETING

I became involved in selling internationally in a somewhat oblique way. Businessmen or tourists visiting New York City would see my commercials for Dial-A-Mattress on television, perhaps in their hotel rooms, and then when they returned to their home country, would remember the 1–800–MATTRESS ("leave off the last 'S' for savings" as our advertising proclaims) number that had appeared on the screen. If they needed a mattress, they would call us—whether it was from Barcelona or Brazil—and order what they needed.

Another kind of sale occurred that really convinced me to go global. One day, a well-spoken gentleman called from Switzerland to order six mattresses. Our Bedding Consultant faxed him descriptions and illustrations of our mattresses, and in a matter of minutes he called back.

He purchased the best mattresses of what we carried—some $6,000 in total—and asked that we deliver them to London. We pointed out that the shipment from the U.S. to England, via DHL air freight, would cost $1,300, but this did not deter him one iota. He wanted the mattresses immediately. It turned out that he was not purchasing the mattresses for himself but for the princess for whom he worked, the daughter of the Aga Khan.

I was absolutely astonished at the international dimension of this transaction and realized all at once that if I could supply mattresses from my warehouse in Long Island City, in New York, to such a cosmopolitan metropolis as London and to such a royal person, I could sell anywhere in the world, anytime, to any person.

You may ask, Why couldn't they simply purchase a mattress in their home countries? Well, it could be for several reasons: No retailer in their country sold the exact mattress as to the size or style that they wanted; or the cost of the mattress in their country might have been prohibitive (and yes, it *is* costly to ship a mattress from one part of the world to another, but surprisingly it might still be less expensive than buying a mattress locally in some countries); or they just might have wanted American-brand merchandise.

American brand names can be seen in virtually every country in the world, and emblazoned on virtually any product. The fact that the product was made in the U.S., or originated there, suggests quality, status, and yes, even freedom. Think of McDonald's or IBM. Think of Ralph Lauren or Coca-Cola. Think of Kodak or James Dean. Walk down any street in Paris or Panama, or in Capetown or Cairo, and you will see American brand names.

After I discovered that I was selling around the world without much direct promotional or advertising effort, although my sales volume was small, I decided to look into the whole area of global marketing. Since then I have come to the conclusion that the question, not only for Dial-A-Mattress, but for all businesses, all sellers of products and service providers, is not *whether* to become involved in global marketing but *how* and *when*.

At this point, you may be saying to yourself that you should skip this section, especially if you have a small operation or if you are just starting out, since your business is simply too minor to engage in a global marketing effort. When you think of international marketing, perhaps visions of such corporate giants as AT&T and IBM dance in your head, and you truly believe that you are too undercapitalized or your business is too immature to attempt foreign sales. And I say to you, think again, because global sales may be the salvation, or certainly the survival, of your business as we enter the twenty-first century.

There is a virtual war taking place among companies and countries attempting to gain the loyalty and the dollars of the consumer. . . perhaps *your* consumer. If you limit your marketing only to one local or even national arena, eventually you may run out of customers, or at least limit the numbers of those customers. Believe me, there is nothing more disappointing and depressing than failing to recognize or gain a new market, unless it is to see someone else secure it. Then you will really become depressed.

Unless you begin to explore telemarketing internationally with a toll-free number now, you will see other companies selling products or services similar to your own in markets in every conceivable country, and they will be making millions. . . and you will not.

If this piece of advice is not enough to frighten you to go global, carefully consider that foreign companies are making inroads on a daily basis into the U.S. market. One of these days you may find your product or service has been usurped by an encroaching company from the European Common Market, and where will you find customers then? At that point you may elect to open new outlets in Eastern Europe or Latin America, or some other emerging market, and you will discover that your competition is already entrenched there, too.

You are *not* too small to go global. I don't care if you sell rice cakes or cuff links, plumbing supplies or cinnamon buns. Telemarketing is a highly complex venture to be sure, and one that takes precision record-keeping and dynamic sales efforts, but I urge you to throw your xenophobia to the winds and begin to think on an international level.

More specifically, there are some direct benefits that you may enjoy by developing a global business, depending, of course, on what country or countries you begin to market to:

- Some countries impose a flat 10-percent tax on telemarketing and fulfillment services engaged in by foreign companies, far less than the tax cost of doing business in the U.S.
- It is not unusual, even for Third World countries, to issue grants or loans for capital investment, training, and even rent for you to start up your business there.

- Some European countries issue a waiver on customs duties for companies from non-European countries.
- There usually is plenty of warehouse and office space available abroad for a relatively low cost, should you need it.
- The labor force is often multilingual and can often be secured at a much lower cost than what is paid as usual wages in the U.S.
- In Western Europe, phone rates have recently been decreased by as much as 20 percent.
- In some foreign countries, products priced below $50 are exempt entirely from import duties.
- Credit cards are now virtually universal (except in Greece where barely two percent of the population have credit cards, and in the new Czech Republic where credit cards are not used), and it makes the entire transaction over the telephone much easier.

What we have attempted to do at Dial-A-Mattress is to establish a toll-free number that we have promoted all over the world. We then advertise our mattresses in a number of media such as the *International Herald Tribune,* in other foreign publications, and on CNN (which is now reaching virtually every major country in the world). These ads tell the customer to call that number and make contact with one of our salespeople in New York City.

We are also in the process of setting up 1–800–MATELAS (French for "mattress"), which we will be advertising in France, in the French-speaking sections of Canada, in Haiti, and in French Guyana.

A gentle warning: Although English is known and spoken by the business community the world over, and differences in languages have diminished with the expansion of the European Common Market in 1992, don't expect that the consumer, who may be calling your toll-free number to order a Christmas ham or a bouquet of roses or an exercise machine in response to your international advertisement or commercial, will necessarily speak English.

When Dial-A-Mattress is about to hire telemarketers, we determine whether they speak any foreign languages. If they do, it is definitely a plus in getting hired. As a result of our language consciousness, we have people who can speak French, Spanish, Italian, German, Portuguese, Russian, and Swahili. If a customer speaks any of those languages, and is calling from Barcelona, for example, he or she is automatically switched over to the Spanish-speaking salesperson. Callers from Rome are routed to the Italian-speaking telemarketer. Having a multilingual staff increases your ability to handle orders from customers from many countries and answer their questions with ease.

Of course, this procedure not only applies to foreign sales but to sales in the U.S. as well. That is why at Dial-A-Mattress we have no hesitancy, for example, in placing advertising in foreign-language publications or on foreign-language television in *this* country. One of the services we provide free of charge for our employees are language classes: It is important for the employees to learn another language, and it is *essential* to us.

What happens if you have a limited staff, or your staff only speaks English, and a call comes in from Japan, for example, and no one speaks Japanese at your call center? My suggestion is that you establish a relationship with a translation or interpreting bureau or agency that has the capacity to handle any language, and an agency that will come to know enough of your business that they will be able to answer your consumer's questions with both alacrity and accuracy.

You may have to spend some time training the personnel at this translation bureau as to the nuances of your business. Then whenever a foreign language call comes in to your company, have it immediately transferred to the translation bureau—and your own telemarketer stays on the line to be able to answer any difficult questions that the translator can't answer. Within minutes, just as if your customer was calling from around the block, the sale should be completed. The translation bureau can be paid either on a per-inquiry basis or a flat monthly fee, whatever can be arranged between you and them.

AT&T also has a wonderful interpreting service for a relatively modest sum (as of this writing about $4.50 per minute, plus a $2.50 service charge per call), through their Language Line Services. A conference call can be set up on demand, consisting of the customer, your sales representative, and the interpreter from AT&T. Their service covers more than 140 languages, and it's ideal for sales efforts that concern medium- or high-priced items.

Perhaps you should also consider the possibility of making an arrangement with a *local* call center in the country where you want to do your telemarketing. In this way, the customer in Lisbon, for example, can call a sales representative who speaks Portuguese, understands the culture, and can identify, perhaps, the very neighborhood where the merchandise is to be shipped or delivered. Generally the customers feel very comfortable with that kind of transaction, since the local sales representatives are familiar with the lifestyles of the consumer and can provide assistance as to colors, styles, sizes, and so on. And once customers have used telemarketing to buy, they usually come back to the telephone again and again to make other purchases.

Note that because of employment practices and local laws, certain countries are limited if you are attempting to establish a 24-hour telemarketing program. For example, neither France nor Belgium will allow women to work between 2 A.M. and 6 A.M.; and in Germany, it is illegal to run any business around-the-clock for 24-hour service.

WHERE TO MARKET?

Although I have been urging you to consider going global, you may be wondering where exactly you should begin, and whether there are any countries to avoid. . . at least at the beginning. First off, let me stress that the best way to go global is to locate an existing product manufacturer or service provider who is already doing business in the country or region that you are interested.

Work with them and you may not have to engage in the extensive research that I am going to suggest. In fact, creating such a global distribution network will enable you to do business in certain foreign countries within a matter of weeks after you make arrangements with local resources, with very little investment on your part.

But in case you have a new or different product or service that is not available in other countries, or if you cannot convince the principal (or any) manufacturer to deal with you, then you must work up the following plan of action.

Before coming to a decision, you *must* engage in some research. If possible, visit the country or countries you are considering and speak to the government officials in charge of trade. Call up other business connections to determine what restrictions there are, if any, regarding your product or service in that country. A visit to the American embassy or consulate in that country is virtually mandatory. Introduce yourself, attempt to meet the Ambassador and explain what you are attempting to do. At that same time, gain as much information as possible as to taxes, duties, shipping, warehousing, and any other factors that might have an impact on your marketing and distributing efforts.

Make additional efforts to determine the following:

1. Is a product or service similar to yours currently being sold in the country you are considering? If so, how does yours differ in price, style, quality, etc.? Can you compete?

2. If you are introducing a new product or service to that country, one that may be unfamiliar to the citizens, how much advertising and/or promotion will it take to explain it so that potential consumers will understand it and want to buy it?

3. Is your product or service only directed to a discrete or niche market, and if so, what are the demographics of that limitation in the country you are considering? Everybody needs soap, for example, but not everybody needs, wants, or can afford a luxury powerboat. Everybody needs clothing,

whatever country they live in, but not everyone needs a baseball mitt.

4. Must you have a local presence and/or address in that country in order to be successful, or can you sell internationally from your home office? (This is what we do at Dial-A-Mattress: We receive the call directly from the foreign country and ship directly to the customer overseas.)

5. How will you handle currency exchange, other than credit card orders?

6. Can you ship your product easily from the U.S., or will you have to bulk-ship to an overseas distribution location? What will these costs be?

7. Is your product especially fragile, such as Waterford crystal or a delicate electronic device? If so, you must build into your budget, and perhaps your sales price, extra moneys for special packing, and shipping costs.

8. Will you be able to compete with foreign local suppliers who are providing the same product or service, especially after you add on custom duties and shipping costs?

9. What are advertising costs in the country that you are considering?

10. Must you adapt, change, or translate your American product or service to make it acceptable to a foreign purchaser? Must you do the same for your advertising or promotion?

11. Should you open a bank account in the country in which you are going to sell, and leave the money in the bank for future promotional, product, and shipping expenses?

Picking a target country is not as difficult as it may appear. After some generic research, you'll determine, for example, such facts as: There over 25 million households in Germany; the population of Brazil alone is 155 million; Chile has the best telephone system in Latin America; businessmen from Thailand have already become steadfast telephone shoppers and Thailand is a booming country as far as telemarketing is concerned; because of their competitive phone rates, Belgium, Denmark, and Ireland are ideal countries in which to establish your own call centers, if you are trying to reach the rest of Europe (and Ireland's corporate taxes are as low as 10 percent); Southeast Asia's economic growth is much greater than that of the U.S.; the Japanese order by telephone tens of millions of dollars worth of products annually from L.L. Bean; and over $5 billion a year—and it's growing—is spent in Australia through direct marketing.

Another point: U.S. dollars are understood almost anywhere in the world, and your offer can usually be in dollars.

In the U.S., visit the embassies or consulates, the tourist offices and the trade offices of the countries that you are interested in doing business with and ply yourself with as many statistics as you can garner. A call, visit, or letter to the U.S. Department of Commerce's Center for International Research in Washington, D.C., will assist you in developing a strategic analysis of all kinds of demographic data for virtually any country in the world. The Office of International Trade of the Small Business Administration will also help you in providing information concerning exporting and other tax and legal questions.

Should you expand into one country at a time, or should you test several markets simultaneously? Of course, your financial situation will often determine just exactly how large or small a marketing effort, and in how many countries, you will make. But all things being equal, I would highly recommend that you attempt to launch your global telemarketing operation in several—or certainly more than one—countries.

Launching in one country might not give you a true or universal result. For example, people in Denmark might not wear turtleneck sweaters—perhaps it's just not the custom—but people in Norway might love them and buy several if the price and style are right. If you try to sell turtlenecks only in Denmark and fail, you might incorrectly assume that they might not sell anywhere in Europe.

If you are already setting up a global telemarketing operation anyway, you should attempt to work around the single-market-at-a-time strategy, and include at least two or three countries to

The Minister for Commercial Affairs
Embassy of the United States of America
David K. Diebold
and
Dial A Mattress Franchise Corporation of New York
cordially invite you to a
Press Conference
on Tuesday 27th June 1989
at the Embassy of the United States of America
Grosvenor Square, London W1

Reply Card Enclosed   *12.00 - 2.00 p.m.*
Upper Brook St. Entrance   *Buffet Luncheon*

PLEASE BRING THIS CARD WITH YOU

The offices of the U.S. State Department will help you do business in foreign countries. When we introduced Dial-A-Mattress in England, we held our press conference at the U.S. Embassy in London. This gave our event more prestige than it would have had if we'd presented it privately, and it encouraged members of the leading media to attend.

test whether you can telemarket your product or service successfully.

You should be aware that 1–800 numbers (or a similar system) have different names in different countries. In France, Italy, Norway, and Denmark, they are called "green numbers"; in Japan, they are known as "auto-collect call"; and in Germany, they are known as the "130 Service."

SPECIFIC MARKETS

Depending on your product or service, I would think that you should explore and research any Latin American country, the emerging Eastern European countries, any country in Europe itself, and all countries in the vast continent of Asia. The days of dictatorships in most countries are over and free-marketing has become the name of the business game throughout the world.

Be careful about trying to telemarket to certain African countries where telephone ownership is still extremely low, unemployment is above 50 percent, and per capita income can be as low as $350 per year.

With the explosion of the cell phone industry, however, telephone systems are now in place in countries that just a decade ago were virtually phoneless. For example, as recently as the late 1980s it was difficult to make a telephone call in the city of Budapest. Just to find a phone was a bit of an accomplishment. Large areas of the city, including businesses and even some government offices, had no phone service at all. This has changed drastically in just a few years and now almost everyone in Budapest has access to telephone service. (Actually, one out of five persons now own a phone in all of Hungary.)

Although it is true that many consumers in foreign countries may never have had the opportunity to purchase something by telephone, that is precisely why the possibilities are limitless. If you begin to experiment with global telemarketing, you may be one of the first telemarketers of your product or service in Moscow or Minsk, or in Baghdad or Brunei.

And don't forget our nearest neighbors with whom we share common borders: Canada, with a population of almost 30 million people, and Mexico, which is nearing a population of 90 million. So strongly did I feel about doing business south of the border, that in 1993, I placed a full-page advertisement in *The New York Times*; it was a letter commending President Clinton for his efforts in trying to get Congress to pass the North American Free Trade Agreement (NAFTA). With more and more technological advances and more people subscribing to telephone service, Mexico could be a virtual gold-mine for the careful but innovative telemarketer.

NAFTA and GATT and other trade agreements being signed, and yet to be signed, will eliminate those taxes, tariffs, and other economic barriers, and will enable all of us to grow globally.

DIRECT MARKETING ON THE INTERNET

At Dial-A-Mattress we have been using and experimenting with the Internet since 1993 as an adjunct to our telemarketing sales efforts. I emphasize the word "adjunct" since the process has not yet been highly profitable for us. However, I recommend that you explore it in conjunction with all of the other methods of advertising that we have discussed in this book.

We have explored the World Wide Web (our address is www.mattress.com), in addition to several other sites on bulletin board services, such as Prodigy, CompuServe, and Bloomberg (which has a site of its own). The WWW is the most user-friendly of all of the Internet services, and allows our customers to call us up on their computers, to receive information about styles, sizes, and prices of our products, accompanied by a variety of illustrations of the mattresses we carry.

If the consumer needs additional information about a particular mattress, for example, he or she can type in the question and we receive it immediately in our computer mailbox. We then reply, giving the consumer the requested information, and suggesting that the computer caller dial our 1–800–MATTRESS number and speak to one of our Bedding Consultants, who will, in turn, complete the sale if possible.

There are problems, however, with Internet sales efforts and you should be aware of them before you invest too much time, money, or hope in their ultimate success for your product or service.

First, you must highly publicize—through advertising and promotion in a variety of media—your Internet call numbers, or else the consumer may never stumble on your home page. Certainly, there are some computer fans who constantly surf the Net and who may find your site accidentally, but these may not necessarily be your potential customers.

Second, the Internet has a problem with targeting an audience. Who, exactly, are the Internet users or surfers, and do they want to buy your product or service? If your market is, for example, affluent males over 60 years of age, or teenage girls who live in the Northeast, or 30-somethings who live in big cities, how do you pinpoint your audience through the Internet?

Traditionally, with other media we can reach specific targets by carefully selecting where we place our advertising or commercials and lock into certain demographic populations such as "drive time" on radio, the MTV audience on television, or the intellectually elite readers of *Scientific American*. But when possibly millions of Internet users around the world see our advertisements on our home page on the WWW, we cannot be sure who these people are, where their interests lie, or whether they really want to buy a mattress.

You may note that there is software being developed that will create a demographic portrait of an Internet user, based on his or her on-line activity.

According to a recent study, only 11 percent of Internetians use it to shop (most people use it for reference and work-related tasks), although a recent Nielsen survey has indicated that more than two million people have purchased something over the Internet during the past several years.

The advantage of the Internet is that it can allow you to provide potential customers with a great deal of easily accessed information about your product or service, at their convenience, at any time of the day or night. Supposing that one night a potential customer wanted to study the prices of all of the nuts, bolts, and screws that you sold. If he knew your home page number, he could call it up at any time and, in the privacy of his own computer, be given the information that he wants and needs—perhaps pages and pages of it—which would perhaps contribute to his decision to ultimately purchase your product or service.

Sound effects, imaginative layouts, "tours" of your company, "walk-through" demonstrations of your product or service, and other special effects can be added to your site to enhance the sales approach. And, by the way, constantly updating your site or sites with new graphics, offers, and other revisions continually signals the Internet user that there is something of interest to him on your site.

Ultimately, you might look into setting up a system whereby your customer can order directly from you by entering into his computer his credit card number in order to make the purchase. There are enormous problems of security with this system, however, and some consumers are wary of attempting to do it. The only safe way to use direct credit-card sales on the Internet is to purchase the necessary software to encode the consumer's credit card number when it arrives at your site, and send it on to a bank where it is then decoded and processed, safeguarding the consumer's number and your company's reputation.

HOW WE DO GLOBAL MARKETING

At Dial-A-Mattress we are setting up formal contractual arrangements and relationships with retailers and manufacturers all over the world. The basic concept, which you might care to apply to your own product or service, is as follows: A customer somewhere in the world sees our international television commercial, or hears our commercials on radio, or spots our advertising in a newspaper or magazine, then dials our 1–800–MATTRESS number and is connected directly with one of our salespeople in New York. If there is a language problem, then the customer is immediately switched to one of our multilingual consultants, who takes the call and arranges for the sale.

The order for the specific mattress is taken, the location it is to be delivered to is determined; the credit card number is noted and verified; and the customer is billed (including shipping charges) for the mattress.

We then contact by telephone or fax, and sometimes both, a retailer or manufacturer *in that country or city*, with whom we have made prior arrangements. The retailer ships the mattress to what is for him a local customer, and the breakdown of profits is as follows:

- Seventy percent of the price that the consumer pays us goes to the foreign retailer or manufacturer, who, in turn, assumes all delivery costs (and, of course, the cost of the mattress).
- Twenty percent goes to Dial-A-Mattress as our charge for referring the sale to the retailer or manufacturer.
- Ten percent also goes to Dial-A-Mattress to cover our advertising and promotional costs, present and future.

What happens, you may ask, if a customer seeing our commercials or reading our advertisements, say in Madrid, goes directly to the retailer there to procure that mattress? The same percentages still apply, since the customer bought the mattress because of our advertisement or commercial, and all other aspects of the sale are exactly the same (with the exception of our salesperson taking the order, as opposed to the salesperson of the retailer).

The only time that the percentages change in our global operation is in the rare possibility that a customer who sees our commercial in a foreign country goes to a retailer, say in London, and wants a mattress shipped to *another* country, say France. In that case, the breakdown of profits is as follows:

- The London retailer retains 20 percent.
- The French retailer/deliverer retains 70 percent.
- Dial-A-Mattress retains 10 percent.

WHY IT WORKS

It is not difficult to discern the actual simplicity and solidity of our global operation. Specifically, we usually do not become involved in the handling—or, more importantly, the expense—of the actual manufacture, warehousing, or delivery of any mattress overseas, so we avoid all of those complications and save all of those expenses. They are provided by the manufacturer or retailer of the respective country. What Dial-A-Mattress provides is our twenty years of marketing know-how, our brand-name—which we have invested tens of millions of dollars to protect and promote—our experience in how to sell mattresses, our knowledge of which mattresses are of the best quality, and our expertly trained Bedding Consultants (our telemarketers).

The only major challenge that Dial-A-Mattress has internationally is to ensure that the retailers we work with carry not only each country's traditional domestic-size mattresses, but also sizes that are specific to America—regardless of where the mattress is manufactured—such as the California King, which is 72" × 84" long, compared to the traditional king-size bed, which is six inches wider and four inches shorter.

Also, if a foreign customer buys an American-size mattress, he or she may want to purchase American-size sheets and other bed linens to accompany his new bed. Arrangements have to be made so that the foreign retailer also stocks enough of these subsidiary bedding items as well.

If you set up a business relationship with a foreign retailer, please make sure that the company understands that *service* is the key ingredient in this telemarketing process. You might consider having all of your foreign retailers and manufacturers sign contracts agreeing to provide your requisite services, such as two-hour delivery on demand; free removal of the old merchandise if desired by the customer; guaranteed comfort exchange if the customer is not satisfied, for any reason, once they receive your new products; and perhaps most importantly, the proverbial service with a smile.

VIEWS OF THE FUTURE

There has been a great deal written recently about the possibilities of re-engineering one's company, and I thoroughly recommend that you look into that kind of restructuring, especially as it relates to telemarketing.

But I ask you to consider taking a strong and careful look not just at your entire business but at individual products that you may be selling, to see if they can be changed or adapted in any way. For example, the explosion of Post-its, those little self-stick slips of removable paper that are now used ubiquitously as page and document markers, came about when the Minnesota Mining & Manufacturing Co. (3M) was looking for a use for a new *weak* glue. And baking soda, an ingredient that is now so pervasive in toothpaste, was introduced in connection with tooth care when the Arm and Hammer Baking Soda people were searching for new ways to expand and capitalize on their product.

If your problem is one of profitability in the products or services that you are telemarketing, don't be too quick to get rid of the product or service until you have analyzed every aspect of it to see if it can serve another use or market, or whether it can be modified in some way that it then becomes, in effect, a new product. Obviously, if you cannot turn bagels into baseballs, or parakeets into parasols, then get rid of the product as quickly as possible and get into something else.

When you are analyzing your business and your product or service—which should be a regular process, as important to you as meeting the payroll and paying your electric bills—ask yourself whether you can run your business differently, in a way that personifies the twenty-first century. Is it possible to eliminate any steps? Can you make or deliver a better product or service? Can you improve customer service all the way around? Can you advertise more effectively? In all of this, the possible redesign of your product or service must be uppermost in your mind. Look for innovations that will reduce costs. Search, search, search. Question, question, question.

Don't be afraid to dream dreams and to allow yourself to see visions of the future.

One dream that I am attempting to put into practice is so all-encompassing that it is exhilarating for me to even think of it, let alone discuss it.

Near my home in New York, there is a small shopping plaza where virtually all of the stores have gone out of business: They were Mom and Pop operations crowded out by huge retail conglomerates that have recently moved nearby.

I am going to put them back into business. . . but with one big difference. In effect, these businesses will now become showrooms, and storage spaces, for their clothing, their beauty supplies, their travel service, or whatever their merchandise or service, and they will be promoted through a central 1–800 number, which I will advertise on television and in print: 1–800–POPULAR. I intend to promote this number nationwide with millions of dollars of advertising.

The process will work as follows: A potential customer decides that they want to take a trip to the Caribbean over the holidays. They will have seen my 1–800–POPULAR number over and over again on television, advertising the fact that if they dial 1–800–POPULAR, they will be connected to a company whereby they can, over the telephone, order *any* product or service they wish, and they will receive high quality, competitive prices, and unparalleled service.

Almost as I write this, I am setting up arrangements to bring the 1–800–POPULAR concept into reality and to do this with hundreds of real estate companies, automobile sellers, appliance stores, and virtually all representatives of the entire retail business in this country. My operators at 1–800–POPULAR will switch the call to the store located closest to the customer, and that store's sales personnel will then handle the sale. At Dial-A-Mattress we will train these store owners how to sell by telephone through our Telemarketing Institute, and we expect that a great amount of the referred 1–800–POPULAR calls will eventually result in sales for these newly established stores. Should a telephone customer care to take a look at the merchandise that he or she wants to purchase, he will be free—even encouraged—to do so, and the sale will be made in the traditional way when the customer arrives at the store.

It is my hope that within a short time, I will have thousands of these small—and not-so-small—businesses, and hundreds of those haunted shopping plazas back in action again, all through the power of telemarketing, basically through my *dream* of 1–800–POPULAR.

There are a few other things that I must get off my chest and share with you in relationship to the future of telemarketing. Make sure that you not only train new employees well, but that they are applying what they learn. Keep going back and retraining everyone in your company. Technology goes through a sea change almost daily, and arenas of marketing are transmogrifying so rapidly that it is difficult to keep up. In order for your telemarketing operation to succeed, your people will have to understand how these new changes can affect your business, and they will have to be trained to the precision of a Swiss watch in order to confront and use this new technology.

I like the slogan that is used for the New York State Lottery: "All you need is a dollar and a dream." Well, you may need slightly more than a dollar to succeed in the telemarketing business, but the dream is there for the taking. Whereas perseverance must become your lifelong partner, dreaming must become your closest friend.

APPENDIX A

FURTHER RESOURCES FROM DIAL-A-MATTRESS

To Purchase This Book by Phone

For information on how to purchase copies of this book by phone, and to find out about discounts on quantity purchases of this book for businesses or schools or groups, call 1–800–DIAL–A–BOOK.

For More Information about Telemarketing

If you want further information about any of the topics in this book, please call us with your specific questions at 1–800–USA–1999.

The Telemarketing Institute

Dial-A-Mattress is about to form the Telemarketing Institute, where we will instruct product and service providers on all the information they need to initiate a telemarketing operation specifically geared to *their* concerns. At the Telemarketing Institute, businesses will learn the elements that have made Dial-A-Mattress successful: rapid delivery, excellent and friendly service, competitive prices, and the art and science of true selling over the phone, not just taking orders like some catalog operations.

The actual training program for the Telemarketing Institute will consist of a number of approaches. Representatives of companies will spend time at our headquarters in New York; "sit in" on our daily meetings afterwards, either in person or via teleconferencing and/or computer; avail themselves of further information and knowledge through a special toll-free number; and generally progress through all of the elements of the Dial-A-Mattress business operation. There will even be electronic testing after each session to ensure that all participants have learned the "secrets" of Dial-A-Mattress's methods. Upon completion of this course of instruction in telemarketing, businesses will have the option of future access to a database of information that is constantly updated by Dial-A-Mattress.

The Telemarketing Institute, headed by myself and a faculty consisting of many of my most experienced, talented, and trusted executives, will be based on our years of trial and error in the telemarketing business. We have proven our method to be successful: It is not just a theoretical concept or hypothetical case history, but a down-to-earth, highly practical process.

While the Institute will provide information and guidance that is specific to your company, this book—used alone or in conjunction with the Institute—will enable you to apply the general principles of the new telemarketing systems and dynamics to your own company or to a company you are thinking of starting. You will learn principles and techniques that Dial-A-Mattress and other experienced telemarketers have tested and proven successful for direct selling using toll-free numbers, which is the fastest-growing area of retailing.

New business technologies are evolving that are changing not only the way consumers spend, but even the very definition of an employee. Corporations are being restructured, and rival companies will both cooperate and compete in the near future. To succeed in business during the last years of the 1990s and into the next century, executives must be willing to let go of old, ineffective methods and adopt newer, technologically efficient ways. Telemarketing is one of the most important roads to retailing progress.

Whether you are the president of IBM or the owner of a single grocery store, I believe that this book and the Telemarketing Institute can help increase business. In addition, I have always believed that the only way to prove something in business is by trying it. With figures and statistics you can "prove" just about anything, so don't let the bean counters influence you with their allocations, ad budgets and curves. Follow your instincts and plunge in.

For more information about starting a new telemarketing business or information about the Telemarketing Institute, please call 1–800–USA–1999.

APPENDIX B

USEFUL FACTS ABOUT 1–800 SERVICE

- 1–800 toll-free calling was originated by AT&T. With the court-ordered breakup of the AT&T monopoly, the competition began to get into the toll-free number business. MCI began offering 1–800 numbers through its phone service in December 1986, while US Sprint jumped on the bandwagon in early 1988.
- AT&T sprang from the INWARD WATS service, used by large companies to receive collect calls from customers and major suppliers.
- AT&T, which created the 1–800 number in 1967, will control about 65 percent of the toll-free market by 1997, according to a survey by Strategic TeleMedia, a research and consulting firm.
- That same survey predicts 1–800 numbers will generate over many, many billion dollars in sales over the next five years.

Profile of the Toll-Free Market

- The growth of 1–800 numbers has been dramatic. In 1967, three million 1–800 calls were made. In 1995, there were 14 *billion*.
- AT&T toll-free directory operators handle nearly half a million calls daily from consumers.
- One of the major reasons given by people who regularly use 1–800 numbers to purchase what they want: "You make it very easy to shop."
- A demographic profile of the personal 1–800 number buyer is impossible, because they cover such a wide variety of people and professions, including truck drivers, airline pilots, lawyers, doctors, and teachers. There isn't any specific demographic pattern.
- An important point in the development of 1–800 numbers was the creation of the so-called vanity numbers, where words were used instead of numbers to help customers remember the number and/or the product

being offered, such as 1–800–HOLIDAY, 1–800–BUY– A–BOOT, 1–800–DENTIST, 1–800–FLOWERS, and 1–800–4–CAVIAR.

One of the key factors in our success is undoubtedly the combination of our vanity number and our slogan: "Dial 1–800–MATTRESS, and leave off the last 'S' for savings."

- According to a recent survey, the use of 1–800 numbers to help companies improve their customer service has grown significantly over the past 10 years. The first study conducted in 1983 showed that slightly more than one third of the companies used 1–800 numbers. The 1992 profile found that almost two thirds of the companies have now signed on.

- The number-one reason for employing a 1–800 number, according to the companies surveyed, is to increase brand loyalty.

- On average, more than 10,000 products in American shopping centers come with a 1–800 number included.

- Database Services Management Inc. has found that, based on their research, companies are attracted to 1–800 toll-free numbers for one major reason: A 1–800 number gives customers added incentive to call your company rather than your competitors.

- On May 1, 1993, businesses that use inbound 1–800 services, which include most large banks and many community banks, gained the ability to switch long distance carriers without having to leave their 1–800 number behind.

- In the 1–800 industry, more than half a million U.S. businesses employ more than 1.3 million 1–800 numbers.

- Since the establishment of WATS Marketing of America, in Omaha, Nebraska, the city has become known as the telemarketing capital of the world. The growth of the telemarketing industry has made a major contribution to the prosperity of the city, which now helps to sell billions of dollars worth of products and services by telephone all over the world.

- Both customers and businesses win with 1–800 toll-free number use. The customer benefits by getting a human voice, not having to type out a letter, and by seeing fast action.

- Over half a million American organizations have at least one 1–800 number.

- The growing demand for personal 1–800 numbers follows the pattern of call-forwarding services, personal computers, modems, and answering machines.

- In development for the future is an AT&T system that will allow a caller to take his personal 1–800 number with him wherever he goes. A special pager, attached to a portable phone, will be able to pick up 1–800 calls and prompt the phone to call back and complete the connection.

Service and Providers

- The telephone industry is running out of unused 1–800 numbers, in part because of a sharp increase in toll-free services, like pagers, which have taken most of the almost 8 million possible 1–800 numbers. As a result, the industry agreed to make the prefix 1–888 an additional toll-free number, beginning in April 1996. But the demand was so huge, the starting date had to be moved up to March 1.
- Worried that the remaining 1–800 numbers might have to be rationed before new 1–888 numbers were available in April of 1995, the FCC ordered a freeze on the number of organizations that were allowed to draw 1–800 numbers directly from a central base. The following week, 113,000 numbers were claimed—*three times* the normal weekly average.
- In August 1995, the FCC capped the total of "800" numbers that could be claimed each week at 30,000.
- Rumors began flying that AT&T and MCI were hoarding 1–800 numbers, fearing the confusion that was expected to occur when the new 1–888 numbers began to be issued.
- Roughly 40 percent of the 135 million to 140 million calls that go through the AT&T network on a typical business day are 1–800 calls.
- According to a study by market research firm Deloitte & Touche, technological aspects (line rental and equipment use) cost about 25–32 cents per call.
- Do you know that you can use a 1–800 for teleconferencing? The AT&T teleconferencing service (1–800–232–1234) connects you with as many people as you may need, whenever you need them, wherever they are. . . anywhere in the world.
- AT&T publishes a directory of 1–800 numbers for consumers. The directory contains more than 60,000 listings for everything from adoption services to retirement communities.
- With the creation of the AT&T Worldwide Network, it became pos-

sible for a business to advertise a single 1–800 number anywhere in the nation.

- There is a software program developed by a New Jersey–based company, A.C.S. Software Division, that will perform an alphabetical translation of your phone number into a household word. This is very useful if you're searching for a 1–800 vanity number. Call 1–800–DIAL–WORD.
- Pacific Bell has instituted a special "Custom 800" service that enables people to take their 1–800 number(s) with them wherever they go. (This is particularly beneficial for salespeople, who avoid losing business by having their old 1–800 number transferred to their new place of business.) The client calls the same number and speaks to the same salesperson, but the firm may be different.
- Sprint Business hopes to lure businesses away from their current telephone carrier. They have just expanded their 1–800 service to 40 countries, 24 hours a day. For businesses whose access to international markets is limited, this service could more than double their international sales. Call 1–800–816–REAL.
- JBS Associates, a check-authorization company, was founded in 1974, in a basement, with one 1–800 telephone line. Today the company annually receives about 20 million calls to verify over $6 billion in checks for over 40,000 retailers in the U.S. and Canada. JBS now has numerous 1–800 telephone lines, which are available to retailers 24 hours a day.
- A new checks-by-phone system may prove to be invaluable to 1–800 users. The On-Line Distribution Co. Inc. has established a program which allows consumers without credit cards to place orders using their checking or savings accounts. (Call John Hunter for more information: 1–800–951–5500.)
- IBM offers Fortune magazine readers the opportunity to hear testimonials from users of their new AS/400 Advances System, which significantly decreases response time and transaction time—resulting in lower support costs. IBM urges readers to call 1–800–IBM–3333, ext. BA135.
- Evidently the two systems—the computer and the 1–800 number—do not negate each other, but rather complement each other.
- World Data Delivery Systems Inc. of Harper Woods, Michigan, didn't exist before company founders, in 1990, realized they could

combine advanced facsimile services with 1–800 toll-free calling to build a whole new business line.

- If you can't figure out what computer program is right for your business, try calling SoftSearch at 1–800–667–6503. The company has a database of nearly every one of the more-than-70,000 computer programs currently available. For a fee, SoftSearch will compile a database on a particular program and provide a demo copy, along with various articles and background information. It can also compile all programs available for a particular purpose, from screenwriting to inventory control. The company is based in Vancouver, British Columbia.

Fraud and Security

- With the coming of age on the information highway, computer hackers have learned how to tap into companies' 1–800 toll-free services and make calls, which the companies will have to pay for. This method of phone fraud is a multibillion dollar industry. Hackers break into a company's private branch exchange, find out the codes for the lines the company uses, and often place them on computer bulletin boards where anybody with access to a modem can read.

  In recent years, Mitsubishi International was hit with charges for $430,000; Love's Country Stores in Oklahoma was billed $75,000; and Dodger Industries, a clothing manufacturer, was billed $35,000.

  1–800 fraud or not, most long-distance carriers insist that the companies foot the bill, on the assumption that if they were more careful in the first place, hackers wouldn't be able to break into their system. To that end, a new software called Fraud-Fighter, which monitors all calls and alerts owners to any unusual activity, was created.

- Watch for overuse of 1–800 numbers. "These services can lead to insidious employee telephone fraud, as friends call them free on the company's number," explains Bill Schwartz of Xtend Communications, a New York–based consulting firm. "Arrange it so incoming 1–800 calls can't be transferred to other lines."

- The FCC has allowed a few companies to ask for a fee for 1–800 calls, as long as the caller also approves it. However, while most companies make an announcement regarding price, some do not, and customers don't know what they're being charged until a whopper of a phone bill arrives. (A Kansas City family received a bill for $195 for calls the son had made to a phone-sex line; and a college in Missouri had to deal with a bill for $20,000 for calls made from dormitory phones.)

Charges often begin after the introductory message, when the caller is asked to press a button on their touch-tone phone. That, in the eyes of the law, constitutes consent, and it starts the meter running.

Another way for these unethical companies to engage in fraud is to send you a check for $5 through the mail to be put toward services offered by a specific 1–800 number. The fine print on the check states that by signing the check you agree to be billed for the service.

If a consumer receives such an incorrect bill, they can call their long-distance carrier and "dispute it." While each long-distance company handles the matter differently, the rule of thumb seems to be that they will forgive you the first time it occurs, *if* you've never called this type of number before. However, they will not overlook it a second time.

- Major Appliance Consumer Action Panel helps consumers resolve problems about major appliances by advising them how to initiate a complaint against a store or manufacturer. It also sponsors a mediation panel to help resolve disputes. Call 1–800–621–0477.
- NHTSA Auto Safety Hotline provides detailed information on vehicles and equipment that have been recalled or are under investigation for safety-related problems. Call 1–800–424–9393. *Today Show* weatherman Willard Scott can be heard on the recording.
- Water Test provides free consultation on water-testing and contaminants in water. It sends kits for bottling and mailing your tap water to them for laboratory testing. Call 1–800–426–8378.

Quick Sales Tips

- Controversial radio host Howard Stern, in addition to a reputation for insults, is known for delivering results for telemarketers. In addition to Dial-A-Mattress, Brother Electronics, Nutri-System Weight Loss Centers, and AIWA have been experiencing great sales success from buying spots on Stern's show. Spots sell for $1,200 to $1,500 each, making them among the most expensive in the market.

- One of the strongest aspects of telemarketing is that you can test a possible selling script within a short time to see if it works. After an hour or so of inbound calls, the script can then be changed (as to approach, offer, price, delivery time, etc.,) until you find the offer and the approach that best communicate the virtues of your product or service.
- An article in *Incentive Magazine* listed mistakes that telemarketers make in their sales efforts: 1) failing to make the offer; 2) treating all customers the same way; 3) having unreasonably high expectations.
- When hiring potential telemarketers, a good time and way to screen them is to listen to their pronunciation, diction, and overall telephone demeanor *when they call for an interview*.
- One of the best ways to build confidence in your telephone sales representatives is to provide them with as much product knowledge and information as possible.
- When selecting a vanity number (a phone number that spells the name of your company or your slogan, like 1–800–MATTRESS) for a telemarketing campaign, it must have a *minimum* of seven letters. But if your company name or product exceeds that number, you can still use it. For example, if a health food store wanted the number 1–800–NUTRITION, only the first seven letters, NUTRITI, equate to the number. As the consumer dials the entire nine letters, the last two letters O-N are automatically discarded, yet the call is routed to the store.
- Similarly, if you are afraid that your customer cannot spell your vanity number correctly, you can purchase "incorrect" vanity numbers as well. At Dial-A-Mattress, we own the 1–800 vanity numbers for MATTRESS, MATRESS, MATRRESS, and so on. This way you will never lose a call. . . and an eventual sale.
- To be able to deal directly by 1–800 numbers, big companies can communicate with consumers on a smaller, more intimate way, which has been found to promote customer satisfaction. It is easier and cheaper to keep your consumer than it is to seek out and sell to those you don't know.
- Customers are coming to expect toll-free complaint lines. Marketers who don't offer them may be at a competitive disadvantage.
- In establishing a blueprint for telemarketing success, it's essential that you analyze the financial benefit from an average hour of inbound calls. If the profit from the sale exceeds the cost (overhead, salaries,

cost per lead, etc.) for that hour, then the program is worth developing or continuing.

- Small, new, and home-based businesses are often surprised at the low cost of AT&T's Starterline. AT&T markets Starterline to businesses that would use a 1–800 service for less than three hours a month.
- If you are a mid-size company, where your total telecommunications budget is between $5,000 and $85,000 per month, AT&T has a special service called UNIPLAN, which lets you combine your domestic and international long distance, switched or dedicated 1–800 service, and corporate calling cards for volume discounts.

Personal Facts

- With personal 1–800 service, parent and child can avoid the awkward moment when the operator says "So-and-so is calling—will you accept the charges?"
- MCI offers a way to ease any mother's fears. It offers a new Personal 1–800 service, which charges her $5 per month for a 1–800 area code, the same thing businesses have done for 25 years.
- A new service by AT&T is "1–800 True Ties." It allows your child, friend, or whoever you wish, to call you while you pick up the charges. Call 1–800–850–TIES.
- You can make arrangements to take lessons in virtually any language in the world by dialing a 1–800 toll-free number listed in the AT&T directory.
- Need someone to give a speech at your fund raising dinner or your local PTA meeting? There are over 25 bureaus listed in the *AT&T Consumer Shoppers' Guide* ($13.50). To purchase a copy, call 1–800–426–8686. The AT&T directory includes 1–800 numbers of companies using AT&T, Sprint and MCI.
- Having an argument or dispute with you neighbor? Your boss? Your mate? There are over 30 arbitration and mediation services listed in the 1–800 telephone directory.

Food and Drink Facts

- For gift-giving, there's Cheesecake City at 1–800–CHEESECAKE. They will deliver freshly made cheesecake to anyone, anywhere in the

U.S. Some of the flavors include original white chocolate, pecan truffle, and super fudge chunk. For the calorie conscious, there are somewhat more healthful low-fat assortments as well. (The actual number is 1–800–CHEESEC. The telephone ignores the extra three letters.)

- Nationwide Gift Liquor Service has liqueurs, wines, champagnes, and hard liquor delivered anywhere in the U.S., where legal, within four working days. Call 1–800–243–3787 or 1–800–SPIRITS.

- You can have a live lobster overnighted to your doorstep simply by dialing a 1–800 number.

- During one promotion using their 1–800 number, the Nutra-Sweet Corporation figured they'd receive about 540,000 calls during the five-week promotion period. They ended up receiving almost three times that number.

- Launched in 1989 as part of Burger King's customer relations department, the 1–800 service department employs physically challenged people to answer calls and enter information into a data bank, which is used in marketing and operations. It is estimated they receive up to 4,000 calls a day on their 1–800 number service.

- In 1992, Pepsi Cola sent a mailing to over one million Diet Coke drinkers inviting them to call their 1–800 number and "talk" to Ray Charles, the spokesperson for Diet Pepsi. Over a half-million people called, and the company won a prestigious "Golden Echo" award from The Direct Marketing Association.

- In 1993, the Coca-Cola Company teamed up with various professional football players to create "Monsters of the Gridiron," a Halloween promotion offering 11 million prizes through a 1–800 interactive number and special codes found on Coca-Cola products. More than 36 million calls were recorded during the contest. Total cost of the calls to Coca-Cola: about $8.3 billion.

Government and Ecological Calls

- When Connecticut was deep in a recession in the early '90s and wanted to entice new businesses to its shores, it set up a toll-free 1–800 number with information about tax breaks, business loans, and other monetary advantages that came with moving to the state. During the first four weeks the number was in existence, over 3,000 calls were received from interested parties.

- U.S. Savings Bonds are advertised as good ways to earn good rates for college savings. You can call 1–800–4–US–BOND for current rate information.
- U.S. Consumer Product Safety Commission receives complaints related to product safety and answers questions on product and chemical safety. Call 1–800–638–2772. Actor James Earl Jones' voice can be heard on the recording.
- The Housing Discrimination Hotline helps callers nationwide to file complaints arising from discrimination because of race, color, sex, religion, or national origin, while trying to rent or buying living quarters. Call 1–800–424–8590.
- The Department of Energy's Energy Efficiency & Renewable Energy Clearinghouse (1–800–523–2929) provides answers about saving money on energy costs and energy-saving products, as well as technical or financial energy questions.
- The Nuclear Regulatory Commission (NRC) has established a toll-free hotline (1–800–952–9674) listing its upcoming meetings at locations throughout the United States.
- If you witness a crime, but don't want to get involved, the We Tip Hotline, 1–800–78–CRIME, will take down your statement without divulging your identity. They will then pass the information on to the proper authorities.
- Other numbers on the We Tip Network include 1–800–47–ARSON to inform police about suspicious fires.
- You can call 1–800–87–FRAUD to report scams on welfare fraud, worker's compensation abuse, or any other fraudulent act.
- During the primaries in 1992, both Ross Perot and Jerry Brown gave politics a new twist when they began to advertise 1–800 services. At Jerry Brown's 1–800 service, calls were answered only by live agents.
- Compu-Call often handles telephone fundraising for operations such as public broadcasting stations.
- Savings Bonds Rate-Line has a prerecorded message that provides up-to-date information on U.S. Savings Bonds, including current rate of interest. Call 1–800–872–6637.
- Working Assets is a long-distance telephone company with a conscience: They donate one percent of their customers' billings to nonprofit organizations they select. They offer a calling card at competitive rates, which means that every time the user dials the 1–800 access number, they donate money to charity. Call 1–800–788–8588.

- The Environmental Defense Fund offers a free brochure of everyday products that are being made from recycled materials to consumers who call 1–800-CALL–EDF.
- ECO-DEPOSITS at South Shore Bank is working to apply business discipline to "sustainable development." This is touted as "IRAs that make sense for you *and* the environment." Call 1–800–669–7725.
- 20/20 Vision is a service that sends one postcard monthly to subscribers, describing the best 20-minute action one can take to preserve peace and protect the environment. A subscription or brochure is available at 1–800–669–1782.
- Calling 1–800–320–APIE gets you American Pie (Public Information on the Environment). This group provides you with information on environmental concerns, ranging from water to household waste to grass and garden procedures.
- The Environmental Protection Agency (EPA) Safe Drinking Water Hotline can be contacted by dialing 1–800–426–4791. This hotline is to help officials and residents understand the rules and programs that have been created in answer to the Safe Drinking and Water Act Amendments of 1986.
- The National Response Center (1–800–523–2929) serves as a clearinghouse for any environmental problem or issue, from chemical spills to legal violations. (The Center requests that you provide as much information as possible when you call, so the operators can best determine where to direct your inquiry.)

Global Concerns

Though 1–800 services still account for only a small percentage of international telephone calls, many businesses, including mail-order companies, airlines, travel agencies, and management consulting firms, are beginning to use the service to gain a foothold in foreign markets without having to open a branch.

- 1–800 service is an AT&T invention and an American phenomenon. In Japan, toll-free calling was introduced only a couple of years ago.
- Outside of the U.S., the country with the highest population of toll-free calls is Canada, where the volume exceeds 20 percent of all calls made.

- In a recent study of telemarketing in the United Kingdom, it was determined that growth is not necessarily going to come from new customers, but from lingering relationships with old customers.
- AT&T international 1–800 service now allows people in 64 countries to call 1–800 numbers in the U.S.
- Clients living abroad who did business with U.S. companies once had to pay to call these companies' 1–800 numbers. Now AT&T's new USADirect 800 Service enables customers in over 130 countries to call U.S. companies' existing 1–800 numbers toll free. For more information, companies can call 1–800–655–1441, ext. 903.
- When a foreign-speaking caller dials an international 1–800 number, AT&T's Language Line Services kicks in. This provides a 24-hour interpretation of the 1–800 number's service in over 140 languages.
- With the aid of an international 1–800 number, Myrtle Beach Golf Holiday, a nonprofit group that promotes golf vacations in South Carolina, has received calls from such countries as Sweden, Norway, Denmark, Ireland, Japan, and the Netherlands.
- The service 1–800–GIFT–LINE gives you information on various national gift-sending networks. Possibilities include fresh flowers, balloon bouquets, and gift baskets.
- *Condé Nast Traveler* recently started a new hotline. If readers dial 1–800–WORLD24, they can order either the *January 1990–May 1995 Traveler Index* (helpful in planning trips) or reprints of articles from the magazine.
- UNZ & Company is a 115-year-old firm dedicated to making it easier for U.S. companies to comply with export regulations. It is the leading supplier of export forms, education, information, and training. Products include international trade forms and labels, yearly catalog and reference books, regulatory publications, and periodic alerts on upcoming or new legislation impacting the trade community. It can be reached at 1–800–631–3098.

The Wide World of Products

- A unique film service uses 1–800 numbers to its advantage. Unlike the ubiquitous Blockbuster or Palmer corner video rental stores, Home Film Festival relies on print advertising and 1–800 numbers to attract potential purchasers to their 208-page *1995 Home Film Festival Guide*. It contains descriptions and reviews of 2,600 foreign films, independents, limited releases, and documentaries available for mail-order purchase at a 10 percent discount. Call 1–800–258–3456.

- In the fall of 1994, in conjunction with the re-release of the 1964 Oscar-winning film *My Fair Lady,* CBS Video and 1–800 Flowers offered a "My Fair Lady Bouquet" promotion on various online services. The bouquet, a special floral arrangement, was made available on Prodigy, CompuServe, and the Bloomberg Financial Network.

- Big Sur Tapes offers an extensive audio collection of writers and thinkers, such as Joseph Campbell, Anais Nin, Aldous Huxley, and Carlos Casteneda. This company sells its audios through its catalog only, thus cutting the costs of overhead of setting up a retail location. Its advertisements tell interested people that they can obtain a catalog by calling 1–800–688–5512.

- Artist Access is a network of independent recording artists on the Internet. They market themselves by offering a catalog and CD sampler at 1–800–341–4505.

- While you are probably familiar with baseball's museum in Cooperstown, NY, you might not be able to make a list of other halls of fame in North America. A new book, *The Volvo Guide to Halls of Fame* (Living Planet Press, $12.95), profiles more than 1,000 of these halls of fame, honoring everything from Barbie dolls to questionable medical devices. It can be ordered by calling 1–800– 345–6665.

- Magazines are setting up Internet services by the dozen. But to access potential subscribers who are away from their terminals, they advertise using 1–800 numbers. For example, *New York* magazine offers a CompuServe service featuring movie reviews and events, timetables, photos, and clips. The reader subscribes to the service by dialing 1–800–535–1168 for a start-up kick.

- Using telemarketing as one of its principal ways to sell renewal subscriptions, *Natural History,* the magazine of the American Museum of Natural History (in New York City), has increased its circulation from 430,00 to 510,000.

- Delta Air Lines has more than 1,000 separate 1–800 lines in use throughout the country at their various sales offices.

- Carnival Cruise Lines has been in business 20 years. The "Fun Ships" of Carnival now carry more passengers than any other line in the world. Most of their success is due to AT&T's 1–800 service, which provides 384 incoming lines for reservations and administrative calls from travel agents in Canada, Mexico, and the Bahamas.

- Through 1–800–HERSHEY, tourists can access information about the hours of operation, admission, and events at Hershey Park, ZooAmerica, North American Wildlife Park, and Hershey Park Arena and Stadium. The 1–800 service also offers convenient lodging, reservations, and information, and even provides a weather report.

- Bed-and-breakfast inns have caught on to the advantages of using 1–800 numbers in their advertising. These numbers add one more dimension of ease of use and low cost to would-be vacationers planning an escape to the country or shore. Some of these inns include Columns by the Sea, in Cape May, NJ (1–800–691–6030) and the RedClover Inn, in Killington, VT (1–800–752–0571).

- The U.S. Dept. of Agriculture has set up a Forest Fall Color Hotline. Starting at the end of August, the recorded message gives frequent updates describing the changing leaf colors in forests throughout the U.S. and tells callers when each area is approaching its peak colors. It also provides 1–800 numbers that people can call to find out the peak viewing locations for specific states. Eighteen states currently have such Fall Foliage Hotlines: AL, CT, DE, KY, ME, MD, MA, MN, NH, NY, NC, PA, RI, TN, VT, VA, WV, and WI.

- Afraid of your rental car breaking down in a lonely, isolated spot? Not to worry if you rented the car from Avis. The Avis Rent-A-Car company's emergency nationwide 1–800 number will route all calls to the nearest Avis road station where help can be dispatched. According to company officials, this service is the first of its kind offered by the rental car industry. (Now all you have to do is hope you break down near a telephone.)

- The International Star Registry in New York, a 1–800 service that names stars in the sky after individuals and sells the documents certifying this, estimates it sold over $6,000,000 worth of stars, for naming purposes, during a seven-year period.

- Dial-A-Gift is a nationwide service that delivers baskets anywhere within 24 hours: fruit baskets, wine and champagne, cheese, cakes, bouquets of helium balloons, and frozen steaks. Call 1–800–453–0428.

- 1–800–FLOWERS has literally seen its business blossom since its founding 11 years ago. Today it has 130 stores, and sales for this year are expected to hit $200 million, mostly through telemarketing.

1–800–FLOWERS offers fresh flowers, wreaths, and bouquets, as well as silk and dried arrangements, which they will deliver locally, nationally, or internationally. They provide next-day delivery in most cases, in the continental U.S.

- Radio Shack has run ads in newspapers and magazines that feature a single product, such as its voice-activated microcassette recorder, along with details about its quality and performance. When customers call Radio Shack's 1–800 number, they hear the locations of stores nearest them, and they can also order the advertised item. It's like a mini-version of the catalog.

- For customers living miles away from the nearest Body Shop, the famous company offers a free mail-order catalog, listing its soaps, lotions, and toiletries. Call 1–800–541–2535.

- Chubb takes the innovative route when it comes to 1–800 numbers. It does not offer merely information on insurance, but a complimentary video about protecting your antiques collection. By asking a specific marketing target—antiques collectors—to call 1–800–CHUBB–08, Chubb is conducting smart business.

- DeBeers Diamonds offers a guide that explains how to judge a diamond's quality and value, and lists the closest diamond jewelers. Call 1–800–77–GLICK.

- The famous Birkenstock shoe company now offers an 18-page catalog at 1–800–247–5748, a number customers can also contact for mail-order repair service.

- Buck Coggins is the owner of a small hunting and fishing store known as Hoot's Outdoors in Albermarle, NC. But being small hasn't stopped Coggins from thinking big. He and his five employees have conducted wholesale and public business in the U.S. via a 1–800 number for years. Later, AT&T suggested using an international service for toll-free calls from Canada over regular U.S. domestic lines.

- Toll-free 1–800 numbers can provide customers with a wide range of information and assistance on anything from recalled automobiles to renewable energy.

- The biggest users of 1–800 numbers are travel companies, information services, and media-related organizations.

- Recently, during an airline promotion program, the number of toll-free calls was, for the first time in history, more than 50 percent of all AT&T calls made for that month.

- 1–800 service has sparked entire industries. Catalog company customers use 1–800 numbers as their invitation to shop 24 hours-a-day. Spiegel and its subsidiary Eddie Bauer together posted $2 billion in sales in 1991, of which 90 percent was made via 1–800 service.

- Between 1983 and 1989, catalog sales for products as diverse as tuxedos and garden hoses rose an incredible 93 percent, thanks in large part to the inclusion of 1–800 toll-free numbers in the catalogs.
- Some 30-minute television infomercials, selling products or services that range from $29.95 to $495, have been known to generate 20,000 to 30,000 inbound calls, during each broadcast.

Funny Stories

- Once during a field trip, a Boy Scout became separated from his troop. While he couldn't remember the name of the hotel where his group was staying, he did recall the nationwide reservations number for Holiday Inn: 1–800–HOLIDAY. The scouts weren't staying at a local Holiday Inn, but a company operator called every hotel in town until she found where the boy belonged.
- The General Electric 1–800 Answer Center once received a call from a little boy who put his marbles into a GE ice maker. "It was sort of an experiment," he tried to explain. The boy was trying to get his marbles out of the ice maker before his mom came home.
- The 1–800 customer service department at General Electric is often asked if it's safe to drink water that collects in a dehumidifier, and if the racks in the refrigerator can be removed and used for barbecuing. (In both cases, the answer is a resounding NO.)
- The Drackett Company received a 1–800 call from a man wondering if Windex glass cleaner (made by Drackett) was harmful to reptiles. (It isn't.) It seems he accidentally sprayed his pet lizards while cleaning.
- For anyone who has been annoyed by a television evangelist comes an unlikely hero. Edward Johnson didn't approve of his mother sending money to these folks, so he simply programmed his home computer to automatically dial the Rev. Jerry Falwell's 1–800 number every 30 seconds, continuously. This went on for over nine months before he was found out. It was estimated the computer made 500,000 phone calls—at a cost of nearly $1 each.
- The IBM Personal Systems HelpCenter is still chuckling about this one: A technician was answering some very technical questions on a 1–800 toll-free number about a customer's personal PS/2 computer.

In the middle of the conversation, the caller's mother summoned him to dinner. The caller, who turned out to be a ten-year-old boy, screamed back: "I can't come down now, Mom. I'm talking to IBM."

- One of the most common questions IBM's 1–800 HelpCenter receives is what to do when a cat has knocked a cup of coffee into a computer keyboard. Answer: Shake it out and blow dry.
- Not all 1–800 lines have been successful. Kellogg's Cereals had one on a trial basis, but discontinued it after receiving hundreds of call from children asking to speak to "Tony the Tiger" (the spokesman for Sugar Frosted Flakes).
- On an Ash Wednesday at the beginning of Lent, General Mills received over two hundred 1–800 calls an hour on its customer service line asking for microwave directions for its Gorton's frozen-fish selections. Soon after, the company installed an automated voice-response system to answer such requests.
- 1–800 phone operators at the Whirlpool Customer Assistance department are trained to explain to customers how to safely open their Whirlpool ovens if they become accidentally locked while in use. (Every Christmas season, the Center receives a large volume of frantic 1–800 calls from customers who have accidentally locked their ovens with a holiday dinner inside.)
- A company named Tele-Cake International sells cakes by phone. The most outrageous request it ever received on its 1–800 toll-free line was for a life-size birthday cake in the shape of a belly dancer.

Business to Business Connection (Yellow Pages/Fed Ex)

- The *AT&T National Shoppers' Guide* is the most widely circulated Yellow Pages in the United States. To place an ad, dial 1–800–562-2255. To order a copy of the *Guide,* dial 1–800–426-8686. It has entries ranging from   Abortion Services to the Wildlife Safari Zoo.
- When the Chicago River flooded offices in the downtown business district in the early 1990s, Con Edison requested 1–800 numbers for three emergency lines. The numbers were up and running in a matter of hours.
- One of Goodyear Tire & Rubber's more than 200 toll-free 1–800 lines serves as a 24-hours-a-day, 7-days-a-week "rescue line" for commercial truck tire blow-outs. This line receives about 2,000 calls a month.

- Polaroid has started a campaign to let retailers know about possible business uses for their Polaroid cameras. Urging them to call 1–800–348–5287, ext. 794, for a free brochure, Polaroid tells retailers to hand out instant shots of their merchandise, such as jewelry and furniture, so that customers can study the potential purchase at home.
- In a daring marketing move, Federal Express is offering free copies of its FedEx Ship software for Windows or Macintosh to consumers calling 1–800–GO–FEDEX. The software enables shippers to use their modems to connect directly to FedEx. They can create and print shipping labels, maintain a customer database, schedule pickups, and track and confirm delivery of packages.

Medical and Health Facts

- 1–800 Service helps AT&T provide world-class service to its customers. And it helps AT&T customers provide world-class service of their own. U.S. Healthcare provided a 1–800 toll-free number through which consumers could inquire about a widely watched television broadcast that featured then-First Lady Barbara Bush and other celebrities promoting the cause of literacy.
- There is a special 1–800 number for the deaf and other disabled persons, where they can get help placing local, long distance, collect, calling card, and third number calls (1–800–855–1155).
- Health Professionals International, based in Winnetka, IL, finds that 1–800 toll-free service keeps the company one step ahead of its competition by using the service to receive 1–800 toll-free calls from 19 countries.
- The Los Angeles riots in 1991 affected almost everyone—in some way—nationwide. For PRN, a Michigan-based pharmaceutical supplier, the rioting forced the closing of their California office. But because of AT&T's 1–800 service, PRN remained in business. Through AT&T's 800 Assurance Policy—which guarantees to reroute calls to a designated location within 30 minutes—PRN was able to send all L.A. calls to Michigan, and, company officers say, no sales were lost and no medicine failed to be shipped during the emergency.
- Lifeline Systems supplies information on emergency response programs and telephone systems for the elderly, the handicapped, and

those at high medical risk. Call 1–800–451–0525.

- 1–800 numbers check hearing now! 1–800–222–3277 gives you a local number to call for an automated screening recording. You'll get four tones to listen for with each ear. If you count just one or two, it's appointment time. The hearing screening number is open 9 A.M. to 5 P.M.

- The National Mental Health Association, 1–800–969–6642, provides brochures on stress, depression, schizophrenia, and other mental health problems.

- The Centers for Disease Control National AIDS Hotline, 1–800–342–AIDS, provides the latest information available about the prevention and treatment of the AIDS virus.

- The National Headache Foundation (NHF), 1–800–843–2256, offers information about various kinds of headaches and treatments, and also provides a list of headache specialists who are NHF members.

- National Parkinson Foundation sends free literature on Parkinson's disease, answers questions on symptoms, and refers callers to local support groups. Call 1–800–327–4545.

- Alzheimer's Association sends free information packets on Alzheimer's disease and provides phone numbers and contacts of local chapters with support group information. Call 1–800–621–0379.

- Shriners Hospital Referral Line provides information on and applications for free hospital care at one of the Shriners' 22 hospitals for children up to 18 years old who need orthopedic care or burn treatment. Call 1–800–282–9161.

- AMC Cancer Information Line has a professional staff that offers free crisis counseling to cancer patients, family members, and friends. It provides information on all aspects of cancer. Call 1–800–525–3777.

- Child Find is a national nonprofit organization that assists in locating missing children. They receive calls from parents who wish to report a missing child, and from those who have seen an abducted child. Call 1–800–426–5678.

- National Child Abuse Hotline provides immediate crisis intervention and information on legal assistance, runaway shelters, counseling groups, and parental organizations within a caller's area. Call 1–800–422–4453.

- One of the most important toll-free phone lines deals with children in trouble. It's called The Missing and Exploited Children Hotline,

1–800–THE–LOST. This line is to report a missing child, a child you may have seen whose picture is printed on milk cartons or posters.

- Runaway Hotline relays messages from runaways to parents. It also serves as a nationwide information and referral center for runaways needing food, shelter, medical assistance, counseling, and related services. Call 1–800–231–6946.

- American Council of the Blind provides services for the blind and visually impaired, including information and referral, legal advocacy, and legislative monitoring. Call 1–800–424–8666.

- In a first for the pet care industry, SmithKline Beecham's Animal Health Unit uses an interactive phone service to direct consumers to nearby veterinarians. Actress Loretta Swit does their 30-second spots, which include 1–800 numbers at the end.

- Petfinders is a nonprofit membership organization that provides lost and found information on pets, and travel information for people taking their pet on a trip. If someone finds a lost pet but cannot house it, the organization guarantees payment to kennels, and also to veterinarians in case of injury. Call 1–800–223–4747.

The Future of 1–800

There are now billions of 1–800 calls annually, most of these business-oriented, and the figure is growing geometrically. Based on the total number of minutes employed, AT&T reports the following percentage of uses of 1–800 numbers:

Sales/Order Taking	49%
Product Inquiries	21%
Employees/Internal Use	19%
Reservations	5%
Customer Reports	3%
Hotline	2%
Credit Card Authorization	1%

As life becomes more complex and people begin to rely more heavily on shopping by phone, primarily to save time and gain convenience, the Sales/Order Taking percentage of 1–800 use will continue to soar.

INDEX

A.C.S. Software Division, 260
Accumaster Services Personal
    Computer software, 43–44
Advanced training, 93–96
Advertising, 12, 138–45
    agency, vs. self-created, 123–25
    amount spent on, and staffing
        needs, 37
    banners, 144
    billboard, 140–42
    brand names in, 110
    campaign, planning, 112–13
    co-op, 110–12
    customers and, 113–23
    cutting costs of, 145–49
    direct mail, 142–43
    hard-sell, 106
    market for good or service, and
        type of, 139
    product or service, defining in,
        128–32
    remnant or stand-by, 147–48
    self-created advertising, 124–33
    television, 133–38
    toll-free number as, 109–10
    trade-out, 159
    videotape, 144–45
    where to advertise, 133–38
    with no cash, 149–50
    Yellow Pages, 144
Agazziz, Louis, 52
Albrecht, Karl, 78
Alcoholic beverages, available on
    1–800 lines, 265
American Express, 35

American Pie, 267
Annoying customers, 89–90
Answering machines, 107–8
Arm and Hammer Baking Soda,
    252
AT&T, 10, 42, 264
    Accumaster Services Personal
        Computer software, 43–44
    Language Line Services, 241
    requesting toll-free hook-up, 20

Barragan, Luis, 162–63
Bencin, Richard L., 79
Bill of lading, 170
Brandon, Joel, 49–50
Burger King, 265
Burnout, preventing, 96–99
Business, future of, 227–28
Business libraries, 42
Buying services, 226

Callbacks, 100
Call Center Magazine, 42, 44
Carlson, Chester, 51
Carson, Johnny, 151
Catalogs, listing product or services
    in, 226
Celebrity endorsement, 136–37
Checks-by-phone system, 260
Closer question, 85–86
Coca-Cola, 265
College Furniture Discounters, 4
Commissioned salespeople
    advanced training and, 94
    burnout and, 97

Communication(s)
distributors and manufacturers and, 219–26
importance of skilled, 54
meetings
to explore ideas, 206–13
to share information, 205–6
open door policy, 217–18
pagers, 213–17
Comparison chart, of products and competition, 66–67
Comparison list, 11–12
Comparison shopping, 66
Competition, knowledge of, 66–67
Computer program, setting up, 43–44, 67–71
data categories, 68–70
Conde Nast Traveler, 268
Confirmation of orders, 198–201
Consumer Behavior (Schiffman and Kanuk), 204
Conversation, tailoring to the customer, 77–81
Cooperative advertising, 110–12
Corporate policy manual, 64–65
Corporation, defined, 32
Crank phone calls, 64, 78–79, 95
Crazy Eddie, 106
Credit card payment, 35, 43, 185–86
CUC International, 226
Custom 800 service, 260
Customer(s)
adapting to style of, 80–81
annoying or impolite, 89–90
building satisfied, 103–4
creating a team between telemarketer and, 87–88
credo (L.L. Bean), 71
determining wants of, 81–84

describing appropriate products, 82–83
qualifiers, 81–82
dissatisfied, 90–91
ending conversations with reluctant, 99–100
objections, dealing with, 84–87
positive feelings and, 102–3
preferences, establishing, 64, 67
relationship, building, 71
respecting, 72, 75, 78, 90, 229
stalling by, 88
tailoring conversation to, 77–81
Customer data, gathering, 79
Customer service
guidelines, 225
renewed focus on, 103–4
retail consumer stories, 222–24
survey ranking businesses on, 161–62

Damaged merchandise, 170
covered in policy manual, 65
Data
categories, for computerized program, 68–70
efficient gathering of, 79
keeping track of, 42–44
Database, of previous transactions, 43
Davidow, William H., 105
Dear customer letters, 65
Delivery, 178–201
bettering the competition, 165–66
as computerized category, 70
confirming order before, 198–201
costs and charges, 164, 181–82
credit card payments, 185–86
do's and don'ts, 182–83
drivers operations daily log, 184–85

drivers' operator, 183–84
driver's primary duties, 191–95
efficiency of, 163
equipment and supplies, 195–96
handling delays in, 92–93
late, 188–89
loading procedures, 196–97
no one home to accept, 186–88
on approval, 169
options, offering, 91–92
outside services, 197–98
problem with merchandise delivered, 188
profitability and, 162–63
routes, 189–92
scheduling, 189
sequence, 191–95
shipping and messengers, 163–64
trucking firms, 164
Delivery service, outside, 197–98
Dentists, 25–26
Dial-A-Mattress
advertising, 140
annual sales, 1988–1995, 16
customer service, 161–62, 223–25
delivery operation, 178–79
discount coupon, 277
distribution, 167–68, 176
galleries, 159–60
history of, 1–15
international sales and, 251
Internet and, 247
meetings
directors', 205–6
to explore ideas, 206–9
open door policy, 217–18
quality control, 168–69
resources from, 255–56
sales training, 60–64, 87

Direct-mail, 142–43
responses, 39
Direct marketing, on the internet, 247–48
Discounts, covered in policy manual, 65
Discover Card, 35
Dispatcher, 183
Dispatching report, 186–87
Dissatisfied customers, 90–91
Distribution center, 167–68
inventory and, 176–77
space requirements for, 177–78
Distributor, storing merchandise with, 45–46
Donahue, Phil, 152
Drivers
equipment and supplies for, 195–96
loading procedures, 196–97
primary duties of, 191–95
Driver's daily log, 183–85
Drivers' operator, 183–84
Drucker, Peter F., 59, 227
Dunham, Jean Dollar, 223

ECO-DEPOSITS, 267
Ecological calls, 266
Economic downturns, 99
888 toll-free calling, 22
Emotions, controlling, 75
Empathy, 75
Environmental Protection Agency, 267
"Exclusive" merchandise, 66–67
Expansion, 47–53
Expert advice, 40–42

Feedback, 18
Food gifts, available on 1–800 line, 264–65
Fraud, 33, 261–62

Galleries, 159–60
GATT, 247
Gift-sending networks, 268
Gillispie, 223
Global concerns, 267–68
Global sales, 240–47
Goethe, 51
Going public, 32
Government calls, 265–66
Graebel Van Lines Company, 225
Grassano, Jennifer, 94
Guarantees, covered in policy man-
      ual, 65

Health facts, 274–76
Hierarchy of needs, 128–29
Howard Rubenstein Associates, 154

IBM, 16, 225, 260
Ideas, exploring, 206–13
Impolite customers, 89–90
Inbound telemarketing, 60. See also
      Telemarketing
Incentives, 132–33
Information, sharing throughout
      company, 205–6
Information Database, 42
In Search of Excellence (Peters and
      Waterman), 161
Installation, 193
International sales, 240–41
International Toll-Free Service,
      21–22
Internet, direct marketing on,
      247–48
Inventory, 45–46, 98
   availability of, 43
   computing how much to order,
      174–75
   control, 175–76
   distribution and, 176–78

purchasing, 173–74
   space requirements and, 171–73
Invoice number, 170
Item number, 70

JBS Associates, 260
Jobbing, 11
Johnson & Johnson, 212–13

Kanuk, Leslie Lazar, 204
Kinkos, 23

L.L. Bean, , 16–18, 71, 222
Lands' End, 223
Late delivery, 188–89
Leadership, 53–58
Leads, tracking, 69
Leaflets, 158
Legal issues, 32–35
Letterman, Dave, 152
Letzt, Harry, 73–74
Listening skills, 72–74, 86, 90
   persuasive listening, 74–76
Loading procedures, 196–97

Made in America (Walton), 1
Major Appliance Consumer Action
      Panel, 262
Malone, Michael S., 105
Management: Tasks, Responsibilities,
      Practices (Drucker), 59
Manufacturers, 219–22
   storing merchandise with, 45–46
Marketing, 59
   see also Telemarketing
   strategies, and customer service,
      104
Maslow, Abraham, 128
MasterCard, 35
Mazursky, Paul, 154
MCI, 20

Medical facts, 274–76
Meetings
    directors', 205–6
    to explore ideas, 206–13
    to share information, 205–6
Merchandise category, 68–69
Merchandise return form, 170
Minnesota Mining &
        Manufacturing, 252
Money-back guarantee, 33–34
Morris, Daniel, 49–50
Myrtle Beach Golf Holiday, 268

NAFTA, 247
Napoleon I, 227
National Response Center, 267
Nationwide Gift Liquor Service, 265
Negative publicity, 157
NHTSA Auto Safety Hotline, 262
Non-listening habits, 76
Nooney, Greg, 13
Nordstrom, 63
Nutra-Sweet, 265

Objections, to sales presentation
    dealing with, 84–87
        three-step dialogue, 85–86
    making a product special to
        customer, 93
    spouse objection, 91–92
1–800 POPULAR, 253–54
1–800 service
    business to business connection,
        273
    food and drink facts, 264–65
    fraud and security, 261–62
    funny stories, 272–73
    future of, 276
    global concerns, 267–68
    government and ecological calls,
        265–67

lasting impression of, 40
medical and health facts, 274–76
obtaining, 20–22
personal facts, 264
profile of toll-free market, 257–61
quick sales tips, 262–64
selecting a product or service for,
        22–30
types of, 27–29
unique products offered on,
        268–72
useful facts about, 257–76
volume discounts, 21
On-Line Distribution Co. Inc.,
        260
Open door policy, 217–18
Order entry, 43
Outbound telemarketing, 52–53,
        60. See also Telemarketing

Pacific Bell, 260
Pagers, 213–17
Partnership, 31–32
Payment form, 70
Pepsi Cola, 265
Per inquiry basis, 146
Personal 1–800 service, 264
Personal Traits Important to a
        Business Proprietor, 55
Peters, Thomas J., 161
Peters, Tom, 19
Picking slip, 191
Pleasant Company, The, 223
Policy manual. See Corporate policy
        manual
PR agency, 154–55
Press release, 156–57
Product development, sales involve-
        ment with, 99
Product line
    describing to customer, 82–83

Product line (*cont.*)
  developing description list of,
      83–84
  recurrent products, 23–24
  salespeople's knowledge of, 23,
      66–67
  videotape of, 26
Promotion, 150–57
  promotional videos, 144–45
Psychological health, 97
Psychological qualities, of product
      or service, 83
Publicity, 150–57
  suggestions, 155–56
Public relations agency, 154–55
Purchasing, 173–74
Purchase order, 175
  number, 170

Qualifiers, 81–82
Quality, of product or service,
      22–23
Quality control, 168–69
  meetings, sales involvement
      with, 99

Receiving, 170–71
Recessions, 99
Recurrent products, 23–24
Re-engineering Your Business
      (Morris and Brandon), 50
Referrals, 163
Rejection, dealing with, 95
Remnant advertising space,
      147–48
Rennenburg, Maureen, 94
Reordering inventory, 174–75
Respecting customers, 72, 75, 78, 90
Rest and relaxation, 96–97
Retraining classes, 94–95
Return authorization tag, 171

Return policy, 169, 170
  covered in policy manual, 65
Role playing
  in sales training, 89

Sales calls
  see also Telemarketing
  recording, 94
Sales history, and inventory, 173
Sales income, recession and, 99
Salesperson code, 68
Sales support, ongoing, 93–96
Scheduling deliveries, 189
Schiffman, Leon G., 204
Schwartz, Bill, 261
Screening applicants, 33
Scripts, 43
  adding variety to, 98–99
  providing suggested, 101–3
Security, 261–62
Seidenberg, Richard, 73–74
Selling techniques. *See*
      Telemarketing
Service
  business, selecting, 22–30
  describing to customer, 82–83
Service Corps of Retired
      Executives, 41
Sexual harassment, 33
Shareholders, 32
Shipping order, 170
Shipping restrictions, 33
Siegel, Mira, 74
SKU, 173–74
  number, 170
  total "movement" of, 174
Small Business Administration, 41
Smiling, 77
SoftSearch, 261
Software, telemarketing, 44
Sole proprietorship, 31

Space requirements, for inventory, 171–73
Spirit of service, 78
Spouse objection, handling, 91–92
Sprint, 20
Sprint Business, 260
Staffing, 36–40
  calculating needs for, 37–39
  screening applicants, 33
  sufficient amount of, to prevent burnout, 98
Staging area, 170
Stalling, by customer, 88
Stand-by advertising space, 147–48
Starterline, 264
Stern, Howard, 12, 262
Stock. *See* Inventory
Storage, 45–46. *See also* Inventory
Storage principles, 171
Strategic Telemarketing (Bencin), 79
Subleasing warehouse space, 46
Superintendent of Documents, U.S. Government Printing Office, 41–42
Supplier, storing merchandise with, 45–46

Target Marketing, 44
Team Methodology, 64
Telecheck Service, 35
Telemarketer
  see also Telemarketing
  adapting to customer's style, 80–81
  ideal, qualities of, 79
  smiling on the phone, 77
  voice of, 79–80
Telemarketing, 16–18
  see also Customer(s); Listening skills
  blue-chip companies and, 225

company overview and objectives, 60
customer interaction, 61
customer objections, response to, 84–87
expanding an existing business, 47–53
expert advice, obtaining, 40–42
follow-up calls, 63
future of, 227
glossary of products and services in, 61–62
keeping track of data, 42–44
key techniques for, 72–81
  focusing, 76–77
  listening, 72–76, 86
  tailoring conversation to the customer, 77–81
leadership, 53–58
  important personal traits, 56–57
managers and directors, sales calls by, 63
mistakes made in, 263
personal development, 62
product line-up, 60–61
"psychology of a winner," 63–64
sales training program and, 60
selling concept of to manufacturers and suppliers, 221–22
staffing an operation, 36–40
starting a business, 31–35
  legal issues, 32–35
  legal types of businesses, 31–32
tailoring conversation to the customer, 77–81
troubleshooting, 201–3
turning calls into sales, 64
Telemarketing Magazine, 42, 44
Television advertising, 133–38

Testimonials, 136–37
3M, 252
Three-step dialogue, 85–86
Thriving in Chaos (Peters), 19
Toll-free
    market, profile of. *See under*
        1–800 service
    number, as advertisement, 109
    purchases, American consumers
        and, 17
Trade-out advertising, 159
Training, advanced, 93–96
Troubleshooting, 201–3
20/20 Vision, 267

UNIPLAN, 264
Unique products available, 268–72
United Parcel Service, 63
UNZ & Company, 268

Vanity phone number, 10–11, 20
    lasting impression of, 40
Videos, promotional, 144–45
Visa, 35

Vicens, Joe, 8–14, 214
Virtual Corporation (Davidow and
        Malone), 105
Voice quality, of telemarketer,
        79–80

Wal-Mart, 48, 223
Walton, Sam, 1, 48
Warehouse, subleasing space to sup-
        pliers, 46
Waterman, Robert H. Jr., 161
Water Test, 262
WATS Marketing of America, 258
Weather, and increased telephone
        sales, 40
Wiersema, Fred, 161
World Data Delivery Systems Inc.,
        260–61

Xtend Communications, 261

Yellow Pages, 144

Zip code, 79

Call 1-800-MATTRESS
now and receive . . .

Special Savings

$25 Off

Mattress & Box
Spring Set from

DIAL-A-MATTRESS
1- 800- MATTRESS SM

LEAVE OFF THE LAST 'S' FOR SAVINGS

Terms and Conditions:

This certificate must be mentioned at time of order and
presented to driver at time of delivery. Cannot be combined
with any other offer. Limit one coupon per order. Not valid
on prior sales. Merchandise subject to availability. May not
be available in all areas. Subject to franchisee participation.
Void where prohibited.   HC1